CAKE ICING
& DECORATION

MARGUERITE PATTEN

PAUL HAMLYN

Contents

© Copyright Paul Hamlyn Limited 1965

Reprinted 1967, 1968

THE HAMLYN PUBLISHING GROUP LTD

HAMLYN HOUSE · THE CENTRE · FELTHAM · MIDDLESEX

Printed in Czechoslovakia by Svoboda, Prague

T 1881

Introduction

This is a book which I have much enjoyed writing and I hope you will have equal pleasure in using it.

It is a well-known fact, appreciated by good cooks and by enthusiastic families, that the look of food has a great bearing on its appeal. Probably in no field of cooking is appearance more important than in the presentation of cakes, biscuits, etc.

To ice perfectly takes many months of practice, a great deal of patience and a natural artistic skill, but even beginners can achieve really interesting-looking cakes by the more simple methods described in the first part of the book.

Do not be unduly depressed if your first efforts at piping and icing are not as professional as you might wish. Persevere, and with each cake you will notice a very definite improvement.

I am extremely grateful to the Home Economists who have helped in producing pictures and would like to record my particular thanks to the *Australian Woman's Weekly* and to the Australian Gas Light Company for initiating me into the secrets of the unbelievably beautiful method of decorating in that country. It was not possible to bring home the various wonderful cakes to photograph here, but I would like to assure readers who have not seen them, that when moulded flowers were used on a cake in Australia, one almost felt you could pick them, they were so realistic. *See colour plates 17 and 18.*

To all who read and use this book, I wish success and enjoyment in your work to make food look really exciting.

Weights and Measures

English weights and measures have been used throughout this book.
3 teaspoonfuls equal 1 tablespoon.
The average English teacup is ¼ pint or 1 gill.
The average English breakfast cup is ½ pint or 2 gills.
When cups are mentioned in recipes they refer to a B.S.I. measuring cup which holds ½ pint or 10 fluid ounces. The B.S.I. standard tablespoon measures 1 fluid ounce.
In case it is wished to translate any of the weights and measures into their American, Australian, Canadian or French counterparts, the following tables give a comparison.

LIQUID A MEASURE

The most important difference to be noted is that the American and Canadian pint is 16 fluid ounces, as opposed to the British Imperial pint, which is 20 fluid ounces. The American ½-pint measuring cup is therefore actually equivalent to two-fifths of a British Imperial pint.
In Australia 1 pint is generally 16 fluid ounces, although in some of the States 20 fluid ounces are used.

SOLID MEASURE

English	American or Australian
1 lb. Butter or other fat	2 cups
1 lb. Four	4 cups
1 lb. Granulated or Castor Sugar	2 cups
1 lb. Icing or Confectioners' Sugar	3 cups
1 lb. Brown (moist) Sugar	2½ cups
1 lb. Golden Syrup or Treacle	1 cup
1 lb. Rice	2 cups
1 lb. Dried Fruit	2 cups
1 lb. Chopped Meat (finely packed)	2 cups
1 lb. Lentils or Split Peas	2 cups
1 lb. Coffee (unground)	2½ cups
1 lb. Soft Breadcrumbs	4 cups
½ oz. Flour	1 level tablespoon*
1 oz. Flour	1 heaped tablespoon
1 oz. Sugar	1 level tablespoon
½ oz. Butter	1 level tablespoon smoothed off
1 oz. Golden Syrup or Treacle	1 level tablespoon
1 oz. Jam or Jelly	1 level tablespoon

* *Must be proper measuring tablespoon*

FRENCH WEIGHTS AND MEASURES

It is difficult to convert to French measures with absolute accuracy, but 1 oz. is equal to approximately 30 grammes, 2 lb. 3 oz. to 1 kilogramme.

For liquid measure, approximately 1¾ English pints may be regarded as equal to 1 litre; 1 demilitre is half a litre, and 1 décilitre is one-tenth of a litre.

Oven Temperatures

	Electricity °Fahrenheit	Gas Regulo	° Centigrade
COOL	225 to 250	0 to ½	107 to 121
VERY SLOW	250 to 275	½ to 1	121 to 135
SLOW	275 to 300	1 to 2	135 to 149
VERY MODERATE	300 to 350	2 to 3	149 to 177
MODERATE	375	4	190
MODERATELY HOT	400	5	204
HOT	425 to 450	6 to 7	218 to 233
VERY HOT	475 to 500	8 to 9	246 to 260

Note: This table is an approximate guide only. Different makes of cooker vary and if you are in any doubt about the setting it is as well to refer to the manufacturer's temperature chart. Australian gas oven temperatures are often in °F. Use 50°F. *less* for gas than electricity.

Care of Icing Equipment

1

1 Icing equipment, particularly pipes, is generally made of metal, and should therefore be dried very carefully after use and put in a warm place before returning to the drawer. This makes certain it does not rust.
2 When you have used an icing pipe, put it to soak immediately in water, otherwise the icing will harden in the pipe and be extremely difficult to remove.

3 Syringes should be washed out very carefully and dried in the same way as the pipes.
4 Nylon or cloth bags should be turned inside out to wash and dried slowly. Do not dry the nylon bags too near strong artificial heat.
5 Take great care that pipes are stored without anything heavy weighing down on top of them, otherwise they speedily become bent and of a poor shape.

To Decorate without Icing

2

1 Cakes can be decorated without icing, by cherries, nuts and a crumble mixture. This is done in baking, see Recipes 36 and 46.
2 By the use of sugar to give a shine or finish.
3 By the use of coconut, see Recipe 11.
4 By syrup or glaze, see Recipes 23—27.

5 Meringues are a very delicious form of decoration as well as a traditional one.
6 Marshmallows.
7 Chocolate in various forms, including chocolate biscuits.
8 Cream.

Various Types of Icing

3

The many different types of icing enable one to produce an amazing variety of decorations on the cakes.
The most simple to use are:
1 Glacé, or as it is often called, water icing, which gives a smooth covering which dries quickly.
2 Butter icing or one of the similar types of soft or semi-soft icings which are equally good for a filling.
3 American frosting which is the icing that hardens on the outside, but remains soft on the inside no matter how long it is kept.
4 Fondant icing which can be used in place of royal icing and produces a hard, very perfect finish. It is also excellent for moulding.
5 Fudge icing which is soft and creamy and ideal for a filling as well as for a coating.
There are other cooked types of icing which are described in this particular chapter, one of

the most effective of these being caramel icing.
6 Marzipan or almond paste produces a perfect 'under-coating' on a cake being decorated with royal, fondant or glacé icing.
7 Royal icing is the most usual for rather rich cakes that need to be stored, and for piping. It can be varied in consistency to produce a softer or harder icing as liked.
In the various recipes and under each section of icing a suggested quantity for coating a certain-sized cake has been given. It must, however, be realized that tastes vary a great deal and the amounts given will produce an average thickness. In many cases you can be more economical; use less and have a thinner icing or use more for a very generous layer.
With regard to the amount left for piping, you will find that, when you begin, you tend to be very much more extravagant with the icing than when you have become an expert.

Cakes without Icing

4

On the following pages there are some simple but interesting ways of decorating cakes without making an icing.

As you will see from the pictures, these produce a more exciting finish than if the cake were left plain.

5 When cakes are better without icing

If a cake has a very attractive appearance when baked, or has a very definite flavour, icing may well detract from both, so never ice a cake unless it will be a great advantage. Never put an icing on the cake unless this will store as long as the cake.

6 Nuts as decoration

Nuts not only give an attractive appearance to a cake, but a pleasant crispness which blends well with soft sponges or a richer fruit cake. The following nuts are the most usual to use:

Almonds

Choose Jordan almonds preferably, since these have the best flavour. These should be blanched by putting into boiling water for approximately 30 seconds. Lift out and when cool enough to handle, remove the skins. If putting on the cake before baking, glaze with egg white, see Recipe 33. If putting on cake after baking, use some jam or icing to make them stick.

Chopped almonds

These are a favourite form of border decoration. Just brush the rim of the cake with jam and sprinkle with nuts.

Split almonds

This means that the nut is split through the centre. Do this carefully so you have two perfect halves.

Shredded or slivered almonds

These are nuts that are cut into thin strips lengthways.

Toasted or browned almonds

This means the almonds are blanched, dried and browned under a moderate grill or in the oven. If they are made very brown, they have a burnt flavour liked by many.

Brazils

A rather large, cumbersome nut for decoration on delicate cakes, unless chopped or grated. To remove the brown skins, heat for a while in the oven, then rub away the skin.

Cashew nuts

These have an attractive shape as well as a good flavour. Use as almonds although they are generally used whole. They need no blanching.

Chestnuts

Generally used as marrons glacés or chestnut cream. To remove the brown skins, boil slit nuts for 10 – 15 minutes. Shell while warm.

Cob nuts

Rarely used as decoration. You will need to skin as brazils.

Hazelnuts

Equally good for decoration as for an ingredient in the cake. Remove the skins as brazils.

Monkey or peanuts

Rarely used for decoration but children will like these so put on to small cakes. The brown skins can generally be removed by rubbing firmly between forefinger and thumb.

Pecan nuts

These are very similar to walnuts and, due to their rather attractive shape, an ideal form of decoration either whole, halved or chopped.

Pistachio nuts

These rather expensive tiny green nuts are ideal for decoration. They should be blanched like almonds. You can, however, use tinted almonds instead, see Recipe 9.

Walnuts

Owing to their attractive shape, these are an ideal form of decoration either whole, halved or chopped.

Nuts for decoration

7 Italian torrone

4 oz. margarine or butter
3 oz. cocoa
5 oz. ground almonds
1 egg
4 oz. castor sugar
2 tablespoons water
2 oz. Marie or semi-sweet
  biscuits
1 oz. glacé cherries
1 oz. walnuts
To decorate:
walnut halves

Cream margarine and cocoa together until soft. Add ground almonds and egg, mix in well. Place sugar and water in a saucepan and dissolve gently. Pour on to cocoa mixture and beat well. Break biscuits into almond-size pieces and add, with chopped cherries and walnuts, to the mixture. Mix in thoroughly. Place in an 8-inch sandwich tin, previously lined with greaseproof paper, smooth with a knife, decorate with walnuts and leave to set in a refrigerator or cold place.
Ease round the edge with a knife and turn out on to a plate.
Serve immediately, or return to the refrigerator until required.

Italian torrone

8 To coat cakes with nuts

It is very usual to coat the sides of a cake with chopped nuts, and this should always be done before you begin icing the top or decorating it in any way.

1 Put the nuts on to greaseproof paper.

2 Brush the sides of the cake either with sieved jam or coat with icing.

Picture 1

3 Hold the top and bottom of the cake rather like a hoop and roll over the nuts so that these adhere to the sides.

4 Turn the cake the right way, and just press the nuts firmly against the sides with a palette knife.

Picture 2

5 This shows the finished result with the top of the cake decorated and piped with a soft butter icing such as described in Recipe 101.

6 If the top is also to be coated with nuts, do this AFTER the sides.

Spread top with jam or icing, then spread nuts over top, pressing these firmly afterwards with a palette knife.

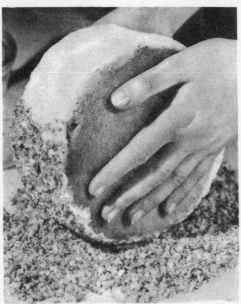

1 Rolling the cake in chopped nuts

2 The sides of the cake coated in nuts

9 To tint nuts

Nuts can be coloured for more decoration. The most suitable are chopped blanched almonds.

1 Put 2 or 3 drops of vegetable colouring on to a plate or saucer.

2 Put the chopped nuts on to the plate and gradually work into the colouring until even.

3 Allow the nuts to dry before using. Tint enough to store in jars for future use.

10 To toast nuts

These give added flavour as well as a particularly crisp texture to cakes.

1 Put the prepared nuts on a flat tray and heat gently under the grill.

2 Turn, and heat the other side.

3 Alternatively, put nuts on baking tray in oven and heat slowly until desired colour.

4 Allow to cool before storing.

11 Coconut for decoration

While one can use grated fresh coconut, desiccated coconut is better because it is dried and does not deteriorate with keeping, on the cake. Coconut can be applied as follows.

1 Over icing. Generally this is put over butter or glacé icing. See Recipes 100 and 53.

2 Over jam. In order to have a smooth finish, the jam should be heated and then sieved.

The pictures under Recipe 15 show the right way to apply this.

3 Before cooking. Top cakes with coconut before cooking so that the coconut browns.

With Methods 1 and 2, the coconut may be used fresh from the packet, or it can be toasted in very much the same way as blanched almonds.

12 To coat a cake with coconut

To apply coconut to sides

Follow the same procedure as with nuts, see Recipe 8, or with smaller cakes, pat the coconut on to the sides with a palette knife.

To apply coconut to top

Lift the coconut on to the tip of a palette knife; pat knife gently to form border round edge or completely cover top of cake.

13 Easter basket

For the eggs:
4—6 eggs
1 packet flavoured cornflour (or 2 half-packets different flavours)
1—2 oz. sugar
1 pint milk
For the cake:
2 eggs
2 oz. castor sugar
1 oz. flour
1 oz. cornflour
¼ teaspoon baking powder
2 oz. desiccated coconut
green colouring
sieved apricot jam
small can mandarin oranges

Pierce a hole in the end of each egg. With a thin skewer break up the yolk and shake the contents out into a bowl and use for scrambled egg or omelette. Rinse the shells under the tap. Make up the flavoured cornflour with the sugar and milk, according to directions on the packet. Carefully pour into the shells and leave to set. Any blancmange that is over can be set in a mould. Whisk the eggs and sugar together for the cake until mixture is thick and leaves a trail. Fold in the sifted flour, cornflour and baking powder. Turn into a well-greased 8½-inch sponge flan tin. Bake for 20 minutes in a moderately hot oven (400°F. — Gas Mark 5). Leave to cool. Colour the coconut pale green, by puting 3 or 4 drops on a plate and working coconut into it. Spread apricot jam around the edge and sides of the flan and roll in the coloured dried coconut.

Drain the juice from the mandarin oranges and moisten the centre of the cake with it. Place the oranges on the bottom of the flan. Arrange the eggs on top. The shells keep the blancmange in good shape, so should be left on till the last minute. Remove the shells before serving and rearrange on top of the oranges.

Easter basket

14 Lamingtons

5 oz. butter
7 oz. castor sugar
vanilla essence
3 eggs
10 oz. flour (with plain flour use 2½ level teaspoons baking powder)
pinch salt
4 tablespoons milk
For the filling:
raspberry jam
For the coating:
7 oz. icing sugar
1 oz. cocoa
3 tablespoons boiling water
6 oz. desiccated coconut

Cream the butter and sugar with a few drops vanilla essence. Add the eggs gradually and beat well. Fold in the sifted flour and salt alternately with the milk. Spread the mixture into a greased 8-inch square cake tin and bake for 50—60 minutes in the centre of a moderate oven (375°F. — Gas Mark 4). Cool and store in an airtight tin. Next day slit the cake through the centre and spread with raspberry jam.

Place the two pieces together again and cut the cake into 2-inch squares. Place the icing sugar in a bowl, make a well in the centre and place the cocoa in this. Pour the boiling water slowly on to it. Stir with a wooden spoon, gradually working in the icing sugar. Add more water if necessary. Keep the icing thin by standing it over hot water.

Put the squares of the cake on to the prongs of a fork or a skewer and dip into the chocolate icing. Allow any excess to drip off. Toss in the coconut. Allow to set standing on a cake tray and store in an airtight tin.

Lamingtons

15 Madeleines

Victoria sandwich 1 (Recipe 30) made with 2 eggs, etc., *or* one-stage method (Recipe 67)

To decorate:
4—5 oz. apricot or raspberry jam
approximately 3 oz. desiccated coconut
glacé cherries
angelica, optional

Make the Victoria sandwich as Recipe 30. It is essential that this mixture is not too soft since you do not wish the cakes to rise in a bump at the top. Half fill approximately 18 well-greased dariole (castle pudding) tins and bake towards the top of a hot oven (425—450°F. — Gas Mark 6—7) for about 12 minutes, until firm and golden brown. Take out of tins.

Put the jam either into a saucepan, or better still into a basin over a pan of hot water. Soften and if apricot jam is very lumpy, either sieve or beat out the whole pieces of fruit.

Picture 1

1 Insert a fine skewer or fork into the base of the cakes, and brush round the sides and over the top with the warm, but not too hot, jam. If you have no pastry brush, then spread with a knife.

Picture 2

2 Put the coconut on to a flat plate or paper.
3 Roll the jam-coated cakes in this, pressing the coconut firmly against the sides with a flat-bladed knife.

Picture 3

4 If you intend decorating with glacé cherries and angelica, do not put too much coconut on the top of the cakes. This ensures the cherry and angelica 'sticking'.

1 Brushing madeleines with jam

2 Coating madeleines with coconut

3 Madeleines decorated with cherries and angelica

16 To use icing sugar in decorative ways

Icing sugar from the packet can be used in various ways to make cakes attractive. It is essential that the icing sugar is smooth before dusting the top of the cake.

1 Keep icing sugar in a dry place to prevent lumps forming.

2 When you open the packet, if you intend to use it dry or in an icing where it must be completely free from lumps, either rub through a sieve with a wooden spoon or roll between two sheets of greaseproof paper and then sieve. The picture shows an even coating of icing sugar dusted on top of a Chocolate butter sponge. Because the sponge is a rich one, you can use Recipe 59.

FILL with butter icing flavoured with chocolate. Then —

1 Put approximately 2—3 tablespoons icing sugar into a small sieve or sugar dredger.

2 Shake evenly over the top of the cake.

3 Do this before lifting on to the serving plate since the icing sugar tends to 'fly' a little bit as you shake.

Chocolate sponge dusted with icing sugar

5 oz. plain flour
1 oz. cocoa
½ level teaspoon salt
2 level teaspoons baking powder
5 oz. brown sugar
2 eggs
3½ fluid oz. (5 tablespoons) corn oil
3½ fluid oz. (5 tablespoons) milk
½ teaspoon vanilla essence
For the syrup:
4 oz. sugar
¼ pint water
2 tablespoons rum, or few drops rum essence

17 Tyrolean chocolate gâteau

Grease and line the bottom of two 8—9-inch sandwich tins or one cake tin with greased paper. Sift all dry ingredients together into a mixing bowl. Whisk the egg yolks, corn oil, milk and flavouring together and add to the dry ingredients. Beat well to form a smooth slack batter. Fold in the stiffly beaten egg whites. Turn the mixture into the prepared tin or tins and bake for about 40 minutes in the centre of a moderate oven (375°F. — Gas Mark 4) for one cake, or just above centre for 25 minutes for two cakes. Turn out and leave to get cold.

Boil the sugar and water briskly for 5 minutes. Remove from the heat and stir in the rum. When the cake is cold, return to the tin, pour the hot syrup over and leave overnight.

Dust freely with icing sugar to decorate. To get the trellis design, press the wire grid from the grill pan or a wire cooling tray over top gently, lift up quickly without 'smudging' the lines.

Tyrolean chocolate gâteau

18 Fancy designs with icing sugar

For a more decorative top with icing sugar:
1 Put a fancy doily on top of the cake.
Picture 1
2 Shake sieved icing sugar over the doily.

Picture 2
3 Lift the doily with one definitive upward movement. In this way the design does not become smudged.

1 Sprinkling icing sugar over the doily

2 Removing the doily to show the design

19 Ordinary sugar as a decoration

Castor sugar can be used to decorate cakes in the same way as icing sugar. It can also be put on the cake before baking to give a delicious crisp texture and attractive glaze. It is particularly useful in giving this decorative coating to small sponge fingers or cakes.

20 Sponge fingers

2 large eggs
3 oz. castor sugar
2 oz. flour (with plain flour use ½ teaspoon baking powder)
little extra sugar

Put the eggs and sugar into a basin and whisk until thick and creamy.
Fold in the sieved flour. Either pipe the mixture on to a flat well greased baking tin (using a cloth bag and a large plain éclair pipe) or put into sponge finger tins, which should be well greased and floured.
Shake castor sugar on top of the cakes, and bake for approximately 7 — 10 minutes near the top of a moderately hot oven (400°F. — Gas Mark 5).

Sponge fingers

21 Syrup for decoration

Syrup is also a means of flavouring a cake and giving it a moist, delicious texture.
The Halva cake below is one example of using syrup, but syrup can be used on any type of light sponge or yeast cake, flavouring it with fruit juice, rum or brandy.

22 Halva cake

6 oz. butter or margarine
6 oz. sugar
½ teaspoon almond essence or grated rind of orange
3 eggs
9 oz. fine semolina
3 oz. ground almonds
3 level teaspoons baking powder
1 oz. split, blanched almonds
3 tablespoons brandy or orange juice
For the syrup:
4 oz. sugar
¼ pint water
1 tablespoon lemon juice
2 tablespoons brandy or wine or orange juice

Cream the butter, sugar and essence or orange rind. Beat in the eggs one at a time. Stir in sifted semolina, ground almonds and baking powder, then stir in the almonds and liquid. Turn into a well-buttered 7-inch round or square cake tin. Bake in a moderately hot oven (400°F. — Gas Mark 5) for 1 hour to 1 hour and 10 minutes.
Make syrup by boiling the sugar and water until thickened (or when a little is dropped into cold water, it forms a soft ball between your thumb and forefinger). Remove from the heat and add lemon juice and brandy, wine of fruit juice.
Pour this hot syrup over the hot cake.

Halva cake

23 Jam, jelly or fruit syrup for glazing cakes

A shiny glaze over the top of a cake makes it look most interesting and also produces a very moist texture.
If you are using canned or frozen fruit in the cake or gâteau, you can use the syrup as the basis for your glaze, see Recipe 25.
If, however, you have no fruit syrup, the recipe with jam or jelly is ideal.

24 To make glaze with jam or jelly

3 level tablespoons jam or jelly
½ level teaspoon arrowroot or cornflour
3 tablespoons water
squeeze lemon juice, optional

The best are apricot, raspberry, or pineapple jams, redcurrant, apple or bramble jelly.
Put the jam into a saucepan, blend the arrowroot or cornflour with the water. Add to the jam and cook gently, stirring all the time, until smooth and clear. Put in lemon juice.

25 To make a glaze with fruit syrup

¼ pint sweetened syrup (from canned or cooked fruit)
1 level teaspoon arrowroot or cornflour

Blend the syrup with the arrowroot or cornflour and boil until thick and clear. If necessary, add 1 or 2 drops of colouring.
This gives a fairly thin syrup, ideal for flans, but if you wish it to set flat on a cake, then double the amount of cornflour or arrowroot. To make a more dense glaze, combine this with 1—2 tablespoons of jam.

26 To apply glaze over glacé or other fruits

Arrange the glacé fruits on the top of the cake, and then very carefully brush the glaze over.

27 To apply glaze to a cake

Allow the glaze to become cool, but not set, and brush over with either a palette knife or pastry brush. Continue to do this until all the glaze is used.

28 Soufflé cake

Victoria sandwich 1, 7-inch quantity (Recipe 30)
Filling and moulds on top:
1 oz. sugar
grated rind ¾ lemon
juice ¾ lemon
1 egg yolk
1 teaspoon gelatine
little warm water
4 tablespoons evaporated milk
1 egg white
Topping:
1 tablespoon crystallized ginger
2 level tablespoons crystallized pineapple
1 oz. citron peel
1 oz. chopped peel
For the glaze:
2 level teaspoons arrowroot or cornflour
2 tablespoons lemon *or* orange juice made up to ¼ pint with water
1 tablespoon sugar

Make and bake the sandwich in two tins. Leave to cool.
Whisk the sugar, lemon rind, lemon juice and egg yolk together in a basin until thick. Dissolve the gelatine in the warm water and whisk the evaporated milk and egg white. Add to the lemon mixture. Pour into seven small wetted, fluted moulds, and the remainder into a flat 7-inch wetted cake tin. Chill.
Chop and mix the crystallized fruits and the peel together.
Remove the soufflés from the moulds when set. Place the round of soufflé mixture between the two layers of cake. Arrange the smaller soufflés on top of the cake. Place the crystallized fruit between the soufflé mixtures.
Make the glaze as the fruit syrup glaze in Recipe 25.
Allow to cool and brush or spread over the top of the cake.

Soufflé cake

29 Amounts of jam, jelly, fruit syrup glaze to allow

Top of 6-inch cake	USE recipe with 3 tablespoons jam, etc., *or* ¼ pint syrup. (Gives rather thick layer.)
Top and sides of 6-inch cake	USE 6 tablespoons jam, etc., *or* ½ pint syrup.
Top of 7-inch cake	USE recipe with 3 tablespoons jam, etc., *or* ¼ pint syrup. (Gives rather thin layer.)
Top and sides of 7-inch cake	USE 6 tablespoons jam, etc., *or* ½ pint syrup.
Top of 8-inch cake	USE 4½ tablespoons jam, etc., *or* ¼ pint and 4 tablespoons syrup.
Top and sides of 8-inch cake	USE 9 tablespoons jam, etc., *or* ¾ pint syrup.
Top of 9—10-inch cake	USE 6 level tablespoons jam, etc., *or* ½ pint syrup.
Top and sides of 9—10-inch cake	USE 12 level tablespoons jam, etc., *or* 1 pint syrup.

30 Victoria sandwich 1

To make for:

two 6—7-inch tins or one deeper tin	USE the weight of 2 eggs in flour (with plain flour use 1 level teaspoon baking powder), margarine and sugar.
two 7—8-inch tins or one deeper tin	USE the weight of 3 eggs in flour (with plain flour use 1½ level teaspoons baking powder), margarine and sugar.
two 8—9-inch tins or one deeper tin	USE the weight of 4 eggs in flour (with plain flour use 2 level teaspoons baking powder), margarine and sugar.

To weigh: Put eggs on one side of the scale pan weigh out ingredients with eggs instead of weights. This makes sure a perfect balance. Sieve flour and baking powder together. Cream margarine and sugar until soft and white. Beat eggs thoroughly in a basin. Add a little beaten egg to the creamed mixture; stir carefully. Add a little flour and stir gently. Continue adding egg and flour until thoroughly mixed.
Grease the tin or tins, and put in the mixture. Spread slightly away from the centre so that the sandwich will be flat when cooked. Bake for about 20 minutes in centre of a moderate oven (375—400°F. — Gas Mark 4—5) when using two 6-inch sandwich tins; 25—30 minutes when using two 7—8-inch sandwich tins; 30—35 minutes when using two 8—9-inch sandwich tins. If using one deep tin, bake in centre of very moderate oven (350°F. — Gas Mark 3) for 40 minutes in a 6-inch cake tin; 50 minutes in a 7—8-inch cake tin; 1 hour in an 8—9-inch cake tin. Test by pressing gently but firmly on top, and if no impression is left by your finger, the cake is ready. Turn on a wire tray to cool. If you tap the tins firmly on the table before turning out, it will loosen the sides and bottom of the cake from the tin.
This can be varied by: allowing 1 teaspoon of instant coffee powder to each 2 oz. flour; allowing approximately ½ oz. cocoa and leaving out the same amount of flour in each 4 oz. flour; OR by adding a few drops of flavouring essence. This applies to the two egg quantity. For larger quantities increase in proportion.

31 Decorations that are cooked with the cake

Some decorations can be put on to the cake before it is baked and the most usual examples are, of course, nuts.

Blanched almonds look most attractive when they come out of the oven. They can be put on before baking, see Recipes 32—34.

Candied peel, as on a Madeira cake, should be put on halfway through cooking to avoid scorching, see Recipe 35.

Crumble mixtures, because of their fat content, can be put on to the cake before baking, see Recipe 36.

32 How to apply nuts to a cake before being cooked

1 Blanch the nuts as Recipe 6.
2 Scatter the nuts on top of the cake, as in

Recipe 34 below, or arrange them in a definite shape to form an attractive design.

33 To glaze nuts before baking

Brush a little egg white carefully over the nuts which gives them an attractive shine.

Some people, however, prefer the nuts to look pale, in which case do not use the egg white.

34 Australian sultana cake

8 oz. butter
8 oz. castor sugar
3 eggs
6 oz. self-raising flour and 6 oz. plain flour (or 12 oz. plain flour with 1¼ level teaspoons baking powder)
pinch salt
6 tablespoons milk
few drops lemon essence or juice
8 oz. sultanas
2 oz. candied citrus peel
1 oz. glacé cherries
2 oz. almonds

Cream butter and sugar well, then beat in eggs gradually. Sift the flours and salt together and add to mixture alternately with milk, essence and prepared fruit, chopping peel and cherries. Put mixture into a greased 8-inch tin, lined on the bottom with paper, and sprinkle the almonds on the top. Bake in the centre of

moderate oven (375°F. — Gas Mark 4) for 45 minutes, then reduce to Gas Mark 2 or 300°F. and bake for approximately another 45 minutes — 1 hour. Remove from tin and leave to cool on wire tray.

An outstanding feature of this Australian sultana cake is its good keeping quality.

Australian sultana cake

35 To use peel in decorating a cake

Plain cakes look particularly attractive with citron or other peel on top. This tends to brown if put on the cake for too long a period.

If it is a large cake which needs a lot of baking, place the peel gently on top of the cake halfway through the cooking period.

36 Crumble toppings

Plain or fruit cakes look most attractive if they have a crumble topping. Never exceed the

proportion of fat as the crumble mixture will become greasy in cooking rather than crisp.

37 To make crumble toppings

1 oz. butter or margarine
2 oz. flour
2 oz. sugar

Rub the margarine into the flour, add the sugar.
Crumble toppings mag be varied as follows:

1 Add ½—1 oz. chopped nuts
2 Add 1 oz. desiccated coconut
3 Add ½—1 teaspoon mixed spice

38 Amounts of crumble topping to allow

Top of 6-inch cake	USE 1 oz. butter, 2 oz. flour, 2 oz. sugar. This gives rather thick layer.
Top of 7-inch cake	USE 1 oz. butter, 2 oz. flour, 2 oz. sugar. This gives fairly thin layer.
Top of 8-inch cake	USE 1½ oz. butter, 3 oz. flour, 3 oz. sugar.
Top of 9-inch cake	USE 2 oz. butter, 4 oz. flour, 4 oz. sugar.

39 How to apply crumble toppings to cakes

Picture 1
Press the crumble gently on top of the cake mixture with a metal spoon.

Picture 2
Be careful how you take the cake out of the tin as the crumble is inclined to be in loose crumbs.

1 Putting crumble topping on cake

2 Cake with crumble topping

40 Meringue toppings on cakes

A meringue mixture gives a very attractive appearance to a cake as well as a special crispness. There is a chapter, beginning at Recipe 406, dealing with meringues, which includes using meringue as a case to be filled.

41 Marshmallow toppings on cakes

Marshmallows give a very attractive look to a cake and they can be varied by toasting, or using white and pink together.

There is a section in this book dealing with marshmallow decorations, see Recipes 241 and 242.

42 Marshmallows

Marshmallows can also be used without extra treatment for a most beautifully simple and yet very effective cake decoration.
Shown *in colour plate 2* are two party cakes:

1 The Happiness tree cake, Recipe 43.
2 Christmas pudding cake, Recipe 44.
These are examples of cakes entirely decorated by marshmallows.

43 Happiness tree cake

Victoria sandwich 1 or 2
(Recipe 30 or 59) made with 2 eggs, etc.
butter icing (Recipe 100) made with 2 oz. butter, 1 tablespoon lemon juice, 8 oz. sieved icing sugar
marshmallow frosting made with 2 oz. white marshmallows, 1 tablespoon milk, 1 egg white, ½ oz. castor sugar
18 pink, 18 white marshmallows, silver glitter dust
thin branch, glue
Christmas ornaments

Make the Victoria sandwich and place in a well-greased, 1-pint heatproof glass or metal measure. Bake in the centre of a very moderate oven (350°F. — Gas Mark 3) for 45—50 minutes. When cold, cover sides of cake with butter icing.
To make marshmallow frosting melt the marshmallows in the milk. Remove from heat and leave to cool. Whisk egg white till fluffy, add sugar then whisk till mixture is shiny and stands in stiff peaks. Fold into the marshmallow mixture and leave to stand for 20—30 minutes. Fill the middle of the 'pot' with the frosting. Press alternate rings of halved pink and white marshmallows into the butter icing.
Sprinkle silver glitter dust on to a small tree branch brushed with glue.
Leave to dry, then stand branch in the middle of the 'pot'. Put a little frosting on the twigs to represent snow and hang with Christmas ornaments at intervals.
Illustrated in colour plate 2

44 Christmas pudding cake

Victoria sandwich 1 or 2
(Recipes 30 or 59) made with 4 eggs, etc.
butter cream (Recipe 100) made with 2 oz. butter, 1 tablespoon lemon juice, 8 oz. sieved icing sugar
To decorate:
approximately 50 dessert marshmallows (10 oz.)
sprig of mistletoe or holly

Make the Victoria sandwich and bake in a well-greased 2½-pint pudding basin in the centre of a very moderate oven (350°F. — Gas Mark 3) for 1½ hours.

When cold, spread with the butter cream and cover with halved marshmallows. Decorate with a sprig of mistletoe or holly.
Illustrated in colour plate 2

39—44 Cakes without icing

45 Different colourings in cooking

By flavouring and colouring the actual cake or biscuit ingredients, you produce a very pleasant harlequin or marbled effect, which often means you need little icing or decoration after.

Examples of this are the Pineapple chocolate sundae cake, Recipe 125, the Battenburg cake, Recipe 321, and the Coffee pinwheels, Recipe 405.

46 Cherries for decoration

In the same way that nuts can be applied to a cake before cooking, so glacé cherries or other glacé fruit can be placed on top. Since they are very heavy, they must be put on to a moderately firm textured cake. In a very light sponge they would sink into the mixture during cooking. If you wish to decorate a light sponge with cherries, therefore, it should be done after cooking or when the cake is three-quarters cooked. Care must be taken, to put them on quickly, otherwise it could cause the cake to sink in the middle.

Maraschino cherries may be used to decorate a cake *after* baking — not before.

47 Cheese cake

4 oz. crushed cornflakes, or cornflake crumbs or crushed digestive biscuits
2 oz. castor sugar
1 rounded teaspoon cinnamon
2 oz. butter
For the filling:
1 lb. cream cheese
2 eggs
4 oz. castor sugar
juice ½ lemon
½ pint sour cream
1 teaspoon vanilla essence
To decorate:
maraschino cherries

Place the crushed cornflakes into a mixing bowl, add sugar and cinnamon and rub in butter. Press into bottom of an 8-inch loose-bottomed cake tin; keep some for decoration. To make the filling, beat the cheese until soft and smooth. Whisk eggs and 3 oz. sugar together until thick, and add to the cheese with lemon juice. Pour into tin. Bake in a moderately hot oven (400°F. — Gas Mark 5) for 30 minutes. Mix sour cream, vanilla essence and remaining 1 oz. sugar together and pour over the top. Return to a very hot oven (475—500°F. — Gas Mark 8—9) for 10 minutes. Cool; refrigerate. Remove 1 hour before serving, take out of tin. Decorate the top and sides with remaining corn-flake mixture. Place rows of cherries across.

Cheese cake

48 Pastry as a decoration

Pastry can be used in decorating, an example being the Hot cross buns below. If making pastry and cakes on the same day, use a lattice design of pastry over a fruit cake.

49 Hot cross buns

1 lb. plain flour
pinch salt
½ oz. yeast
2 oz. castor sugar
½ pint lukewarm milk and water
1 level teaspoon cinnamon
1 level teaspoon nutmeg
3 oz. currants
1 oz. chopped candied peel
2 oz. butter
1 egg
2 oz. short crust pastry made with 2 oz. flour, 1 oz. fat, little water

Sieve half the flour into a mixing bowl with the salt. Cream the yeast with a teaspoon of the sugar and stir in the lukewarm milk and water. Pour into the sieved flour and mix well together. Cover with a clean damp cloth and put in a warm place to 'sponge' for 40 minutes. Sieve the remaining flour and sugar with the cinnamon and nutmeg. Stir in the currants and chopped peel. Melt the butter and beat the egg. Add the dry ingredients to the sponged mixture, pour in the melted butter and beaten egg and mix thoroughly with your hand. Cover again with a damp cloth and put in a warm place to rise for 1—1¼ hours. Turn the dough on to a floured board and cut into sixteen pieces. Shape each piece into a round bun. Place on a well greased and floured baking sheet, allowing room for the buns to spread. Make the pastry. Roll out and cut into narrow strips about 2 inches long. Place a cross of pastry on top of the buns and put in a warm place to prove for about 40 minutes. Bake for 15—20 minutes in a hot oven (450°F. — Gas Mark 7). Five minutes before removing from oven, brush over with a little milk and sugar to glaze.

Hot cross buns

50 To glaze pastry

Pastry used as a cake is often given an attractive shine in the following ways:
1 Lightly beaten egg white is brushed on before baking.

2 A very little milk or water is brushed on the top of the pastry and icing sugar lightly dusted on the top before baking. Do not make the pastry too wet.

Glacé Icing

51 The purpose of glacé or water icing

The main purpose of glacé or water icing is to give a quickly made, smooth coating over cakes.

52 Glacé or water icing

You will find in some recipes that the water for glacé icing is heated. This gives a rather shinier and better appearance to the icing and is to be recommended where you wish to keep the cake a day or two since the shine is inclined to last longer. The amount of water given below is only approximate.

If you are covering a very soft delicate cake, it is better to have the icing slightly softer.
If you wish to make absolutely certain that you get a very neat edge on the icing without it running down the sides of the cake, it is better to make it as stiff as possible and spread with a damp palette knife.

53 Glacé icing

8 oz. icing sugar
approximately 1½ dessertspoons warm water

1 Sieve the icing sugar if it is lumpy, or roll between greaseproof paper.

2 Add the water gradually, or mix in saucepan and gently heat for 1 minute.

54 Advantages of glacé icing

The chief advantage of glacé icing is that it is so easy and quick to make. It is also economical in that you use only a small amount of icing to cover the top of a cake.
It never becomes hard like royal icing.
It can be flavoured and varied a great deal.

The flavourings, Recipe 56, give you an example of how to incorporate different ingredients into the icing, but you can experiment with mixing chocolate and orange; blending the icing sugar with syrup from canned fruit, etc.

55 Disadvantages of glacé icing

The chief disadvantage of glacé icing is that it will not keep indefinitely without cracking, so should never be used on cakes like wedding cakes that are to be kept for a long period. It has very limited use for piping, being suitable only for writing or drawing lines.

56 Flavourings for glacé icing

Almond glacé icing Add a few drops of lemon essence.

Chocolate glacé icing 1 Add 1 good dessertspoon cocoa to the icing and then beat in a knob of butter the size of an acorn, melted.

Chocolate glacé icing 2 You will find it possible to incorporate melted chocolate into glacé icing. On an average use 2 oz. melted chocolate to 8 oz. icing sugar.

Coffee glacé icing Mix with strong coffee instead of water, or with soluble coffee powder, blended with a little warm water.

Lemon glacé icing Mix with lemon juice instead of water.

Mocha glacé icing Add 1 good dessertspoon cocoa to the icing sugar, and use strong coffee instead of water. A small knob of butter, melted, can be added if liked.

Orange glacé icing Mix with orange juice instead of water.

Spiced glacé icing Blend ½ teaspoon mixed spice, ½ teaspoon grated nutmeg and ½ teaspoon cinnamon with the icing sugar.

Vanilla glacé icing Add a few drops of vanilla essence.

57 Amounts of glacé icing to allow

Top of 6-inch cake	USE 4 oz. icing sugar.
Top and sides of 6-inch cake	USE good 8 oz. icing sugar.
Top of 7-inch cake	USE 6 oz. icing sugar.
Top and sides of 7-inch cake	USE good 12 oz. icing sugar.
Top of 8—9-inch cake	USE 8 oz. icing sugar.
Top and sides of 8—9-inch cake	USE 1 lb. icing sugar.
Top of 10—11-inch cake	USE 10—12 oz. icing sugar.
Top and sides of 10—11-inch cake	USE 1¼—1½ lb. icing sugar.

Obviously the depth of the cake determines how much extra icing is needed for the sides.

The quantities above assume the cake to be about 3 inches in depth.

58 Types of cake, etc to coat with glacé icing

Glacé icing is an ideal one to choose for:
Victoria sandwiches or sponge cakes
Genoese pastry

Puff pastry or other pastries
Soft plain cakes, like a Madeira
Biscuits

2 Christmas pudding cake
and Happiness tree cake

3 Iced cherry ring
(See Recipe 66)

4   Child's birthday cake coated with glacé icing   5   Mandarin moka

6   Orange garland cake

59 Victoria sandwich 2 or butter sponge

To make for:

two 6—7-inch tins or one deeper tin	USE 4 oz. flour (with plain flour use 1 level teaspoon baking powder) 4 oz. butter 4 oz. sugar 2 eggs
two 7—8-inch tins or one deeper tin	USE 6 oz. flour (with plain flour use 1½ level teaspoons baking powder) 6 oz. butter 6 oz. sugar 3 eggs
two 8—9-inch tins or one deeper tin	USE 8 oz. flour (with plain flour use 2 level teaspoons baking powder) 8 oz. butter 8 oz. sugar 4 eggs

Sieve the flour, or flour and baking powder. Cream butter and sugar until soft and light. Gradually add the beaten eggs, taking care not to add too quickly otherwise the butter mixture may curdle (separate). If this happens, stir in a little flour. Lastly, fold in the flour with a metal spoon to avoid over-beating. Grease the tin or tins and put in the mixture, spreading slightly away from the centre so that the sandwich will be flat when cooked. Bake for approximately 20 minutes just above centre of a moderate oven (375—400°F. — Gas Mark 4—5) when using two 6—7-inch sandwich tins. For two 7—8-inch sandwich tins, bake for 25—30 minutes. With two 8—9-inch sandwich tins, bake for 30—35 minutes. If using one deep tin, bake in centre of a very moderate oven (350°F. — Gas Mark 3) for 40 minutes for a 6-inch cake tin; 50 minutes for a 7—8-inch cake tin; and 1 hour for a 8—9-inch cake tin. Test by pressing gently but firmly on top, and if no impression is left by your finger the cake is ready. Turn on to a wire tray to cool. To loosen the cake from the sides and bottom of the tin, tap firmly on the table.

This can be varied by: allowing 1 teaspoon of instant coffee powder to each 2 oz. flour; allowing approximately ½ oz. cocoa and leaving out the same amount of flour in each 4 oz.; or by adding a few drops of flavouring essence. This applies to the two-egg quantity. For larger quantities increase in proportion.

Victoria sandwich 2 or butter sponge

60 How to prepare cakes or biscuits for glacé icing

Icing looks much more professional if it is absolutely smooth and clear with no crumbs from the cake or biscuit, so before icing brush away all loose crumbs from the top, or top and sides, of the cake or biscuit with a fairly stiff dry pastry brush. If you want to obtain a truly professional coating, you should brush the pastry or cake with a little egg white. Allow this to dry and then ice. This forms a barrier between the cake and the icing.

61 How to apply glacé icing to cakes

You will find more detailed information on the application of glacé icing under the various headings, but generally speaking it is better to put the amount of icing needed to cover or coat a cake on at one time, then spread. If you put a spoonful of icing on and spread this, then add another spoonful and spread again, lines may form where the icing hardens. *Colour plate 4* shows glacé icing (of the right consistency to coat a Genoese cake, see Recipes 53 and 134) covering a child's birthday cake. It will be used as Recipe 62.

62   To coat large cakes with glacé icing

1 Pour the required amount of icing for the size of cake into the centre. Do not smooth it until you have all the icing from the basin or the saucepan.
2 Have beside you a jug of warm water and a palette knife.
3 Allow the icing to trickle down the sides of the cake. You will often find that the icing, with very little help, coats the whole cake quite easily.
4 Dip the palette knife in the warm water, shake fairly dry, and then use it to spread the icing evenly over the top and sides.
5 For greater details as to neatening sides,

see under royal icing, Recipe 271. You will, however, find glacé icing much easier to handle.
6 Spread very gently so that you do not pick up any crumbs from the cake.
7 For a very good professional coating, it is better to do two thin layers rather than one thick one, allowing the under-coating to dry thoroughly first.
Picture 1 below, shows glacé icing, made with coffee essence, being poured into the centre of the cake.
In picture 2 it has been allowed to trickle down the sides ready for neatening. *Colour plate 4* shows a birthday cake coated in glacé icing.

1 Pouring glacé icing over a large cake

2 Spreading glacé icing with a palette knife

63   To coat small cakes with glacé icing

To coat small cakes with a circle of icing in the centre, see Recipe 73.
To coat just the top of small cakes, work as pictured for the large cake, Recipe 65.
If you want to make a selection of tiny cakes from a slab sponge, which are to be iced only on the top, it is best to coat the whole of the top of the sponge with icing, allow this to set and then cut into shapes afterwards with a warm knife, which does not damage the icing.
If you are coating cup cakes, as described in Recipe 76, you simply pour in spoonfuls of very soft icing which needs no spreading since the paper cases support this.
You may want to coat both the top and sides of little cakes with icing.

The picture with Recipe 221 shows how small cakes are coated with fondant icing; exactly the same technique is used for glacé icing.
1 Put a tray or large dish under the cooling tray to catch any drips.
2 Put the neatly cut shapes of cake on to the cooling tray.
3 Make sure the icing (whatever type is being used) is soft enough to pour.
4 Pour over the cakes, if necessary just helping the icing down the sides with a spoon.
5 Leave until set; remember, though, you can gather up icing from the tray to use again.
6 You may need to put a knife round the base of the little cakes and cut away any untidy surplus of icing.

64   To coat petit fours with glacé icing

Petit fours or very tiny fancy cakes are easier to coat with glacé icing by dipping, rather than pouring the icing over them.
1 Insert a fine skewer or fork into the cakes.
2 Dip them extremely gently into the very soft glacé icing.
3 Stand on wire cooling trays with a large tray or dish underneath so that the surplus icing can be picked up and used again.
For more elaborate designs, i.e. if you have a roll of marzipan on top, or butter icing, to give an attractive shape, you must coat with icing which should be very soft in texture.

Coating petits fours with glacé icing

65 To obtain neat top edges on a cake with glacé icing

Picture 1: Method 1

1 Tie or pin a strong band of greaseproof paper round the sides of the cake. Make sure it is very tight and very firm. Check also that it is a perfect shape. You will find this easier if you use several thicknesses of the greaseproof paper.

2 Make the icing, put on to the top of the cake and spread with a palette knife.

3 Allow to set and harden.

4 Unpin or untie the paper.

5 Work very slowly and carefully and with the help of a knife ease the paper away from the icing edge. Do not do this too roughly otherwise you pull off some of the icing with the paper and spoil the finish.

Picture 2: Method 2

1 Make the icing reasonably stiff.

2 Put on top of the cake, then spread towards the edges with a warmed palette knife.

3 When the top of the cake is covered and the icing is just beginning to stiffen very slightly, take the edge of the knife round the cake, removing any surplus icing. Do this before the icing hardens, otherwise you will crack glacé icing.

1 First method of obtaining neat edges on top of a cake with glacé icing

2 Second method of obtaining neat edges on top of a cake with glacé icing

66 To apply decorations to a cake

Glacé cherries or other decorations, see *colour plate 3*, should be put on to the cake when the icing is beginning to stiffen. If you wait until the icing is quite hard, the decorations will not adhere properly.

If you put these on when the icing is very soft, they will slip out of position.

The picture below shows how a great variety of decorations can be achieved by very simple methods. They are as follows:

1 Leaves of angelica, see Recipe 126 for cutting leaves.

2 Glacé cherries.

3 Chocolate drops cut into shapes, see Recipe 188.

4 Tiny mimosa balls.

5 A very small amount of melted chocolate (this could be achieved by melting a few chocolate drops) put into the centre of the cake with a skewer.

These particular cup cakes are made by the speedy one-stage method suitable for modern quick-creaming margarine and fats. For details of this see Recipe 67.

67 One-stage cup cakes

4 oz. self-raising flour
½ level teaspoon baking powder
4 oz. luxury or softened margarine
4 oz. castor sugar
2 eggs
grated rind of 1 orange or lemon
icing (Recipe 53)
  made with 8 oz. icing sugar, 3 tablespoons orange *or* lemon juice
To decorate as Recipe 66:
mimosa balls
chocolate buttons
angelica 'leaves'
halved glacé cherries

Sieve the baking powder and flour, then put all the ingredients into a mixing bowl and beat with a wooden spoon until well mixed, taking 2—3 minutes. Place heaped teaspoons of the mixture in paper cases.

Bake just about centre of a moderately hot oven (400°F. — Gas Mark 5) for 15—20 minutes. Allow to cool.

Make the icing and put on top of the cup cakes, see Recipe 63.

Decorate as suggested in Recipe 66.

Decorated cup cakes

68 To coat biscuits with glacé icing

It is very important that glacé icing is fairly firm when using to coat biscuits.

If it is too soft, it softens the crisp texture of the biscuit.

1 Arrange the biscuits on a wire cooling tray.

2 Spread or pour the glacé icing over the biscuits.

3 Any surplus icing drips through the cooling tray and can be caught on a plate or flat, clean tray underneath.

69 Black and white Easter bunnies

4 oz. butter
4 oz. castor sugar
1 egg
8 oz. plain flour
1½ oz. preserved stem ginger, chopped
To decorate:
4 oz. icing sugar
1 dessertspoon ginger syrup from jar preserved ginger
water to mix
6 oz. plain chocolate

Cream the butter and sugar together. Beat in the egg, and stir in the flour and then the chopped ginger. Mix well together and turn on to a floured board. Roll out ¼ inch thick, cut out with a rabbit cutter. Place on greased trays and bake until golden brown in a very moderate oven (350°F. — Gas Mark 3) for approximately 15 minutes. Cool on a wire tray. This quantity will make 3 dozen biscuits.

Make icing by mixing icing sugar with ginger syrup and hot water to a thick coating consistency that will coat a wooden spoon smoothly without running off. Break the chocolate and melt in a bowl over hot, but not boiling, water.

When the bunnies are cold, coat half the biscuits with white icing and the other half with the melted chocolate. To prevent the chocolate bunnies from sticking, place on greaseproof paper while the chocolate sets. Make eyes by cutting small triangles of ginger and stick them on the bunnies before the icing or chocolate has set. When the icing and chocolate is quite set, the bunnies' tails may be piped or spooned on. Give the white bunnies chocolate tails and the black bunnies white tails.
See Recipe 72 for illustration.
Note: If you do not like ginger, use sultanas instead and blend icing sugar with all water.

70 Glacé icing for a trickle effect

Many cakes, the Easter tea ring and Orange garland cake below being two examples, look their most decorative if they have a casual trickle of icing down the sides rather than an even coating.

To achieve this:
1 Put all the icing on the top of the cake.
2 Allow it to trickle down the sides.
3 If it runs a little unevenly, shake the cake slightly to encourage a more uniform trickle.

71 Orange garland cake

8 oz. flour (with plain flour use 2 level teaspoons baking powder)
6 oz. butter
6 oz. castor sugar
2 rounded teaspoons grated orange rind
3 eggs
1 oz. candied peel
2 oz. chopped walnuts
1 tablespoon orange juice
To decorate:
glacé icing (Recipe 53) made with 8 oz. icing sugar, 3—4 dessertspoons orange juice
2—3 oz. mixed shelled nuts *
sugar syrup, made with 2 oz. sugar, 1 tablespoon water
* *Halved walnuts, cashew nuts, blanched almonds, unskinned hazelnuts.*

Sift flour. Cream butter, sugar and orange rind until fluffy. Beat in eggs, one at a time, adding a tablespoon of flour mixture with each. Stir in peel, walnuts and orange juice, then add flour. Turn into a greased and paper-lined 7-inch cake tin. Bake in the centre of a very moderate oven (350°F. — Gas Mark 3) for 1¼ hours. Cool on a wire tray.
Blend icing sugar with enough orange juice to give pouring consistency. Pour icing over the top of the cake and let it trickle down the sides. When set, lift on to a serving plate and decorate the top of the cake with a garland of glazed nuts.
To glaze nuts: Arrange on flat dish and brush with the hot sugar and water syrup made by boiling sugar and water for 1—2 minutes.
Illustrated in colour plate 6

Orange garland cake

72 Easter tea ring

8 oz. flour (with plain flour use 2 level teaspoons baking powder)
4 oz. butter
3 oz. castor sugar
2 eggs
2 tablespoons milk
4 tablespoons canned mincemeat
To decorate:
5 oz. icing sugar
hot water
1 oz. sliced roasted almonds
glacé cherries
angelica

Grease an 8-inch ring tin. Sift the flour and baking powder together in a bowl. Rub in butter until like fine breadcrumbs. Add the sugar and stir in beaten eggs, milk and mincemeat. Turn the mixture into the prepared tin and bake in the centre of a moderate oven (375°F. — Gas Mark 4) for 50 minutes until well risen and golden brown. Turn out and cool on a wire tray.

Make a glacé icing with the icing sugar and sufficient hot water to give a thick coating consistency. Pour over the tea ring and allow to run down the sides and decorate with almonds, cherries and angelica.

Easter bunnies and Easter tea ring

73 To produce neat circles of icing on cakes

The Holly buns below are iced in such a way that you get the pleasant contrast of the lightness of the icing and darkness of the cakes. These would not have been nearly so effective if completely coated.

Method 1
1 Make the icing as soft as possible.
2 Put a teaspoonful in the centre of the cakes.
3 Spread with a small warmed knife.
Method 2 (A rather slow one)
1 Put a very tiny plain pastry cutter on top of the little cake.
2 Pour in the glacé icing.
3 Allow it to harden, then lift up the cutter.

74 Holly buns

1 egg
1 oz. castor sugar
1 dessertspoon cocoa
1 oz. flour (with plain flour use ¼ teaspoon baking powder)
1 oz. melted butter or margarine
To decorate:
glacé icing, *vanilla or lemon,* (Recipes 53 and 56) made with 4 oz. icing sugar, etc.
imitation holly leaves and berries

Whisk egg and sugar until firm. Sieve together the cocoa and flour. Fold into mixture. Pour in the melted butter or margarine and fold in *very* lightly. Pour into twelve paper cake cases. Bake in a moderately hot oven (400°F. — Gas Mark 5) for about 10 minutes. Cool on a wire tray.

When cold, decorate with vanilla or lemon glacé icing and the imitation holly leaves and berries. These may be made of marzipan if liked, see Recipe 256, and for this you will need marzipan made with 2 oz. of ground almonds, etc., and a few drops of green and red colouring.

Holly buns

75   To make cup cakes

You can use the following recipes for making cup cakes:
Holly buns — Recipe 74.
Victoria sandwich 1 or 2 — Recipes 30 or 59.
Genoese pastry — Recipe 134.

One-stage cakes — Recipe 67.
Make sure that you only half-fill the paper cases. The cake mixture will rise, but even so it will give you quite a depth of paper to support the icing.

76   To ice cup cakes

As you will see in the picture for Chocolate party cup cakes, Recipe 147, and the Assorted cup cakes, Recipe 67, the basic cakes have a very smooth icing that spreads right to the paper case. This icing should be fairly thick. Make the icing of flowing consistency and pour enough over the cooled cakes to come to the very top of the paper cases.

77   To coat pastry with glacé icing

One very often decorates the top of Vanilla slices with glacé icing. If you are baking the puff pastry in one complete block, then cutting into slices afterwards, it is better to split the pastry through the centre, put in the filling, then cover the whole of the top with icing. Puff pastry is so light and fragile it is likely to crumble, so use rather runny icing. Allow the icing to set, then cut the pastry in fingers with a sharp knife, dipped in hot water, and shaken fairly dry.

The picture shows the filled puff pastry slice completely coated over the top with soft glacé icing. Any design you wish to pipe (and on top of this is a line design in a contrasting colour — for details of drawing lines, etc., see Recipe 87) is piped on to the firmly set icing base so that it does not run. Allow any decorations to set (these are not essential) and then cut as described above.

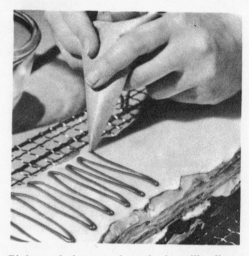

Piping a design on a large iced vanilla slice

78   Puff pastry

8 oz. plain flour
good pinch salt
cold water to mix
few drops lemon juice
7 — 8 oz. fat (more margarine than cooking fat, or all butter)

Sieve flour and salt together. Mix to a rolling consistency with cold water and lemon juice. Roll to oblong shape. Make fat into neat block and place in centre of pastry and fold over it first the bottom section of pastry, and then the top section, so that the fat is quite covered. Turn the dough at right angles, seal edges and carefully 'rib' (i.e. depress it with the rolling pin at intervals, so giving a corrugated effect and equalizing the pressure of air to make certain that the pastry will rise evenly). Roll out. Fold dough into envelope, turn it, seal edges, 'rib' and roll again. Repeat 5 times so making 7 rollings and 7 foldings in all. It will be necessary to put the pastry to rest in a cold place once or twice between rollings to prevent it becoming sticky and soft. Always put to rest before finally rolling and before baking.

79   Vanilla slices (mille-feuilles)

8 oz. *puff pastry* (see above)
cream or confectioner's custard (see below)
glacé icing
jam
chopped nuts

The puff pastry can either be cut into fingers or baked whole as one cake. If baking as a whole cake, put the two rounds of pastry, each about ½-inch thick, into the centre of a very hot oven (475°F. — Gas Mark 8) for a good 10 minutes, then lower to moderately hot (400°F. — Gas Mark 5) and cook until firm and pale brown in colour. Let the pastry get quite cold, then sandwich the two layers together with jam and sweetened cream. Coat sides with more cream; cover with chopped nuts. Cover top with icing and nuts. For individual slices, cut into fingers and bake for 13 minutes. Decorate with cream, icing and nuts.

80   Confectioner's custard (vanilla cream)

Method 1
1 level tablespoon cornflour
¼ pint milk
1 — 2 teaspoons sugar
vanilla essence
2 egg yolks
4 tablespoons whipped cream
Method 2
2 egg yolks
2 tablespoons castor sugar
1 tablespoon cornflour
½ pint milk
1 vanilla pod

Method 1
Blend the cornflour with the milk. Put into saucepan with sugar and vanilla essence and gradually bring to the boil, stirring all the time. Cook until mixture is very thick. Take off the heat and cool slightly. Add the egg yolks and return to the heat for a few minutes, without allowing mixture to boil.
When the mixture is a little cooler, add the whipped cream.

Method 2
Whisk together the egg yolks, sugar and cornflour, then add a little warm milk. Boil remainder of milk with vanilla pod. Remove the pod. Gradually add egg and sugar mixture to boiled milk and then return to heat, warming gradually until the mixture cooks and thickens.
This cream should be thick enough to spread over a cake.

81 More elaborate uses of glacé icing

Although as stated under Recipe 55 glacé icing is not a good one to put on cakes that will be kept for a prolonged period, you can use it in very imaginative ways.

82 Wattle ring

4 oz. butter
4 oz. castor sugar
grated rind 1 lemon
2 eggs
3 oz. cornflour
4 oz. flour (with plain flour use 1 level teaspoon baking powder)
To decorate:
lemon glacé icing (Recipes 53 and 56) made with 1 lb. icing sugar
crystallized or preserved ginger
mimosa balls
angelica

Beat butter and sugar to a cream with the lemon rind. Add the eggs gradually, beating well. Sift in cornflour and beat thoroughly for 5 minutes. Lightly fold in sifted flour. Bake in a greased 8—9-inch border mould or ring tin in the centre of a moderate oven (350—357°F.

— Gas Mark 3—4) for 45 minutes — 1 hour. When cold, ice with the lemon glacé icing, and decorate with a ring of sliced crystallized ginger and a delicate design of wattle sprays using mimosa balls, or pieces of crystallized pineapple, and angelica.

Wattle ring

83 Pineapple 'jiffy' cake

6 oz. plain flour
2 slightly rounded teaspoons baking powder
4 oz. castor sugar
2 oz. melted margarine
1 beaten egg
1 teaspoon vanilla essence
¼ pint milk
For the icing and decoration:
12 oz. sieved icing sugar
3 tablespoons warmed pineapple juice, taken from a can of pineapple chunks
few drops lemon juice
few drops yellow colouring

Sieve the flour and baking powder together in a bowl and add the sugar. Mix together the margarine, egg, vanilla essence and milk. Slowly add this to the dry ingredients and then beat thoroughly for 2 minutes for a smooth batter. Grease and line a 9-inch sandwich tin or an 8-inch square tin. Pour the batter mixture into the tin and bake for 35 minutes in the centre of a moderate oven (375°F. — Gas Mark 4). Remove from tin and cool on a wire rack. Beat the icing sugar, pineapple and lemon juice together until the icing becomes smooth and glossy and coats

the back of the spoon. Mark a line across the centre of the cake and place a narrow strip of foil or greaseproof paper across this line. This will prevent the icing from spreading.
Pour half the icing over one half of the cake, allowing it to coat the side. Add the colouring to the rest of the glacé icing, remove the strip of paper and spread this icing on the other half of the cake.
Decorate with chopped pineapple, as shown in the picture, just as the icing begins to set. Serve the remaining pineapple chunks with the cake as dessert, or the cake alone for tea.

Pineapple 'jiffy' cake

84 To use glacé icing with other forms of decoration

Glacé icing is a very good partner to cream, and in particular to butter or similar icings.

The following recipes give an idea as to its very limited use for piping.

85 Simple piping with glacé icing

Do not attempt to pipe rosettes, stars, etc., with glacé icing. No matter how stiff a texture you make the icing, you will find it will collapse after a short time.

You must, therefore, use it just for simple line designs. Do not make the icing too runny,

otherwise it will be extremely difficult to control the flow as it comes from the pipe. Test by picking some up on the edge of a knife or a spoon, and it should flow very slowly. If it runs very easily, then put in a little more sieved icing sugar.

86 Valentine cake

Victoria sandwich 1 (Recipe 30) using 2 eggs, etc., and flavouring with a few drops vanilla essence *or* grated rind of ½ lemon
For the butter icing:
4 oz. butter or margarine (preferably unsalted)
6 oz. sieved icing sugar
few drops of rose water *or* raspberry flavouring
cochineal
For the glacé icing:
2 oz. icing sugar
squeeze of lemon juice
1 dessertspoon water
To decorate:
sugar forget-me-nots
silver balls
cupid

Grease and line a 6 × 7-inch heart-shaped tin. Make the Victoria sandwich mixture and put into the tin, hollowing out from the centre towards the sides so that the cake will rise evenly. Bake for 45 minutes in the centre of a very moderate oven (350°F. — Gas Mark 3). Prepare butter cream by beating the butter or margarine until soft, adding the sugar by degrees, then beating thoroughly. Stir in the flavouring and a few drops of cochineal. Beat well until icing is evenly coloured. Spread it over the sides and top of the cold cake. Smooth top and 'dab' sides with tip of a table knife, see Recipe 115 for further information on this. Make glacé icing by placing icing sugar, lemon juice and the water in a small saucepan. The icing should coat the back of a wooden spoon thickly. Beat well, adding a little colouring, if liked. Stir over gentle heat for 1 minute. Put icing into syringe, nylon or paper icing bag, see Recipes 274—278, fitted with a No. 1 or 2 writing pipe and write 'February 14th'. Arrange flowers and silver balls alternately around the edge and put cupid in place.

Valentine cake

87 To make lines and words lines with glacé icing

To pipe lines
You will need writing pipe No. 1, 2 or 3.
No. 1 is a very fine pipe and on a large cake could look insignificant.
No. 2 is a good medium-sized pipe for writing.
No. 3 is rather heavy for other than a very large cake.
Insert the pipe into the bag or syringe, see Recipes 274—278. Hold this at the angle one would hold a pencil or a pen. If you are good at drawing, draw the lines with the icing on the cake. If you are not good at drawing and feel you have not a sufficiently straight eye, just scratch the straight lines (with the help of a ruler) with a fine knitting needle or an ordinary needle.

To write words
Exactly the same procedure will be followed. Recipe 284 shows how comparatively simple it is to pipe a greeting in writing when the letters have first been either lightly sketched with a soft pencil or pricked out with a needle.
To form lines without a pipe
It is possible to use the base of a greaseproof paper bag for forming lines without using the pipe.
Make the bag as instructed in Recipe 275.
With a sharp pair of scissors cut a very little from the tip of the bag. It is surprising how large a hole can be made, so cut carefully.
Fill with the icing and trace the lines or writing as described above.

88 To pipe flower petals in glacé icing

Put a small amount of glacé icing into the bag or syringe.
Fit the writing pipe in as shown in Recipes 274—278. Draw one curved line starting from a small sweet, which is to be the centre of the flower. Without lifting the pipe away from the cake, guide it back to the starting point. Pick up the pipe sharply so that you break the icing trail. Take care not to hold it over

the cake before starting the second petal. If you are good at drawing, you will be able to make these simple flowers in a freehand design (see sketch opposite). If, however, you find difficulty in drawing use the technique suggested under piping with royal icing, Recipe 282, and sketch or prick out the petals with a very fine needle or pin before you attempt to pipe.

89   To pipe a broken line design in glacé icing

As you will see on the Daisy chain cake, a broken line design can look most effective and this is a very suitable use for glacé icing. As with the petals, you can prick or sketch the design first. Hold the pipe very near the cake to get a flowing movement of the icing. Lift up very sharply to obtain the complete break in between the lines.

90   Daisy chain cake

Victoria sandwich 2 (Recipe 59) using 4 eggs, etc.
4 tablespoons jam
To decorate:
1¾ lb. sieved icing sugar
1 teaspoon lemon juice
7 tablespoons warm water
pink colouring
green colouring
8 very small round sweets, *or* small round cake decorations for daisy centres

Grease a 9-inch cake tin and line it with greaseproof paper. Make the Victoria sandwich and put the mixture into the prepared tin. Bake for about 1 hour in the centre of a very moderate oven (350°F. — Gas Mark 3).
Split the cake through the centre and sandwich together with the jam, and place on a cooling tray preparatory to icing.
Put the sugar into a saucepan, add lemon juice and sufficient warm water to mix to a coating consistency. Beat well, stirring over gentle heat for one minute. Pour the icing over the cake, reserving about 4 tablespoons for the piping decoration.

Colour one half of the remaining icing pink, and the other half green, see Recipe 91 below, adding a little icing sugar to make the icing stiff enough to stand up in points.
Place sweets at regular intervals round the top of the cake about 1 inch from the edge. Using the pink icing in a small paper icing bag fitted with a No. 1 writing pipe, pipe petals round the daisy centres, see Recipe 88. With the same pipe and a clean bag and the green icing, pipe a broken line between the daisies to form the 'chain', see Recipe 89. For a luxurious look, tie a band of satin ribbon round the sides of the cake.

To pipe flower petals in glacé icing

Daisy chain cake

91   To add colourings to icings

Except in very exceptional circumstances, icing colourings should be pale and delicate.
It is very easy to *over*-colour the icing. If this is done, the only way to lighten it is to add more icing sugar and water, or egg whites or fat, depending on the type of icing. This is wasteful and can be avoided as follows.
Put the point of a fine skewer into the bottle of colouring. Bring out the skewer and you will probably find two or three drops only of the particular colouring required adhering to the metal. If you feel you have too much, then return some to the bottle. When you have one or two drops only on the skewer, shake this into the icing. Beat in thoroughly and then add more until the desired tint is obtained.

92   Choice of colourings

For PALE PINK	Use cochineal.
For YELLOW	Use saffron yellow.
For ORANGE	Use either a true orange colouring or a mixture of saffron yellow and cochineal.
For a real RED	Ask for red colouring NOT cochineal. If you cannot buy it, you must then get your red by using a lot of cochineal and then taking out the purpley red this gives by adding a few drops of saffron yellow.
For GREEN	Use a mixture of blue and yellow. Most people have apple green (a very pale delicate green) or sap green (a darker yellow-green).
For BLUE	Use blue colouring, not easily obtainable.
For PURPLE	Use red and blue mixed.
For BROWN	Use either coffee essence, powdered coffee, chocolate or cocoa.

3 eggs
3 oz. castor sugar
2 oz. flour (with plain flour use ½ level teaspoon baking powder)
1 tablespoon cocoa
For the glacé icing (Recipe 53)
about 8 oz. icing sugar
water to mix (approximately 2 tablespoons)
1 teaspoons cocoa

93 Musical valentines

Grease and flour some small heart-shaped cake tins. Whisk the eggs and sugar until thick, light and fluffy. Carefully fold in the sieved flour and cocoa. Pour into the tins. Bake near the top of a hot oven (425°F. — Gas Mark 5) for about 7 minutes.

Picture 1

Add a little water to the icing sugar and beat well. Spread a little on top of each cake, see Recipe 63.

Allow to become firm. Cover rest of icing to prevent skin forming. Blend the cocoa with a little hot water. Beat into the remaining icing, adding a little more icing sugar to keep a good piping consistency.

Pictures 2 and 3

Decorate the cakes by piping lines and notes of music on to the white icing.

Insert a No. 2 — or if you like a very thick line, a No. 3 — writing pipe into a nylon or paper bag, or into the syringe. Fill with chocolate icing. Hold the pipe over the little cakes and pipe straight lines of icing. If you find difficulty in getting a straight line, this should be marked out first with a very fine knife across the nearly hardened white icing. When the icing completely hardens, you will still have a faint line to guide you.

Allow the chocolate lines to harden, but keep the tip of the pipe covered with damp paper or a cloth so the chocolate icing will not become too crisp to use.

When the lines are quite firm, you can then make your musical signs. If you think these are difficult to do, then prick out the design with a fine needle or pin before piping.

1 Spreading the cakes with glacé icing

2 Piping the musical designs with chocolate glacé icing

3 The completed Musical valentines

94 Feathering with glacé icing

Feathering, which is a most attractive design, is admirably suited to glacé icing.

Small biscuits can be feathered and the design of the feathering can be varied in a number of ways.

You can use either a writing pipe or a skewer as can be seen from the pictures opposite.

This is one occasion in decorating when the basic ground work icing should not be allowed to dry. If it should become too dry, you do not get that pleasant soft flowing-together which is a characteristic of good feathering.

95　Step-by-step feather icing

1 Make the glacé icing.

2 Remove part of the icing and either tint, see colouring Recipe 92, or colour and flavour with chocolate, see Recipes 93 or 56.

3 Cover the top of the cake, little cakes or biscuits with the basic groundwork of icing.

Picture 1

4 Insert the coloured icing into the bag or syringe and, using a No. 1 writing pipe, draw lines across the cake, cakes or biscuits. If you do not wish to use a pipe, then dip a fine skewer or knitting needle into the coloured or chocolate icing and, when it is thoroughly coated, draw lines across the cake in just the same way as they are piped. This is not a difficult procedure.

Picture 2

5 Take a clean skewer or knitting needle and drag the coloured icing across the cake.

Continue doing this until you have a simple feather design over the cake.

If you wish the feathering to flow all one way, work as shown in this picture, where you see the lines being drawn across in the same direction.

Picture 3

6 A very attractive effect is created if instead of pulling all the lines to the left or to the right, the first lines are pulled to the left and then the other lines to the right.

Picture 4

This shows finished cake completely feathered.

1　Piping lines in coloured icing across iced cake

2　Drawing skewer across in same direction

3　Drawing skewer across in opposite direction

4　The completed cake with feather icing

96　To make a circular design in feather icing

The same idea can be used for a circular design. Draw a spiral on the cake with white icing on a coloured ground or the other way round. When the spiral is complete, drag the skewer away from the centre to the edge to give the delicate tracing.

The circular design makes almost a spider's web effect.

97　To use jelly for feather icing

Instead of glacé icing, you can use redcurrant or apple jelly.

The jelly is melted with a very little water.

Allow to become cool, but keep sufficiently soft to handle.

It is used in exactly the same way as glacé icing.

98 Points to remember when using glacé icing

1 Get the right consistency for easy control.
2 It is not an icing that will keep for a prolonged period.

3 It is not an icing to use for elaborate piping.
4 It is an icing that can be flavoured and coloured in a diversity of ways.

Butter and Similar Icings

99

The only real butter icing, or butter cream, is that made with butter an icing sugar. There are other similar types of icing which are loosely called 'butter' icing.

The use of margarine or some of the vegetable fats produces a very pleasant soft icing and there are many recipes here using these. Various flavourings and colourings may be added.

100 Butter icing or butter cream

2 oz. butter
3—4 oz. sieved icing sugar
flavouring as required

1 Cream the butter until very soft and white. DO NOT warm it.

2 Work in the sugar and flavouring. To make a firmer icing, use the larger quantity of sugar.

101 Butter icing using modern margarine and cooking fat

Because of the high quality of margarine and the lightness of modern whipped-up cooking fats, it is possible to use these in soft icing such as a butter icing.

Many of the recipes in this book give the quantity of margarine or cooking fat to use, but if you want to use your own recipe, exactly the same amount as butter is needed.

102 How to vary the consistency of butter icing

The consistency of butter icing can be varied a great deal.
When a little fruit juice is added it immediately becomes softer. If it becomes too soft, this can be remedied by adding more icing sugar.
You will find that in recipes in this book the consistency of butter icings varies considerably.

You need a firm icing to give you a rather crisp filling or coating. A soft icing is often better to spread round the sides of a cake if you are coating in nuts, etc., afterwards.
A fairly firm icing is best for piping.
A rather soft, delicate-textured butter icing is more suitable to fill and cover a delicate sponge.

103 To flavour butter icing

Caramel

Beat 3 oz. margarine. Add approximately four tablespoons caramel and 9 oz. sieved icing sugar, alternately, beating the mixture to keep it smooth and fluffy.
Note: To make the caramel, put 8 oz. granulated sugar and $\frac{1}{4}$ pint water into a small strong pan and stir over gentle heat until the sugar has dissolved. Bring to the boil and boil to a rich golden brown. Use as required. Surplus caramel can always be stored in a bottle and kept for future use.

Chocolate

Add a good dessertspoon of chocolate powder or 1 oz. melted chocolate and a few drops vanilla essence to basic butter icing, Recipe 100.

Coconut

Allow 1 oz. desiccated coconut to each 2 oz. butter. Because this is rather dry, use the minimum quantity of icing sugar.

Coffee

Work in a good dessertspoon of coffee essence or one teaspoon soluble powder dissolved in two teaspoons water. Do this gradually or the mixture will curdle.

Lemon

Add two teaspoons finely grated lemon rind and gradually beat in one dessertspoon lemon juice.

Orange

Use three teaspoons finely grated orange rind and gradually beat in one dessertspoon orange juice.

Rum

Add few drops rum essence or about one dessertspoon rum.

Vanilla

Add half a teaspoon vanilla essence.

104 The purpose of butter icing

Butter icing is used firstly as a filling. It is also an excellent coating and very good for piping.

105 Advantages of butter and similar icings

Butter icing keeps. It is therefore wiser to put butter icing into a cake rather than cream if you know you want it to last a day or so.

It is extremely easy to pipe with butter icing providing you have made it the right con-sistency. It is therefore an excellent icing for beginners to pipe with.

It lends itself to a great variety of flavourings. Those given are the basic ones, but you can be very adventurous by adding liqueurs, etc.

106 Disadvantages of butter icings

In very hot weather, butter icing can become rather sticky and greasy looking. This can be remedied by a higher proportion of icing sugar. If you add too much liquid to butter icing in the form of fruit juice or coffee, it can curdle. The moment this starts to happen you should add a little more icing sugar. If, however, it has become very stiff, it is hard to remedy.

107 Amounts of butter icing to use

Top of 6-inch cake	USE 2 oz. butter, etc.
Top and filling of 6-inch cake	USE 4 oz. butter, etc.
Top, filling and sides of 6-inch cake	USE 6—8 oz. butter, etc.
Top of 7-inch cake	USE 3 oz. butter, etc.
Top and filling of 7-inch cake	USE 6 oz. butter, etc.
Top, filling and sides of 7-inch cake	USE 9—12 oz. butter, etc.
Top of 8-inch cake	USE 4 oz. butter, etc.
Top and filling of 8-inch cake	USE 8 oz. butter, etc.
Top, filling and sides of 8-inch cake	USE 12 oz.—1 lb. butter, etc.
Top of 9-inch cake	USE 5—6 oz. butter, etc.
Top and filling of 9-inch cake	USE 10—12 oz. butter, etc.
Top, filling and sides of 9-inch cake	USE 15—18 oz. butter, etc.
Top of 10-inch cake	USE 6—7 oz. butter, etc.
Top and filling of 10-inch cake	USE 12—14 oz. butter, etc.
Top, filling and sides of 10-inch cake	USE 1 lb.—1 lb. 5 oz. butter, etc.
Top of 11-inch cake	USE 7—8 oz. butter, etc.

Piping takes rather more butter icing than you might imagine and it is very difficult to gener-alize about amounts.

If you wish a simple, rather narrow piped edge round the cake, allow approximately half as much butter icing as you have allowed for the top. The above quantities assume that you are requiring a moderately generous filling or coating of icing.

The depth of the cake also determines the amount used — the figures above are for a cake of approximately 3-inches in depth.

108 Types of cake to fill and decorate with butter icing

Victoria sandwich is, of course, admirably suited to being decorated with butter icings.

Genoese sponge is another cake that is often decorated with it.

109 To prepare a cake for butter or similar icings

Quite often you find that with a delicate sponge cake the butter icing is difficult to spread. The reason for this may well be that the icing is a little too stiff.

Obviously the weather plays a part in softening the icing to some extent, as well as the pro-portion of sugar used and the amount of hard work put into the process of creaming. If you find the butter icing is breaking the sponge cake, then add just a very little extra fruit juice, water or milk to give a consistency that spreads easily. Do not warm the butter icing otherwise it will look oily, but you can use a warm knife.

110 To prepare a cake for piping with butter or similar icings

It is advisable to spread a very little butter icing round the rim of the cake, or over the cake before attempting to pipe, thus giving a good base. Naturally, if you have already used a base of glacé icing or jam, this will not be necessary.

111 Butterfly cakes

4 oz. margarine
4 oz. castor sugar
6 oz. flour (with plain flour
  use 2 level teaspoons baking
  powder) *
2 eggs
a little milk, if necessary
For the vanilla cream icing:
2 oz. margarine
4 oz. sieved icing sugar
few drops vanilla essence
For the chocolate icing:
add 1 oz. chocolate powder
To decorate:
sieved icing sugar
few walnuts
little angelica
glacé cherries
* *There is a fairly high ratio of
  flour and baking powder to
  make cakes rise in a peak*

Cream margarine and sugar until light and fluffy. Sieve flour and baking powder. Add the sieved flour and eggs alternately to the creamed mixture. Stir gently OR put in all beaten eggs gradually, and then fold in the flour. If necessary add a little milk to obtain a dropping consistency. Half-fill 12 — 18 well-greased patty tins and bake in a hot oven (425 — 450°F. — Gas Mark 6 — 7) for 12 — 15 minutes. Cool on a wire tray.
Make vanilla cream icing, Recipe 100. Cut off peaks of cakes and halve them to form wings.

Picture 1 (No piping)
Place a good teaspoonful of icing on each cake. Place 'wings' in position in the icing and finally decorate with a dusting of icing sugar.
Picture 2 (Piped)
Add the chocolate powder to half the vanilla cream icing. Place cream icings in paper or nylon icing bags or syringes with a large rosette nozzle, see Recipe 280, and pipe rosettes over the cut surface of the little cakes. Replace 'wings' and finally decorate with chopped walnuts, angelica and glacé cherries.

1 Butterfly cakes without piping

2 Butterfly cakes with piping

112   To decorate by means of marking butter icing

Because butter icing has such a definite texture, it is possible to create a very pleasing appearance without the bother of piping.
The cakes in the two following recipes illustrate this point.
Recipe 113 has been decorated by drawing a small knife across the icing to give this even ridged effect.
Recipe 114 has been decorated by moving the prongs of a fork in a wavy line over a similar type of icing, in this particular case one made with lard.

113   Coffee nut layer gâteau

Victoria sandwich 2 (Recipe 59)
coffee butter icing (Recipe 100
  and 103), made with 6 oz.
  butter, etc.
2 oz. chopped walnuts
few grapes

Make the Victoria sandwich and bake in a 2 lb. loaf tin for approximately 1 hour. When quite cold split in three layers. Make the butter icing, put half into a basin and add the chopped walnuts to this.

Sandwich the three layers of cake together with this. Spread the remaining butter icing over the top and sides of the cake. Mark into ridges with a small tea knife and press halved pipped grapes on top.

Coffee nut layer gâteau

114 Danish biscuit layer cake

6 oz. lard *
3 oz. cocoa
8 oz. icing sugar
3 tablespoons canned of fresh cream *or* evaporated milk
1 egg yolk
8 oz. plain square or oblong biscuits
To decorate:
glacé cherries
angelica
* *Margarine or butter could be used.*

Line a square 6-inch cake tin with a piece of greaseproof paper. Melt the lard slowly in a bowl over a saucepan of boiling water. Sieve the cocoa and icing sugar and add gradually to lard, stirring constantly. Remove the bowl from the heat. Add the cream and egg yolk. Pour a thin layer of the chocolate mixture into the prepared tin. Cover with a layer of biscuits.

Repeat these two layers, beginning and ending with chocolate mixture.
Leave in a cold place to set for about 1 hour. Remove from the tin. Mark the top with a fork, moving it across the icing in a wavy line, and decorate with cherries and angelica. Serve thinly sliced.
Illustrated in colour plate 15

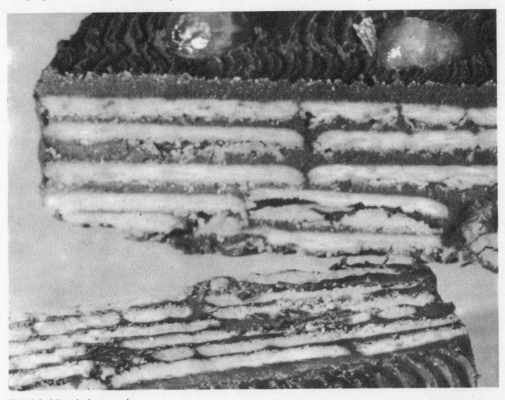

Danish biscuit layer cake

115 To get a 'picked-up' effect with butter icing

In exactly the same way as you can use royal icing for a 'picked-up' or 'snow' effect, so you can do the same with butter or similar types of icing, see picture under Recipe 300.
This method of decoration is carried out by using:
(a) A small knife
Sweep the point of the knife over the icing and at the same time lift it in peaks. Do not try to do this evenly since it creates a much more effective result if it is slightly uneven.
(b) A fork
Sweep the prongs of a fork through the icing in a similar way.
(c) The handle of a teaspoon
Sweep this over the icing in a similar way.

116 Gingerbread special

8 oz. flour (with plain flour use 2 level teaspoons baking powder)
1—2 teaspoons ground ginger
pinch of salt
3 oz. butter or margarine
8 oz. golden syrup or black treacle
1 egg
4 tablespoons milk
2 oz. demerara sugar
For the icing:
4 oz. butter or margarine
6 oz. sieved icing sugar
1 dessertspoon syrup from preserved ginger
To decorate:
small pieces preserved ginger

Grease a tin 9½ inches × 7½ inches across top, and 7½ inches × 5½-inches across base, or an 8-inch square tin. Sieve the flour, ground ginger and salt into a basin. Melt the fat in a saucepan with the syrup or treacle and sugar, but do not let it get too hot. Beat the egg and add it to the milk, then stir all the ingredients together. Put the mixture into the tin and bake just below the centre of a very moderate oven (325—350°F. — Gas Mark 3) for 45 minutes. Turn on to a cooling tray.
Cream the butter and sugar together until soft, see Recipe 100. Add the ginger syrup gradually to flavour the icing. Spread the icing over the upturned gingerbread, pick up in points, see Recipe 115, and decorate with small pieces of preserved ginger.

Gingerbread special

117 Lattice design

A very attractive lattice design can be produced by combining butter or other icing (cream can be used instead) and various coloured jams. Use a No. 2 or 3 writing pipe. Insert this into the bag or syringe. Make sure the icing or cream is stiff enough to hold its shape but soft enough to flow.

Mark the lattice design with a knife over the top of the cake, then pipe either straight or slightly wavy lines following the marks. Fill the centres with various coloured jams or jellies. The easiest way to do this neatly and economically is to put the jam into a piping bag or syringe and pipe this into the spaces. If the jam is very stiff, it should be beaten with a small quantity of water. It should not be used warm.

When the jam has been put into position, pipe butter icing or cream round the edge of the cake to give a neat wavy border.

Lattice design on top of a cake in butter icing

118 To coat cakes smoothly with butter or similar icing

It is possible to use these icings for spreading smoothly over cakes. Make certain the icing is not too stiff. Put it all on top of the cake, then spread over the top and round the sides as described and illustrated for royal icing, see Recipe 271.

119 Mandarin moka

Victoria sandwich 1 (Recipe 30) made with 3 eggs
For the filling:
1½ oz. cornflour
4 teaspoons instant coffee
¾ pint milk
For the icing:
5 oz. margarine
5 oz. castor or icing sugar
2 11-oz. cans mandarin oranges
3 oz. chopped walnuts
To decorate:
16 walnut halves

Grease and line two 12 × 9-inch Swiss roll tins. Make and bake the cakes as Recipe 30, dividing the mixture between the tins.

Remove carefully from the tins and allow to cool. Blend the cornflour and coffee together with a little of the milk and boil the remainder. Add to the cornflour and coffee paste, return to the heat, bring to the boil, stirring continuously. Allow to cool.

Beat the margarine and sugar together until white and creamy. Add the cornflour mixture very gradually to the butter icing and beat until light and fluffy. Keeping about 42 segments for decoration, chop oranges and fold into half the coffee mock cream, together with the chopped walnuts.

Cut each slab of sponge in two, crosswise. Layer the mandarin mixture between the squares of sponge. Cover the top and sides with rest of coffee cream, spread smoothly. Decorate with mandarins and halved walnuts. *Illustrated below and in colour plate 5.*

Mandarin moka

7 Ratafia cake

8 Chocolate filled Swiss roll

120 Orange surprise

4 oz. margarine
4 oz. castor sugar
2 eggs
4 oz. flour (with plain flour
use 1 level teaspoon baking
powder)
For the icing:
3 oz. margarine
5 oz. icing sugar
few drops orange colouring
grated rind ½ orange
1 orange
To decorate:
orange slices *or* angelica

Cream margarine and sugar together. Beat in eggs. Sieve flour and baking powder together and add to the mixture. Bake in two 7-inch tins for 20—25 minutes in a moderately hot oven (400°F. — Gas Mark 5).
Cream margarine and icing sugar together for the icing. Add the grated orange rind and a few drops of orange colouring to match or tone with the orange skin. Cut the orange in half, scoop out flesh and chop. Add to a third of the orange icing and sandwich cakes together. Cover top and sides of cake with orange flavoured icing. Place a nightlight in the centre of the cake with the orange shell over it. Cut the remaining half orange shell or angelica into small diamond shapes and decorate the cake. Small candles can also be placed around the edge for a birthday cake.

Orange surprise

121 Effective decoration with unpiped butter icing

As shown in the following pictures, it is quite possible to get a very effective decoration with butter icing without elaborate piping. To give the slightly crisp effect shown in the Apple shower cake and the Christmas tree cake, use a higher percentage of icing sugar.

122 Apple shower cake

5 eggs
10 oz. castor sugar
1 tablespoon orange flower
water or 1 tablespoon grated
orange rind
¼ teaspoon salt
6 oz. plain flour
For the filling:
½ oz. gelatine
2 tablespoons water
6 tart dessert apples
3 oz. sugar
1 orange
2 oz. toasted hazelnuts,
chopped
To ice and decorate:
4 oz. butter
8 oz. icing sugar
grated rind ½ orange
6 pared, cored, halved and
poached dessert apples
angelica

Separate yolks from whites, beat yolks with 5 oz. sugar and flavouring over a pan of hot water, away from the stove, until thick and white. Whip the egg whites very stiffly with the salt, fold in the remaining sugar and mix well. Combine egg whites and egg yolk mixture alternately with the sifted flour and turn into a greased and floured 9-inch cake tin. Bake in a very moderate to moderate oven (350—375°F. — Gas Mark 3—4) for 1 hour. Turn out and cool. Turn on to a serving plate and cut a piece 4 inches in diameter from the centre of the cake and put to one side.

Dissolve gelatine in water. Core and chop the apples coarsely; cook in covered pan with the sugar, juice from the orange and rind from half the orange, until tender. Remove rind and sieve apples. Mix together the dissolved gelatine, apple purée and nuts and pour into the centre of the cake and allow to set.
Cream butter, sugar and orange rind until white and fluffy. Place small cake on top of the apple filling and cover the entire cake with icing.
Finally, decorate with poached apples and angelica leaves.

Apple shower cake

123 Christmas tree cake

Genoese sponge (Recipe 134) baked in large oblong tin
coffee butter icing (Recipes 100 and 103) made with 4 oz. butter, etc.
chocolate butter icing (Recipes 100 and 103) made with ½—1 oz. butter, etc.

Bake the cake. Cut out a simple Christmas tree and tub design in paper to fit the cake. Lay it over the oblong cake and cut round with a sharp knife. The pieces left can either be used for a trifle, or to make tiny petit fours.

Cover the tub with the chocolate butter icing, smoothing it carefully. Cover the tree with the coffee butter icing and then mark with a fork. Lift on to a cake board and decorate with candles.

124 Chocolate peppermint cream cake

8 oz. butter or margarine
11 oz. castor sugar
12 oz. flour (with plain flour use 3 level teaspoons baking powder)
3 eggs
1 egg yolk
¼ pint milk
1 teaspoon vanilla essence
3 oz. plain chocolate
Chocolate peppermint butter icing:
4 oz. plain chocolate
2 oz. butter
12 oz. icing sugar
few drops peppermint essence
4 tablespoons boiling water

Grease a 9-inch tin and line it with greaseproof paper. Beat the fat until soft, add the sugar and beat until the mixture is light in colour and fluffy in texture. Sieve the flour. Add the eggs one at a time with a little of the sieved flour, stir then beat thoroughly. Add the egg yolk and the milk and a little flour, beat again. Stir in remaining flour, the flavouring and the melted chocolate. Mix thoroughly, but do not beat. Turn the mixture into the prepared tin, smooth level with a palette or table knife and bake in centre of moderate oven for 1¼ hours (375°F. — Gas Mark 4). Allow to cool and then decorate.

Melt the chocolate with the fat in a bowl over a saucepan of very hot water. Remove from the heat and add the icing sugar, essence and water gradually, beating until smooth but not stiff. When the cake is cold split horizontally and spread half the icing between the layers. Place the cake on the cake board. Use the remaining icing to cover the top of the cake. Swirl the icing with a knife. A birthday message may be written on a paper flag affixed to a cocktail stick and speared into the icing. Tie the ribbon (backed with greaseproof paper) around the cake. For a birthday cake, arrange candles round board.

Chocolate peppermint cream cake

125 Pineapple chocolate sundae cake

6 oz. margarine or butter
6 oz. sugar
3 eggs
4 oz. flour (with plain flour use 1 level teaspoon baking powder)
For the pineapple section:
1 packet pineapple flavoured blancmange
or 1¼ oz. plain cornflour and a few drops pineapple essence
For the chocolate section:
1 packet chocolate flavoured blancmange
To decorate:
chocolate butter icing (Recipes 100 and 103) made with 4 oz. butter, etc.
10 blanched hazelnuts
angelica

Cream the margarine or butter and sugar. Gradually beat in the eggs and stir in the flour. Divide the mixture in half.
Into one half blend the pineapple flavoured blancmange or cornflour and pineapple essence. Into the other blend the chocolate flavoured blancmange. Grease and flour a 1½–2-lb. loaf tin. Put in the two cake mixtures, adding a little pineapple then a little chocolate.
Bake in the centre of a moderate oven (375°F. — Gas Mark 4) for approximately 45–50 minutes. Allow to cool.
Make the butter icing. Cover the cold cake with this. Spread into a ridged design with a knife and decorate with blanched hazelnuts and tiny leaves of angelica.
To blanch hazelnuts, see Recipe 6.

Pineapple chocolate sundae cake

126 To make angelica leaves

Cut strips of angelica.
If the angelica is very sugary, soak for a short time in warm water and dry.

Cut tiny diamonds. The least wasteful way to do this is shown in Diagram 1 below. It can also be done as shown in Diagram 2.

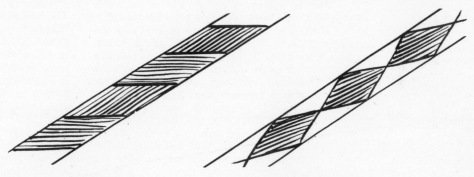

1 To make angelica leaves

2 To make angelica leaves

127 To obtain a line effect with butter icing

The slightly spiral line effect shown in the cake below is easily achieved.
Cover the cake with the butter icing and then use a tea knife or very slender palette knife.

Make a sweep from the centre to the edge of the cake and then follow this line all round. This is difficult to do round the sides, so straight lines are generally better.

128 Chocolate peppermint layer cake

3 oz. plain block chocolate
2 tablespoons milk
4 oz. flour (with plain flour use 1 level teaspoon baking powder)
4 oz. butter or margarine
4 oz. castor sugar
2 eggs
few drops vanilla essence
For the butter cream icing:
3 oz. butter or margarine
8 oz. sieved icing sugar
4 teaspoons hot milk
few drops peppermint essence
a little green colouring
To decorate:
3 'ring' mints

Dissolve the shredded or grated chocolate in the milk over gentle heat and stir to a smooth cream. Sieve the flour. Beat the butter and sugar until soft and light in colour and fluffy in texture. Add the eggs one at a time together with a tablespoon of flour. Beat well after each addition. Add the chocolate mixture and essence, and stir in the remainder of the flour. Do this lightly and avoid beating. Divide the mixture evenly between two greased and floured or lined 7-inch sandwich tins. Smooth level; bake just above centre of moderate oven (375°F. — Gas Mark 4) for 25 minutes. For the icing, beat the butter until soft, add half the sugar and beat well. Add hot milk, essence, colouring and remainder of sugar. Stir, then beat until smooth.
Spread one cake with a little of the icing, place other cake on top. Cover sides and top with remainder of icing. Mark with a round-bladed or very narrow palette knife, see Recipe 127; decorate centre with upright 'ring' mints supported by a peak of icing.

Chocolate peppermint layer cake

129 To obtain a broken line effect with butter icing

The best way to do this, is really just to spread the butter icing roughly over the cake. It often forms quite pleasing lines itself, but if you wish to follow a definite design, as in the Chocolate log below, it is advisable to push it very gently with a knife.

130 Fatless sponge

To make for:

two 6 — 7-inch sandwich tins	USE 2 eggs 2 — 2½ oz. castor sugar 2 oz. flour (with plain flour use ½ teaspoon baking powder) 1 dessertspoon hot water
two 7 — 8-inch sandwich tins	USE 3 eggs 3 — 4 oz. castor sugar 3 oz. flour (with plain flour use ½ teaspoon baking powder) 1 tablespoon hot water
two 9 — 10-inch sandwich tins	USE 4 eggs 4 — 5 oz. castor sugar 4 oz. flour (with plain flour use 1 teaspoon baking powder) 2 tablespoons hot water

Put the eggs and sugar into a basin and whisk hard until thick. You will get a lighter result if NOT whisked over hot water. FOLD in the well-sieved flour carefully and gently with a metal spoon. FOLD in the water. Grease and flour, or grease and coat with equal quantities of flour and sugar, two sandwich tins. Divide the mixture between them, spread evenly and bake for 12 — 14 minutes near the top of a really hot oven. With gas, heat the oven at Gas Mark 7 — 8 and then turn to Gas Mark 6 when the cakes go in. With electricity heat to 450°F. and then turn to 425°F. when the cakes go in.

Test by pressing gently but firmly in the centre of the cakes. When firm, they are cooked. Take out of oven, leave for a minute, tap tins sharply, then turn on to a wire cooling tray. COOL AWAY FROM DRAUGHT.

If you wish to bake in one deep tin, allow approximately 25 — 30 minutes in the centre of a moderate oven.

Note: 1 oz. melted butter or margarine can be added with the water if the cakes are to be kept for a day or two.

Flavourings — quantities for a two-egg sponge
Add 1 teaspoon instant coffee powder;
or omit ½ oz. flour, substituting ½ oz. cocoa
or add a few drops flavouring essence.
For larger quantities increase in proportion.

131 Chocolate log

recipe as *fatless sponge* (Recipe 130) using 3 eggs
substitute 1 tablespoon cocoa for ½ oz. of flour
vanilla butter cream (Recipes 100 and 103) made with 4 oz. butter, etc.
1 level dessertspoon cocoa
To decorate:
sprigs of holly

Grease and line a Swiss roll tin. Make the sponge as Recipe 130, adding flour and cocoa instead of only flour. Pour into the prepared tin. Bake in a hot oven (425°F. — Gas Mark 6) for about 10 minutes. When cooked, turn out at once on to a piece of sugared greaseproof paper. If edges are crisp, trim with a sharp knife and carefully roll up so that the grease-proof paper is rolled inside. Allow to cool and then gently unroll. Remove the paper. Make the butter cream. Spread evenly with half the butter cream and roll up again, see Recipe 170. Add the sieved cocoa to remaining vanilla butter cream, and coat the outside of the roll evenly. Draw a fork or knife, see Recipe 112, along to give bark effect; add holly sprigs.

Chocolate log

132 Chocolate raisin log

ingredients as for *chocolate log* (Recipe 131) or *Genoese pastry* (Recipe 134) omitting ½ oz. flour and using ½ oz. cocoa in its place

For the filling:
4 oz. seedless raisins
2 tablespoons rum
1 large can sweetened chestnut purée
4 oz. butter
4 oz. icing sugar
To decorate:
robin
sprig holly

Make and bake the sponge in a Swiss roll tin as Recipe 131. When the cake is cooked, put a piece of greaseproof paper over, and roll. Allow to cool.

Make the filling by placing the raisins in a saucepan and pour over the rum. Bring to the boil and leave until cold. Beat together the chestnut purée, butter and icing sugar until smooth and creamy. Divide mixture in half and add raisins to only one half of the mixture.

Unroll the sponge and spread with the raisin filling. Roll up tightly. Cut off a small piece of one end, diagonally, and place on the side of the log to represent a branch. Cover completely with remaining chestnut cream, smooth and fork line along length of cake, see Recipe 112. Using a No. 2 writing pipe, pipe a whirl on the side branch to look like the marking of a log. Sprinkle with icing sugar and decorate with a robin and a sprig of holly.

Chocolate raisin log

133 To pipe with butter icing

As already mentioned, butter icing is suitable for simple piping. The following pictures show some of the ways in which it can be used.

Picture 1
This shows the use of butter icing in writing. This is extremely easy since butter icing never flows as freely as glacé icing and so you have perfect control.

Do not make the icing too stiff for writing, otherwise it may break halfway through a letter.

Hold the pipe near to the cake and get a very definite flow in your movement.

Also in Picture 1 will be seen a simple lattice effect with butter icing.

The same pipe, i.e. No. 1, 2 or 3, is used for this and lines are drawn first in one way and then in another.

Around the edge is a simple design using a 5-star pipe.

The new aluminium icing syringe illustrated is good for butter icing since it helps to keep it cool.

Picture 2
This also shows piping with butter icing, again in lattice work.

The cake to the left of the icing syringe has been piped with the 5-star pipe; the small circular cake in the front with an 8-star, which is rather more delicate.

1 Writing with butter icing

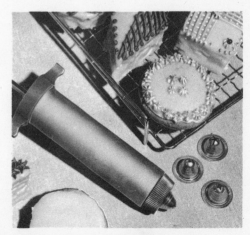

2 Small cakes piped with butter icing

134 Genoese sponge or pastry

To make for:

two 6—7-inch sandwich tins or one 8 × 6-inch tin	USE 2 large eggs 2½—3 oz. castor sugar 2 oz. flour (with plain flour use ½ teaspoon baking powder) 2—2½ oz. melted butter, allowed to cool
two 7—8-inch sandwich tins or one 10 × 8-inch tin	USE 3 large eggs 4 oz. castor sugar 3 oz. flour (with plain flour use ½ teaspoon baking powder) 3—4 oz. melted butter, allowed to cool
two 8—9-inch sandwich tins or one 12 × 10-inch tin	USE 4 large eggs 5—6 oz. castor sugar 4 oz. flour (with plain flour use 1 teaspoon baking powder) 4—5 oz. melted butter, allowed to cool

Put the eggs and sugar into a basin. Stand over a saucepan of hot water. Whisk together until thick. Take the basin off the heat and continue to whisk until the egg is cold. Fold in the flour, with the baking powder if used, then the melted butter. This can be used like the fatless sponge for a sandwich cake, in which case grease and flour or line two sandwich tins and bake as below, for approximately 12 minutes, or since Genoese pastry is so often used for tiny cakes, line one large tin with greased and floured greaseproof paper and bake at the top of a moderately hot oven (400°F. — Gas Mark 5) for approximately 14 minutes until firm and pale gold in colour. Turn out of tin straight away. Cut into various shapes and cover with butter or similar icing and decorate with chopped nuts.

135 Iced Genoese sponge

Genoese sponge or pastry (Recipe 134) made with 3 eggs
To decorate:
coffee butter icing (Recipe 100) made with 9—12 oz. butter
2—3 oz. chopped blanched almonds
For piping:
chocolate butter icing (Recipe 103) made with 1½—2 oz. butter

Genoese sponge, or, as it is often called, Genoese pastry, is very suitable for decorating with butter icing since the soft consistency of butter icing blends well with the delicate texture of Genoese pastry.

If baking the Genoese sponge in one tin, split through the centre and sandwich with some of the coffee butter icing. Spread the sides of the cake with more of the coffee butter icing and roll in the chopped nuts, see Recipe 8. If preferred, the nuts can be lightly toasted before using. Make sure they are allowed to become absolutely cold.

Spread the remainder of the coffee butter icing over the top of the cake and mark into eight or desired number of portions.

Fit an 8-star pipe into either a cloth, paper or nylon bag or syringe.

In order to get the border design as shown, you can pipe a length of ribbon with the 8-star pipe round one section, then turn the pipe upright and press out a star. Turn the pipe on its side again, make another ribbon, then another star. Another method is to pipe a ribbon right the way round the cake, and then to pipe the stars on at regular intervals on top afterwards.

Iced Genoese sponge

136 Bûche de Noël

This is made in exactly the same way as the Chocolate log, Recipe 131, except that pieces of glacé fruits are mixed in with the butter cream for filling.

The chocolate butter icing is piped and not spread over the cake. For the rather fine line of piping, choose the small border pipe. For thicker piping use either the 5, 6 or 8 star pipe. You will find that piping uses more butter icing than just spreading, so increase the amount of chocolate butter icing by a quarter to a half.

137 Raspberry heart cake

Victoria sandwich (Recipe 30 or 59)* made with 2 eggs, etc. butter, etc.
For the icing:
raspberry butter icing (Recipe 100) made with 6—9 oz. butter, etc., raspberry essence and cochineal
For the piping and decoration:
raspberry butter icing, made with 2 oz. butter, etc., raspberry essence and cochineal
2 oz. chopped, blanched almonds
6 glacé cherries
* To give very fine texture, use 3 oz. flour (use 1 teaspoon baking powder with plain flour) and 1 packet raspberry flavoured blancmange

Make and bake the Victoria sandwich in a heart-shaped tin.

When cooked, spread the sides with part of the butter icing. You cannot roll this particular shape in the nuts, so put the cake on a piece of greaseproof paper and pat the nuts against the sides with a palette knife.

Spread the rest of the icing on top. As the picture illustrates, this is a particularly soft butter icing, so use the minimum quantity of icing sugar.

For the very simple piping round the edge, use either a large 6 or 8 star pipe and pipe stars close together to form a neat border. Cut glacé cherries into quarters and press these against the border.

Raspberry heart cake

138 Jamaican gâteau

Make *Raspberry heart cake* (Recipe 137) using a pineapple flavoured blancmange
For the filling:
pineapple butter icing (Recipe 100) * made with 3 oz. butter, etc.
3—4 oz. chopped, canned or glacé pineapple
For the piping:
pineapple butter icing made with 3 oz. butter, etc.
sieved icing sugar
* Made by adding a few drops of pineapple essence and saffron yellow colouring

Split the heart-shaped cake through the centre and spread the base portion with butter icing and pineapple.

Cut the top in half down the centre to make two wings. Dust these with a little sieved icing sugar and press in position, rising slightly from the centre.

Pipe a band of butter icing down the centre with a No. 8 star pipe to give a slightly ribbon effect. If you pipe the line for about 1 inch, pressing out towards the end, you will have a slightly raised effect. Do this continually, giving the effect of looped ribbon. The same piping, slightly smaller, is used round the edge to give a neat border.

Jamaican gâteau

139 Chestnut cream cake

6 oz. margarine or butter
6 oz. castor sugar
6 oz. flour (with plain flour use 1½ level teaspoons baking powder)
3 eggs
a few drops vanilla essence
For the filling and decoration:
5 oz. butter or margarine
10 oz. sieved icing sugar
8 oz. can chestnut purée
4 oz. plain chocolate, grated
sieved icing sugar

Grease and line two sandwich tins, one 8 inch and one 7 inch. Cream margarine and sugar until the mixture is light and fluffy. Sieve the flour. Add the eggs one at a time with a little sieved flour, if mixture looks life curdling. Stir in the rest of sieved flour and flavouring thoroughly, but do not beat. Divide mixture between tins, with two thirds in the larger.

Bake the smaller one for 20—25 minutes and the larger for 25—30 minutes just above centre of moderate to moderately hot oven (375°F. — Gas Mark 4—5). Ovens vary, so check with instruction book the temperature for baking a Victoria sandwich. Beat far until soft, add sugar gradually, then the chestnut purée and grated chocolate. Spread nearly two thirds of this filling on the cooled 8-inch cake. Cut the 7-inch cake into eight pieces and place these a little apart on top of the filling. Put the remaining filling into an icing bag with a large rose or star pipe and pipe rosettes between the slices of cake. Finish with a rosette in the centre of the cake. Dredge with icing sugar.

Chestnut cream cake

140 French Easter cake — Joyeux Pâques

Genoese sponge (Recipe 134) made with 4 eggs, etc.
Coffee crème au beurre (Recipe 141)
To decorate:
4 oz. nut brittle, obtainable from a sweet-shop, *or* 3 oz. chopped blanched walnuts
For the piping:
glacé icing (Recipe 53) made with 2—3 oz. icing sugar

Make the Genoese sponge and bake in an 8-inch tin. Turn out and cool.
Cut the cake across into two, and sandwich together with a little of the crème. Coat the sides and press the nut brittle round, see Recipe 8. Cover the top. Use remaining crème and a large star pipe to decorate the edge of the cake with rosettes. Pipe the greeting 'Joyeux Pâques' with the white glacé icing, using a No. 2 writing pipe.

French Easter cake — Joyeux Pâques

141 Coffee crème au beurre

12 tablespoons water
4½ oz. loaf sugar
3 egg yolks
6 oz. butter
1 tablespoon coffee essence

Boil the water and sugar together to 230°F. or until it forms a thread from a spoon. Put the egg yolks into a basin and whisk well, adding the sugar and water syrup slowly, and continue whisking until the mixture thickens. Add the softened butter in small pieces, continuing to whisk all the time. Add the coffee essence.

142 Christmas chalet

Victoria sandwich 1 or 2 (Recipe 30 or 59) made with 3 eggs *
butter icing (Recipe 100), made with 1½ oz. cocoa, 8 oz. butter, 1 lb. icing sugar
8 oz. seedless raisins
water to cover
icing sugar
2 small Christmas trees
sprig holly
* *Either plain Victoria sandwich, or omit ½ oz. flour and put in ½ oz. cocoa.*

The picture below shows how butter icing can be used for a very definite piping design. Make the Victoria sandwich and put the mixture into a greased and floured 2 lb. loaf tin and bake in the centre of a very moderate oven (350°F. — Gas Mark 3) for approximately 1¼ hours. Allow cake to cool. Make the butter icing. Cover the raisins with cold water. Bring to the boil and stand for 5 minutes. Drain, dry and chop half the quantity.
Divide the cake into three layers. Put the top layer to one side, and sandwich the other two together with some of the butter icing and half the chopped raisins. Coat the top and sides with butter icing and press the whole raisins against the sides, saving a few for the ends of the roof. Dust well with icing sugar. Sprinkle the remaining chopped raisins on top of the cake.
Cut a strip 1 inch wide from the long side of the remaining layer of cake. Cut the large piece of cake diagonally from corner to corner and lay on top of the butter icing and chopped raisins to form a roof. Spread a little icing over the ends and press over the remaining raisins. The remaining butter icing can either be spread on to the roof and marked with a fork to represent tiles, see Recipe 112, or piped with a syringe or icing bag and a No. 12 pipe. Draw ribbons of butter icing up one side of the roof and down the other, giving the ridged effect by moving the pipe slightly to the left at intervals, see Recipe 279.
From the spare piece of cake, cut off a wedge to form the chimney.
Place in position. Dust the cake with icing sugar, and decorate with the sprig of holly and Christmas trees.
A 'door' can be left in the side of the cake as shown in the picture, if wished.

Christmas chalet

143 Chick choc cake

6 oz. butter or margarine
6 oz. castor sugar
5 oz. flour (with plain flour
   use 1¼ level teaspoons
   baking powder)
1 oz. cornflour
3 eggs
To coat cake and make 'nests':
5 oz. plain chocolate
4 tablespoons water
4 oz. butter or margarine
8 oz. sieved icing sugar
flavouring
To decorate:
2 oz. desiccated coconut
green colouring
1 oz. chopped roasted
   almonds
*For the glacé icing (Recipe
53):*
8 oz. sieved icing sugar
good squeeze lemon juice
2 — 2½ tablespoons water
few drops yellow colouring
small sweet eggs or eggs made
   of marzipan (see below)
3 yellow chicks

Cut up the fat, beat until soft with a wooden spoon. Add the sugar and beat until the mixture is light and fluffy. Sieve the flour and cornflour together. Add the eggs one at a time with a little of the sieved flour, stir, then beat thoroughly. Add the remaining flour, stir in thoroughly but do NOT beat. Divide the mixture evenly between two greased and lined or floured 7-inch sandwich tins. Bake for 25—30 minutes just above centre in a moderate oven (375°F. — Gas Mark 4). To make the chocolate butter icing, shred the chocolate finely with a knife, place in a small saucepan with the water. Stir over gentle heat until smooth, then cool. Beat the fat until soft, then beat in sugar gradually; finally beat in melted chocolate and essence.

Sandwich the cakes together with a little of the icing, spreading the remainder round the sides of the cake, but reserving about two or three tablespoons for decoration.

Add a few drops of green colouring to the coconut, distributing it evenly with a teaspoon. Allow to dry out in a warm place. Mix the coloured coconut and nuts together and press this mixture round the outside of the cake, completely covering the chocolate icing. For the glacé icing, put the sieved icing sugar into a saucepan; add lemon juice. Add water carefully and mix to a coating consistency. Add a few drops of yellow colouring. Beat well, stirring over a gentle heat for 1 minute. Pour the icing over the top of the cake. Allow to set. Using a large star pipe, Recipe 280, fitted into a nylon or cloth bag or icing syringe, and the remaining chocolate butter icing, pipe three circles on the cake to represent nests. Fill with small eggs and put the three chicks in place.

Chick choc cake

144 Marzipan eggs

small quantity *marzipan*
   (Recipes 256, 257 or 258)
various flavourings

Make the marzipan or almond paste into egg shapes and brush on the various colourings with a very fine paint brush. Allow the colourings to dry before using.

145 Candle cake

Victoria sandwich 1 or 2,
   (Recipe 30 or 59) made
   with 2 eggs
1 dessertspoon cocoa
vanilla butter icing (Recipe
   100), made with 3 oz.
   butter, etc.
For the coating:
glacé icing (Recipe 53) made
   with 12 oz. icing sugar
To decorate:
royal icing (Recipe 267)
   made with 1 egg white,
   8 oz. icing sugar
or butter icing (Recipe 100)
   made with 3—4 oz. butter,
   etc.
a little cocoa
approximately 1½ yards bright
   red ribbon
large red candle
star stand for candle
4 sprigs holly leaves

Make and bake the Victoria sandwich, sieving the cocoa with the flour. Cook in two 7-inch sandwich tins and, when cold, sandwich with the butter icing.

Coat top and sides with the glacé icing. For the decoration, put half the butter or royal icing into a basin and blend with a little sieved cocoa.

Using a 5, 6 or 8 star pipe, pipe rosettes of the white icing round edge and base, leaving spaces in between. Fill spaces with chocolate rosettes. With a decoration like this you need exactly the right number of light and dark stars or rosettes, so put a pin at one place to mark the beginning. Then with another pin, go round and prick once to mark the centre of each star or rosette. As you do so, count the number of holes. If you find this will not allow alternate light and dark rosettes, you can very easily go back again and respace the holes.

Tie ribbon round cake; put large red candle in a star holder in the centre; add holly sprigs.

Candle cake

146 Ribbon on cakes

A ribbon is inclined to become rather discoloured with icing, so always put a band of greaseproof paper or foil *under* the ribbon. If exactly the same width, it does not show.

147 Chocolate party cup cakes

2 oz. butter or margarine
2 oz. castor sugar
1 egg
2 oz. flour (with plain flour use ½ teaspoon baking powder)
1 dessertspoon cocoa
few drops milk or warm water
For the piping:
butter icing (Recipe 100) made with 4—5 oz. butter, 6—8 oz. icing sugar and various flavourings *
* *Or use little chocolate to flavour*

Cream the butter and sugar together until light and fluffy. Gradually beat in the whisked egg. Fold in the sieved flour and cocoa, adding a little warm water or milk, if necessary, to give a soft dropping consistency. Put this mixture into eight small paper cake cases and bake for 10—15 minutes in a moderately hot oven (400°F. — Gas Mark 5). Allow to cool and then decorate as follows.

For coating tops:
Use either a small quantity of melted chocolate, see Recipe 189, Chocolate glacé icing, Recipe 56, or White glacé icing, Recipe 53.

Cake 1
Use melted chocolate or chocolate glacé icing for base.
When nearly set, place three halved blanched almonds in position.
Pipe a star of vanilla butter icing and press a mimosa ball or hazelnut in the centre.

Cake 2
Use chocolate glacé icing for the base.
When nearly set, press a halved walnut in the centre. Allow to set and pipe a border of stars in vanilla butter icing.
In the picture these borders were made with an 8 star pipe.

Cake 3
Either leave plain without glacé icing, or put chocolate glacé icing underneath, and allow to become quite hard.
Use either a 5 or 8 star pipe and draw two rather thin lines across the cake.
Using the same pipe, make a looped ribbon design across cake, see Recipe 138, between the straight lines.

Cake 4
Cover cake with glacé icing and allow to set. Using either a 5 or 8 star pipe, make a border round the outside.
To get this particular design, hold the pipe pointing towards the centre and pull down in sharp flat movements all the way round.
Turn the pipe to make the usual tiny star shapes inside.

Cake 5
Using a 5 star pipe or even a 6 star, make alternate lines of chocolate and vanilla butter icing. These can be done one after the other since this type of icing does not run.

Cake 6
The small cake in the picture was not coated first but just given a border of shapes made with a 12 star pipe, the centre star being decorated with a silver ball and pieces of orange slices, obtainable from a sweet-shop.

Cake 7
This can be done with glacé icing first.
The design is done by making lines in vanilla butter icing with a 5 or 8 star pipe, then making the same ribbon design as cake 3, in between. As you can see, you can adjust the size of the loop though using the same pipe. All depends on the amount of icing expressed at one time.

Cake 8
Use a 5, 6, 8 or 12 star pipe. Instead of holding the pipe upright, make it lie rather flatter to the cake. The slightly fan shape is made by using a little pressure at the beginning of the fan and increasing this to get the slightly wider top. Continue like this all round cake. Decorate with a crystallized sweet in the centre.

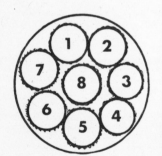

Chocolate party cup cakes

148 Coffee cream soufflé cake

6 oz. castor sugar
4½ oz. plain flour
1¼ level teaspoon baking powder
pinch salt
4 eggs
3 tablespoons oil
3 tablespoons concentrated coffee essence mixed with 4 tablespoons water
pinch of cream of tartar
To fill and decorate:
2½ oz. granulated sugar
4 tablespoons water
2 eggs yolks
6 oz. unsalted butter
4 tablespoons concentrated coffee essence
4 oz. hazelnuts

Sift the castor sugar, flour, baking powder and salt together in a mixing bowl. Separate the eggs and place the egg yolks and oil in the middle. Beat, slowly adding the coffee and water mixture, until quite smooth. Beat the egg whites until stiff, adding the cream of tartar when the egg whites start to froth, and continue until stiff. Fold the flour mixture in carefully and lightly with a metal spoon.

Pour into an ungreased 8 × 4-inch cake tin and place in a very moderate oven (325—350°F. — Gas Mark 3) for about 1 hour.

Test with a skewer before taking out. Leave to cool, upside down, before removing from the cake tin.

Make the butter cream by boiling the sugar and water to the stage that fine threads form on the spoon as you pull it up. Pour this mixture slowly on to the egg yolks in a bowl,

beating with a whisk until it becomes thick, pale and light. Cut the butter into small pieces and add, beating into the mixture until it is smooth and thick in consistency then beat in the coffee essence.

Prepare the hazelnuts by rubbing them in a dry tea towel to get the skins off. Reserve one quarter for decoration, and put the remainder through a nut mill or chop.

Slice the cake in half and spread with a thick layer of the coffee cream. Put the two halves together and spread the sides thinly with coffee cream. Holding the cake by its top and underside, roll the sides, pressing gently, in the plate of ground nuts.

Place on plate and decorate with large piped rosettes of coffee cream round the outer edge, topping each with a hazelnut and filling the centre with hazelnuts.

Coffee cream soufflé cake

149 To pipe the sides of a cake with butter icing

Butter icing is particularly suitable for piping on the sides of a cake because, being soft, you can press the pipe into the cake and control the flow of icing very easily.

Try and put the cake on either a turntable or substitute, Recipe 272, so that you have a good

line of vision, and after piping the top, pipe down the sides and base.

Always work in this order, piping the top and then down to the sides. In this way you are not likely to spoil the sides by bringing your hands over to decorate the top.

150 Ratafia cake

sponge mixture as for *Coffee layer gâteau* (Recipe 174)
coffee butter cream (Recipe 100) made with 4 oz. butter, etc.
100 tiny *ratafias* (Recipe 151)
1 glacé cherry
fresh orange slices or canned mandarin oranges
6 angelica leaves

Make and bake the Coffee sponge as Recipe 174 or bake in one tin in the centre of a very moderate oven (350°F. — Gas Mark 3) for approximately 40 minutes.

Sandwich together with a layer of coffee butter cream, or if making in one tin, split across in two when cold and then sandwich together.

Spread the outside of the cake smoothly with

butter cream and arrange ratafias in rows evenly all over the surface. Pipe the rest of the coffee butter cream in rosettes between the biscuits. Arrange overlapping mandarins or fresh orange slices to form a flower on the top in one corner, with a cherry for the centre, and small angelica leaves.

Illustrated in colour plate 7.

151 Ratafias

1 egg white
few drops almond essence
2½—3 oz. castor sugar
2½ oz. ground almonds

Whisk the egg white lightly. Add the almond essence, then the sugar and ground almonds. Make into tiny balls the size of a hazelnut and put on to a greased and floured tray. Press with your fingers so they flatten and bake for

5—8 minutes only a in very moderate oven (350°F. — Gas Mark 3) till pale golden brown. 1 egg white produces approximately 24 of these tiny ratafias and you can make up a large quantity as they store well in an airtight tin.

152 Chocolate valentine heart

6 oz. butter or margarine
6 oz. castor sugar
3 eggs
8 oz. flour (with plain flour
  use 2 level teaspoons baking
  powder)
1 tablespoon cocoa
little milk or water
To decorate:
butter icing (Recipe 100)
  made with 6 oz. butter,
  8 oz. sieved icing sugar
1 dessertspoon cocoa
few drops vanilla essence
little cochineal
glacé icing (Recipe 53) made
  with 4 oz. icing sugar, 1
  tablespoon water, few drops
  cochineal

Cream the fat and sugar until light and fluffy. Beat in the lightly beaten eggs. Fold in the sieved flour and cocoa, adding sufficient warm water or milk to form a soft dropping consistency. Divide into two greased heart-shaped tins. Bake just above the centre of a moderate oven (375°F. — Gas Mark 4) for approximately 30—35 minutes. Cool on a wire tray.

Make the butter cream by beating all the butter and all the icing sugar together. To one quarter add the cocoa and vanilla essence and beat well. To the remaining three-quarters add a little cochineal to give the required pale pink colouring.

Make the glacé icing and add a little cochineal. Sandwich the two heart-shaped cakes together, using pink butter icing.

Spread the glacé icing over the top of the cake and allow to set, see Recipe 66.

Use the chocolate butter icing and a No. 2 or 3 writing pipe to begin with. Pipe a heart shape on top of the cake. This may be quite difficult to draw, so the easiest method is to cut out a heart shape in greaseproof paper, lay it in position on the top of the *set* icing and then make the line just outside the edge of the greaseproof paper. Lift the paper up carefully without smudging the icing.

The line of dots can be put on after the heart shaped line, since you will hold the pipe fairly high to get these and just squeeze out a very little butter icing with the same No. 2 or 3 writing pipe. Still using chocolate butter icing, change to a 5, 6, 8 or 12 star pipe and pipe the border of stars.

Use the pink butter icing for piping round the centre and base of the sides with a similar star pipe.

Chocolate valentine heart

153 Butter or similar icings flavoured with honey

The previous pages have given the basic butter or similar icings with various flavourings. The addition of honey is another way of varying flavour and texture. It is used in the same way.

154 Honey buns

4 oz. margarine
4 oz. castor sugar
2 eggs
4 oz. flour (with plain flour
  use 1 level teaspoon baking
  powder)
For the honey icing:
3 oz. margarine
8 oz. icing sugar, sieved
3 level tablespoons honey
1 tablespoon lemon juice
To decorate:
walnut halves

Cream the margarine and sugar together until very light. Beat in the eggs, one at a time, adding a little sieved flour with the second egg. Fold in the remaining sieved flour. Place heaped teaspoons of the mixture in bun cases or bun tins brushed inside with melted margarine. Bake in a hot oven (425°F. — Gas Mark 6), near the top, for 15 minutes. Cool on a wire tray.

Cream the margarine and half the icing sugar together until very light. Stir in the honey, lemon juice and the remaining icing sugar. Beat until smooth and light.

Spread the icing on top of the buns. Swirl with the point of a knife and place half a walnut in the centre of each.

Honey buns

155　Honey cradle cake

4 oz. margarine or fat
8 oz. castor sugar
6 level tablespoons honey
4 egg whites
10 oz. plain flour
pinch salt
pinch cream of tartar
2 level teaspoons baking
　powder
approximately ¼ pint milk
honey and lemon filling
　(Recipe 156):
lemon icing made with 1 egg
　white, 12 oz. icing sugar,
　2 tablespoons lemon juice
To decorate:
satin ribbon 2 inches wide
two 10-inch doilies

Cream the fat, sugar and honey until light and fluffy. Beat in egg whites, one at a time. Sieve dry ingredients together and fold into creamed mixture. Stir in milk to give a soft dropping consistency. Divide mixture between two greased and lined 8-inch sandwich tins and bake above the centre of a moderate oven (375°F. — Gas Mark 4) for 30 minutes. When cold, sandwich the two cakes together with honey and lemon filling. Whisk the egg white, add the icing sugar and lemon juice to make the lemon icing. Beat until smooth and stiff enough to stand in peaks. Put the icing on the top and sides of the cake, see Recipe 271, and leave to set.

Tie 2-inch-wide band of ribbon round cake. Cut out the centre of one doily and stick the edging to the sides of the cake with icing to form a frill. Cut the other doily across and place one half over one end of the cake to represent a hood. Secure with a little icing. With a No. 8 star pipe, make a border round the top of the cake as Recipe 138. Pipe tiny rosettes with the same pipe to outline the pillow shape. Add tiny bows of narrow ribbon at the sides of the 'hood' if wished.

Honey cradle cake

156　Honey and lemon filling

2 oz. butter
3 oz. icing sugar
1 tablespoon honey
1 teaspoon finely grated
　lemon rind

Cream the butter and sugar together. Beat in the honey and lemon rind. The combination of lemon and honey makes a very pleasant change from the usual butter icing.

Satin Icing

157　The purpose of satin icing

Satin icing may be used in place of butter or royal icing or as a substitute for almond paste.

158　To make satin icing

For the syrup:
2 oz. margarine
juice 2 lemons *or* 4 table-
　spoons pure lemon juice
1 lb. sieved icing sugar
For thickening and kneading:
4 — 8 oz. icing sugar (depend-
　ing on size of lemons used)

1 Place the margarine and lemon juice in a saucepan.
2 Stir over a low heat until margarine melts.
3 Add 8 oz. of the sieved icing sugar and again stir over a low heat, WITHOUT SIMMER-ING, until the sugar is almost dissolved.
4 Then cook for 2 MINUTES ONLY, from the time the mixture begins to simmer gently at the sides of the saucepan until it boils gently all over the surface. (IMPORTANT: Time the mixture very carefully at this stage, for if it is over-boiled the paste will become too hard to manipulate and may crystallize.)
5 Remove from the heat and stir in the remaining 8 oz. of sieved icing sugar and beat well with a wooden spoon.

6 Pour into a bowl and again beat well, scraping mixture from the sides with knife.
7 Gradually add extra sieved icing sugar, to make the mixture the consistency of soft dough, working it in with the wooden spoon.
8 When sufficient icing sugar has been worked in and the dough is even, turn the mixture out on to a pastry board dusted with icing sugar.
9 Knead until the mixture becomes smooth and white — the longer you knead, the whiter it becomes.
10 Unless the satin icing is to be used immediately, wrap it in greaseproof paper and store in an airtight tin or put in a polythene bag and store in a cool, dry place.
11 Knead the icing a little before use.

159 To colour satin icing

If you wish to colour the whole batch of satin icing, add two or three drops of the required colour to the syrup. Beat this in evenly until the right shade is obtained before adding the extra sugar to thicken. If after thickening and kneading you require a deeper shade, add one or two drops more colouring, and knead in well until the colour is evenly distributed.

If you wish to use several colours, divide the icing, once prepared (i.e. thickened and kneaded) and colour each piece with a few drops of the appropriate colouring, kneading in well.

160 Advantages of satin icing

Satin icing has the advantage of being easy to roll out, rather like marzipan, and it is therefore far less difficult for a beginner to get a really smooth layer over the cake.

It also is sufficiently thick to use on cakes without almond paste if you so desire.

It is not only a coating icing, it is an icing that can be moulded. An example of this is the moulding for petals, opposite. It will keep for several weeks if wrapped in greaseproof paper and stored in an airtight tin or if kept in a polythene bag and stored in a cool dry place.

161 Disadvantage of satin icing

The only disadvantage could be that some people will find this a little thick and, in consequence, slightly sweet.

This can be remedied by thinning it down a little and using it almost as a glacé icing if wished. You cannot, of course, make it too thin if you are going to roll and cut into strips or circles.

162 Types of cakes suitable for satin icing

Most types of cake are suitable for covering with satin icing. Because it is a firm icing it tends to be better on a firm sponge such as a Victoria sandwich or a fruit cake.

163 To coat with satin icing

Satin icing is rolled out in exactly the same way as almond paste. You will make a round for the top and leave enough for the sides. After rolling the satin icing into a large strip to cover the sides of the cake, divide it into two or more lengths. As satin icing is softer than the normal almond paste, this method is better than making one long strip.

164 To ice small cake with satin icing

Roll the satin icing out fairly thinly. Using a fluted pastry cutter, the same size as the cakes to be iced, cut out rounds of satin icing.

Spread the cakes with sieved apricot jam. Then press the satin icing gently down on top of the small cakes and decorate as wished.

165 To ice biscuits with satin icing

Roll out the satin icing fairly thinly.

Using biscuit cutters, cut out shapes to correspond with the shapes of the biscuits to be iced. Spread the tops of the biscuits with sieved apricot jam and press the satin icing gently on the top. Biscuits can also be sandwiched together with the satin icing in between, using sieved apricot jam to hold them firmly together.

166 Cup final cake

Victoria sandwich 1 (Recipe 30), made with 2 eggs
satin icing (Recipe 158) made with 2 oz. margarine
apricot jam
2—3 drops colouring

Make and bake sandwich in deep 8—9-inch tin. Prepare satin icing.

Place the cake on a cake board. Brush top and sides of cake with hot sieved apricot jam. Roll out one third of the satin icing into a long strip to cover the sides of the cake. Trim off the rough edges, roll up like bandage; cover sides, unrolling icing as you move round cake.

Colour two thirds of the remaining icing with two or three drops of colouring. Use the appropriate colour for the particular football team. Roll out into a long strip 3-inches wide, trim off the rough edges. Pleat round top of the cake to form the outer ring of a rosette. Roll out the uncoloured satin icing and cut a strip 2½ inches wide, pleat on the cake to form inner ring of the rosette. Roll out remaining uncoloured icing into strip about 1 inch wide, trim; cut to form two ribbons with pointed ends. Place plain ends of the ribbons between the two pleated parts of the rosette and allow them to hang over the side of the cake.

Cover the centre with a flat round disc of the coloured satin icing to complete the rosette.

Cup final cake

167 To mould with satin icing

Because satin icing is soft and pliable, it can be moulded into tiny animals, which are admirable for children's cakes, etc.

It can also be moulded into small flowers, either by pulling the icing into the shape required, or by a series of petals as shown in the pictures below.

Picture 1

Flatten a little of the satin icing out thinly with the forefinger of the right hand against the back of the left hand.

Make the required number of petals like this.

Picture 2

Make the centre of the flower by moulding a petal round a knitting needle or skewer.

Picture 3

Add the next petal and mould rather loosely.

Picture 4

Continue like this, bending the outer petals in an artistic and realistic shape until the flower is complete.

Picture 5

This shows a cake decorated with the completed flowers, and also leaves of green satin icing, moulded and marked in a similar way. When the flowers are completed, you can put a tiny mimosa ball in the centre, but with roses this is not necessary.

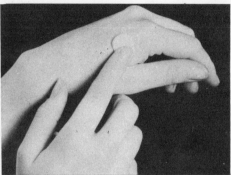

1 To make the petals

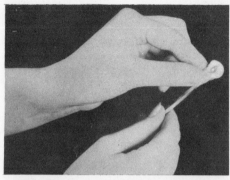

2 To make the centre of the rose

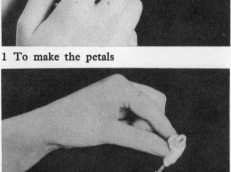

3 Adding the petals

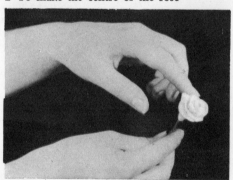

4 The completed rose

5 Cake covered with satin icing decorated with moulded roses

168   Candle party cake

Swiss roll:
4 oz. margarine
4 oz. castor sugar
2 eggs
4 oz. self-raising flour
2 tablespoons apricot jam
Satin icing:
2 oz. margarine
4 tablespoons lemon juice
1½ lb. icing sugar, sieved
red and yellow colouring
hot sieved apricot jam

Cream the margarine and sugar together until very light. Beat in the eggs one at a time, adding a little flour with the second. Fold in the remaining flour. Place the mixture in a Swiss roll tin, brushed and lined with grease-proof paper to come above the sides of the tin. Bake in a hot oven (425°F. — Gas Mark 6), on second shelf from top, for 10—12 minutes. Turn out on to sugared greaseproof paper, a little larger than the Swiss roll. Carefully remove the paper from the roll. Cut off the outer edge with a sharp knife. Spread with the hot jam. Roll up carefully, then wrap round with sugared paper. Leave to set with the paper round it for 2—3 minutes. Remove paper and cool on a wire tray.

Melt the margarine with the lemon juice in a saucepan over a low heat. Stir in 8 oz. icing sugar. Return to a very low heat until sugar has dissolved and mixture begins to bubble. Cook for *2 minutes only* (time cooking *very* carefully at this stage). Remove from heat and gradually stir in another 8 oz. icing sugar; beat well with a wooden spoon until cooled slightly. Knead well on a board using more icing sugar to make a smooth, pliable 'dough'.

Trim ends of Swiss roll. Cut a slice diagonally from one end to make a sloping top for the candle and scoop out some of the cake from this end to make a hollow for the flame.

Colour one half of the icing red and the other half yellow, kneading in the colour a drop at a time. Roll out the red icing into a long strip with icing sugar. Brush the Swiss roll and 6-inch cake board with apricot jam. Cover the sides and top of the Swiss roll with the red icing. Form two small pieces of icing and stick on the side for the candle drips. Smooth over the candle with the fingers to make it shine. Roll the yellow icing out thinly and cover the cake board. Place the candle in the centre of the board and cover the base with a thin strip of yellow icing to represent the candle holder. A handle for the candlestick, matches and a face on the candle (eyes, nose and mouth) can be moulded from yellow icing. The flame is made from a heart-shaped piece of yellow and red icing moulded on to a cocktail stick and secured on top of the candle.

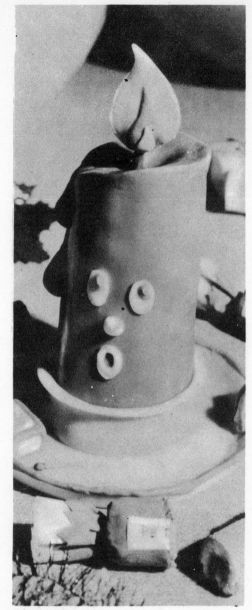

Candle party cake

169   Easter Sunday bonnet

sponge as *Humpty Dumpty cake* (Recipe 375)
satin icing (Recipe 158), made with 1½ lb. icing sugar
apricot jam
To decorate:
1½ yards blue ribbon
fluffy birds
artificial flowers

Make the sponge as Recipe 375 and bake in a prepared 8-inch sandwich tin in a very moderate oven (300—350°F. — Gas Mark 2—3) for 35—45 minutes. Cool.
Make the satin icing, Recipe 158.
Brush the top and sides of the cake with hot sieved apricot jam. Roll out one third of the satin icing into a circle large enough to cover the top of the cake. Place on top and trim off any surplus. Roll out a long strip of satin icing for the sides of the cake. Roll this up like a bandage, then cover the sides of the cake. Roll out the remainder of the satin icing into a long strip and trim with a pastry cutter or wheel. Pleat or fold it round the outside edge of a cake board. Lift the cake on to this so that it stands out round the bottom edge of the cake. Tie a large bow of ribbon round the cake and decorate the top with birds and flowers.

Easter Sunday bonnet

9   Chocolate surprise cake

10 Coffee layer gâteau

To Fill a Swiss Roll

Jam or butter icing are ideal for filling a Swiss roll. Make the fatless sponge, Recipe 134, using 2 eggs etc., for a small Swiss roll tin and 3 eggs, etc., for a large one.

For a chocolate Swiss roll omit ½ oz. flour and add one tablespoon cocoa.

Step-by-step directions for filling a Swiss roll are given here.

Picture 1
This shows how the sponge looks when it comes from the oven.

Picture 2
This shows sponge turned out on sugared paper. Greaseproof paper is being removed.

Picture 3
The crisp edges are being cut away.

Picture 4
If filling with jam, you will spread the warm jam over the sponge and roll. If filling with butter cream, you will roll the sponge round greaseproof paper. This prevents it breaking. You can use foil, but great care must be taken not to leave the sponge wrapped for a very long period, for foil holds the heat and you will remove the skin from the sponge.

Picture 5
This shows butter cream spread on the un-rolled, cooled sponge, together with fresh fruits, if liked.

Picture 6
The completed roll.
Illustrated in colour plate 8.

1 The baked Swiss roll

2 Removing the greaseproof paper

3 Trimming the crisp edges

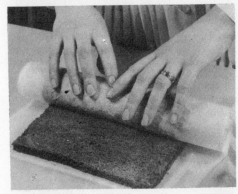

4 Rolling in greaseproof for buttercream filling

5 Spread roll being covered with fruit

6 The filled Swiss roll

Glacé Fudge Icing

171

This is like a soft cream, but has a very high ratio of icing sugar to margarine, which gives a very crisp texture. It is ideal for filling or coating a cake, but it is a little firm to use for piping unless really hard pressure is applied. For the basic recipe see Spring cake below.

172 Spring cake

8 oz. margarine
8 oz. castor sugar
finely grated rind of 1 lemon and 1 orange
4 eggs
8 oz. flour (with plain flour use 2 level teaspoons baking powder)
almond paste (Recipe 256) made with 2 oz. ground almonds
red, green and blue culinary colourings
For the filling:
3—4 heaped tablespoons lemon curd
For the glacé fudge icing:
4 oz. margarine
3 tablespoons lemon and orange juice
1 lb. sieved icing sugar
few drops pale green colouring
To decorate:
3—4 heaped tablespoons desiccated coconut
mimosa balls
1 yard narrow ribbon, mauve or yellow
1 9-inch cake board, optional

Cream the margarine and sugar together until light and fluffy. Beat in the grated rinds. Beat in the eggs one at a time until no traces remain, adding a little sieved flour with the second. Fold in the remaining flour. Divide equally between two greased and lined 8-inch tins. Smooth the tops and bake in the centre of a moderate oven (375°F. — Gas Mark 4) for 35—40 minutes. Cool. Make the almond paste and divide into four portions. Colour each portion respectively red, green and blue, leaving a fourth portion uncoloured (yellow), working in the colourings a drop at a time and kneading well. Roll the red, yellow and blue portions out thinly and cut into rounds with the smallest fluted pastry cutter. Roll the green portion out and cut into leaf shapes, marking veins with a knife. Cut a number of thin strips for stems. Cut the cakes open crossways and sandwich all together again with lemon curd. If using a cake board, spread a little lemon curd on this, and press the layered cakes down gently on to this. Melt the margarine with the fruit juices over moderate heat and, when just boiling, remove and beat in sugar and a few drops of colouring. Cool a little and beat again. Pour this over the centre of the cake and allow to flow down the sides, spreading where necessary with a warmed palette knife. Press coconut on to sides with palette knife.
Arrange a circle of overlapping rounds of almond paste round the top edge and press another circle round the base, with mimosa balls between. Arrange a group of rounds on top to represent flowers, adding leaves and stems and pressing mimosa balls into the centre of each flower.
Tie a ribbon bow round the sides of the cake.

Spring cake

To Combine Icings

173

Very often the best result is obtained from combining more than one type of icing.
Butter cream blends with either glacé icing or any of the cooked icings and the recipe below (colour picture 10) utilizes this combination of icings to give not only an attractive-looking cake, but a cake which has a good contrast in textures.

174 Coffee layer gâteau

For the sponge:
4 oz. margarine
4 oz. castor sugar
2 eggs
4 oz. flour (with plain flour use 1 teaspoon baking powder)
2 teaspoons instant coffee
3 tablespoons milk
For the mocha butter cream:
2 level teaspoons instant coffee
4 oz. icing sugar
2 oz. butter
1 level tablespoon cocoa
Coffee frosting:
1 lb. loaf sugar
¼ pint water
2 egg whites
2 teaspoons instant coffee
1 tablespoon hot water
To decorate:
24 halved walnuts

Cream the margarine and sugar, beat in the eggs gradually.
Fold in the sifted flour, baking powder and instant coffee alternately with the milk. Pour into two greased 7-inch sandwich tins and spread evenly. Bake in a moderately hot oven (375°F. — Gas Mark 4) for 25—30 minutes until firm. Allow to cool.
Beat all the ingredients for the mocha butter cream together.
Cut the two sandwiches across in half and sandwich together with the mocha butter cream.

Heat sugar and water for the frosting gently until dissolved.
Boil syrup until temperature of 240°F. or a firm ball when tested by dropping a little in water. Beat egg whites until stiff. Remove syrup from heat and allow to cool slightly. Pour over the egg whites, beating well and adding the coffee dissolved in the hot water. Beat until of a thick coating consistency.
Pour over cake smoothly, decorate with a fork by pulling up in peaks. Finish the edge with halves of shelled walnuts.
Illustrated in colour plate 10.

To Cut Cakes for Filling

175

In many recipes you will be instructed to cut the sandwich cake through the centre, see Coffee gâteau above, Recipe 174. This can be done with a knife, but there is often a tendency to get an uneven cut, i.e. the cake is deeper at one side than the other. If you use a very firm piece of cotton and hold it either side of the cake, you pull this firmly across (rather like a piece of wire cutting through cheese) and get a very straight even cut.

Cream and Cottage Cheese

176

Many people are very fond of a slightly subtle combination of sweet and savoury and the very plain type of cream cheese spread, used on a cake, gives a rather more interesting flavour than an ordinary type of butter or similar icing, which is more usual.

177 Advantages of using cream cheese for decoration

This does not become quite so sticky and greasy looking in hot weather and it has got the great advantage that it possesses a rather unusual taste.

178 Disadvantage of using cream cheese in decoration

Some people may not like the delicate cheese flavour; it is something of an acquired taste.

179 Types of cake for decorating with cream cheese

This type of topping blends well with a rather plain cake and it also blends extremely well with fruit-topped cakes, i.e. you can spread or pipe a plain sponge with cream cheese, and top it with fresh strawberries or raspberries.
The cream cheese spread can be softened by adding a little fresh cream, see Recipe 181 below, which makes it easier to spread on a very light sponge.
You can use it as in Recipe 182 (Philly sandwich cake) with icing sugar to give an alternative to an ordinary butter icing.

180 Amounts of cream cheese to use

Top of 6-inch cake	USE 3 oz. cream cheese
Top and filling of 6-inch cake	USE 6 oz. cream cheese
Top of 7-inch cake	USE 4 oz. cream cheese
Top and filling of 7-inch cake	USE 8 oz. cream cheese
Top of 8-inch cake	USE 5 oz. cream cheese
Top and filling of 8-inch cake	USE 10 oz. cream cheese

To combine icings 174
To cut cakes for filling 175
Cream and cottage cheese 176—180

181 Chocolate and raspberry nut cakes

For the plain cake:
3 oz. margarine
6 oz. castor sugar
1 egg
½ teaspoon vanilla essence
8 oz. flour (with plain flour use 2 level teaspoons baking powder)
¼ pint milk
For the topping:
⅛ pint cream
1½ packets, about 4½ oz., cream cheese spread
2 tablespoons raspberry jam
2 oz. chopped walnuts
For the chocolate cake:
3 oz. margarine
6 oz. castor sugar
1 egg
½ teaspoon vanilla essence
6 oz. flour (with plain flour use 2 level teaspoons baking powder, with self-raising flour use ½ level teaspoon baking powder)
2 oz. chocolate powder
¼ pint milk
Topping for chocolate cake:
4 tablespoons cream
1½ packets, about 4½ oz., cream cheese spread
2 tablespoons pineapple jam
chocolate shavings

With either type of cake, cream together the margarine and sugar until light and fluffy. Add the beaten egg and vanilla essence, the sieved dry ingredients and the milk. Put into a greased and floured 8-inch square tin. Bake in the centre of a moderate oven (375°F. — Gas Mark 4) for 25—30 minutes.

Picture 1
This shows the chocolate cake being topped with the cream cheese mixture. Make this by beating the cream until it is thick, then adding the cheese spread. Fold in the pineapple jam and spread this mixture over the cooled cake. Cut the cake into 9—12 pieces and sprinkle the chocolate shavings over the top.

Picture 2
This shows the grated chocolate being put on to the chocolate cakes. The Raspberry nut cakes have already been decorated as follows: Beat the cream until it thickens, then add the cheese spread and fold in the raspberry jam. Spread this mixture over the cooled cake, and sprinkle the top with chopped walnuts. Cut cake into 9—12 pieces.
Note: The cake mixture (chocolate or plain) can be made in two 8-inch round cake tins and baked as for the square tin. Sandwich together with either of the toppings.
The completed cakes are illustrated in colour plate 11.

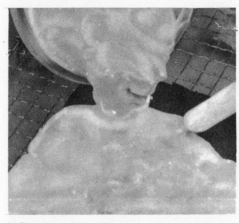
1 Covering cake with cream cheese topping

2 Decorating the chocolate cakes

182 Philly sandwich cake

For the sponge:
4 oz. margarine
4 oz. castor sugar
2 eggs
4 oz. flour (with plain flour use 1 level teaspoon baking powder)
For the filling and icing:
3 oz. cream cheese spread
14 oz. icing sugar
1—2 dessertspoons lemon juice
To decorate:
silver balls
strips of angelica

Cream the margarine and sugar until light and fluffy. Add egg gradually to avoid curdling and beat in well after each addition. Fold in (not beat) the flour and mix in thoroughly. Divide the mixture evenly between two lightly greased and floured 7-inch sandwich tins and bake in the centre of a moderately hot oven (375°F. — Gas Mark 4) for 25—30 minutes. Allow to cool.
Cream the cheese spread until smooth. Gradu-ally work in very carefully sieved icing sugar and lastly add lemon juice. Using two-thirds of the cheese icing, spread and smooth over tops of both layers and sandwich together.
Mark a 5-inch circle on the top of the cake, see Recipe 284. Using a nylon or paper icing bag or syringe, and a rose pipe and rest of cheese icing, fill the circle with rosettes. Top each rosette with a silver ball and arrange 1-inch strips of angelica round the border.

Philly sandwich cake

183 Chocolate mushroom cake

4 oz. margarine
4 oz. castor sugar
2 eggs
4 oz. flour (with plain flour use 1 level teaspoon baking powder)
For the icing:
1½ oz. chocolate
3 oz. cream cheese spread
1 teaspoon instant coffee powder
7 oz. sieved icing sugar
To decorate:
6 oz. chocolate drops
egg white
castor sugar

Cream together the margarine and sugar until light and fluffy. Beat in the eggs, then fold in the flour sieved with the baking powder. Bake in two 7-inch greased sandwich tins above centre of a moderate oven (375°F. — Gas Mark 4) for 15—20 minutes.

Grate or break chocolate into small pieces (or use extra chocolate drops). Melt in a basin over hot water. Beat well together with the cream cheese spread, instant coffee and icing sugar. Sandwich the cakes together with approximately one third of the icing and cover the top and sides with the remainder, keeping one tablespoon for decoration.

Take half the chocolate drops, brush the tops with white of egg and sprinkle with castor sugar. Allow to dry for ½ hour.

Decorate the top of the cake with alternate rows of plain and sugared drops, placing drops in icing at an angle.

Leave a few of each for the side of the cake. Put remaining chocolate butter icing into a icing bag or syringe with a rose or star pipe and pipe neat edges round top and base.

Chocolate mushroom cake

184 Cottage cheese for decorating cakes

Cottage cheese can also be used for decorating cakes. Handle as little as possible since you are inclined to make the cheese separate into a very hard tough curd if you over-handle.

Condensed Milk Fondant Icing

185

This is a fondant icing rather similar in taste to the cooked one, see Recipe 219, but it never becomes quite so hard and brittle. It is very good for plain cakes, since it is very sweet.

186 Coffee fondant cake

6 oz. flour (with plain flour use 1 level teaspoon baking powder)
1½ dessertspoons soluble coffee powder
6 oz. margarine
6 oz. castor sugar
3 eggs
Fondant icing:
8 oz. sieved icing sugar
1 tablespoon lemon juice
2 tablespoons sweetened condensed milk
To decorate:
4 oz. desiccated coconut

Sift together the dry ingredients. Cream together the fat and sugar until light and fluffy. Beat in the eggs one at a time. Quickly fold in the dry ingredients and turn into a greased and lined 6—7-inch cake tin. Bake in a very moderate oven (350°F. — Gas Mark 3) for about 1 hour. Cool. Beat the icing sugar and flavouring into the sweetened condensed milk until smooth and creamy. Cover cake with fondant icing and desiccated coconut (Recipe 12).

Coffee fondant cake

187 Points to remember with butter and similar icings

Be careful when adding liquid to this type of icing that the mixture does not curdle.

Beat the butter, or other fat used, well, so that you get a smooth, light texture as well as an attractive appearance.

Use this icing for filling and decorating.

Remember, if correctly made, this icing pipes extremely well. If it is inclined to be soft and not holding its shape in piping, add a little extra sieved icing sugar. If it is inclined to be stiff and therefore difficult to pipe, either add a little extra butter or other fat and cream well, or put in a very small quantity of milk, fruit juice or other liquid.

Chocolate Decorations and Icing

188 Easy chocolate decorations to combine with butter icing

Uncooked chocolate can form the basis of an attractive decoration on cakes and it combines extremely well with butter and similar icings. Remember plain chocolate is better to use than milk, since its flavour is more definite.

An ordinary bar of chocolate can be grated to use either for sprinkling on the top of the cake, see Recipe 235, or for coating the sides. Small chocolate drops, either plain or milk, can be cut into pieces for decoration. In order to get a clean cut use a really firm knife.

Picture 1

This shows bars of chocolate cut into triangles to use as a decoration on a gâteau.

Picture 2

This shows these bars forming a 'sun-ray' effect. The sides of this cake are coated with butter icing, then rolled in chocolate vermicelli or grated chocolate. The top of the cake is decorated with rosettes of butter icing, and the triangles of chocolate pressed into this, the centre being filled with a large rosette and a sugar flower pressed on top.

Picture 3

This shows a similar cake, the top decorated with portions of flaked chocolate bars and a chocolate drop placed in the centre.

Picture 4

This shows the flaky bars being crushed for rather coarse chocolate for sprinkling over the top of cakes.

If you wish to make this coarse flake with ordinary bars of chocolate, bring a sharp knife down the side of the bars to form large thin pieces. A more professional way of making chocolate chips is to melt chocolate couverture or plain chocolate, pour it on to a flat tin or marble slab and then drag a sharp knife across the chocolate when firm. With practice you can get curls of chocolate.

1 Cutting chocolate triangles

2 Cake decorated with chocolate triangles

3 Cake decorated with flaked chocolate bars

4 Crushing flaked chocolate for decoration

189 To use melted chocolate for icing

Chocolate icing is a great favourite with most people and it can be made either as below, or simply by melting chocolate, which naturally hardens again to become fairly brittle. This makes an admirable coating on a cake and can be used for piping, if wished.

190 Advantages of using chocolate for icing

Melted chocolate, or a melted chocolate icing, is very simple to make as it does not need many other ingredients and its flavour is excellent and popular.

191 Disadvantage of using chocolate for icing

You can overheat the chocolate which will make it lose its glaze and change its texture.

192 Types of cake suitable for chocolate icing

Chocolate icing combines rather better with plain, chocolate, orange or coffee flavoured sponge cakes than with richer cakes such as fruit cakes.

193 Melted chocolate icing 1

2 oz. chocolate
1 tablespoon cold milk
1 tablespoon cold water
4 oz. sieved icing sugar

1 Place the chocolate together with the milk and water in a basin over a pan half full of water, making sure the basin rests firmly on the rim of the pan.
2 Bring the water in the pan to the boil, and then remove from the heat.
3 Allow the chocolate to melt slowly.
4 Stir in the sieved icing sugar.
5 Add a little more icing sugar, or water, if necessary to form the right consistency.

194 Melted chocolate icing 2

1 Put the broken chocolate into a basin and melt it as given in the icing above, Recipe 193.
2 A few drops of oil or a very tiny knob of butter helps to keep the icing very glacé.
3 The real secret is not to use too much heat in melting.

195 Amounts of melted chocolate icing to use

For top of a 6-inch cake:	USE 1 oz. chocolate
Icing 1	2 oz. icing sugar, etc.
Icing 2	USE 3 oz. chocolate
For top of a 7-inch cake:	USE 1½ oz. chocolate
Icing 1	3 oz. icing sugar, etc.
Icing 2	USE 4½ oz. chocolate
For top of an 8—9-inch cake:	USE 2 oz. chocolate
Icing 1	4 oz. icing sugar, etc.
Icing 2	USE 6 oz. chocolate

196 Choice of chocolate for melted chocolate icing

It is best, if possible, to try to procure the real chocolate couverture. If this is unobtainable, use block chocolate, either plain or milk.

197 Sachertorte

scant 5 oz. flour
6 eggs
5 oz. chocolate
1 tablespoon water
5 oz. butter
5 oz. icing sugar
little apricot jam
melted chocolate icing (Recipe 193) made with 4—6 oz. melted chocolate

Sift the flour twice. Separate egg yolks and whites. Break chocolate into small pieces, add a tablespoon water and put in a warm place to melt. Cream butter with 4 oz. sugar, add egg yolks gradually. Add the melted chocolate (which must be soft but not hot) and stir well. Whisk egg whites until stiff, whisk in remaining 1 oz. sugar. Fold stiffly beaten egg whites into the butter and chocolate mixture, alternately with the flour. Bake in a greased and floured 9-inch tin in the centre of a moderate oven (375°F. — Gas Mark 4) for 50—60 minutes. When cold, spread with warmed apricot jam and chocolate icing.
For an even richer cake, split through the middle. Fill and coat sides with chocolate butter icing (Recipe 100, made with 12 oz. butter) and chocolate vermicelli. When the top chocolate has set, put a little melted chocolate into a piping bag or syringe with a No. 1 or 2 writing pipe and pipe the word 'Sacher' across.

Sachertorte

2 oz. butter or margarine
¼ pint water
pinch salt
vanilla essence
3 oz. plain flour
2 large eggs
thick cream
melted chocolate icing (Recipe 193) made with 2 oz. chocolate, 4 oz. icing sugar, etc.

Chocolate icing is often used for éclairs; here are step-by-step directions for making them.

Picture 1
1 Place the fat, cold water, salt and vanilla essence in a pan.
2 Heat the water to boiling point making sure that the fat has melted.
Picture 2
3 Immediately add all the flour.
4 Remove from heat and beat until mixture forms a smooth ball and leaves the sides.
5 Allow to cool.
Picture 3
6 Beat in the eggs.
Picture 4
7 Place in a piping bag fitted with a ¾-inch plain meringue pipe.
8 Pipe the mixture in even lengths on to a greased baking tray.
Picture 5
9 Bake for approximately 25 minutes in a hot oven (425—450°F. — Gas Mark 6—7).

DO NOT OPEN THE OVEN DOOR BEFORE THIS TIME.
It is also important that the éclair cases are cooked until quite crisp on the sides.
Picture 6
10 Immediately slit open with scissors. See pictures, Recipes 181 and 198.
11 Allow to cool.
Picture 7
12 Whip the cream.
13 Place in a piping bag fitted with a large meringue star pipe.
14 Fill the éclairs with the cream.
Picture 8
15 Place the chocolate with the milk and water in a basin over a pan of water.
16 Bring the water in the pan to the boil, then remove from heat.
17 Allow the chocolate to melt slowly.
Picture 9
18 Stir in the sieved icing sugar.
Picture 10
19 Top the éclairs with the chocolate icing.

1 Melting the fat in the water

2 Beating mixture after flour has been added

3 Beating the eggs into the cooled mixture

4 Piping mixture on to a greased baking tray

5 The baked éclairs

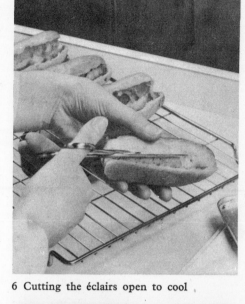

6 Cutting the éclairs open to cool

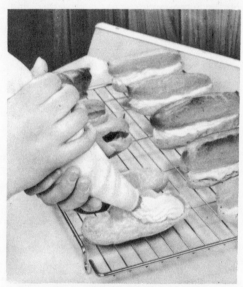

7 Filling the éclairs with piped cream

8 Melting the chocolate in milk and water

9 Adding the sieved icing sugar

10 Coating the éclairs with chocolate icing

Chocolate vermicelli	Obtainable all ready to use.
Grated or heated chocolate	See pictures, Recipes 181 and 198.
Chocolate drops	See picture, Recipe 183.
Cut bars of chocolate	See pictures 1 and 2 under Recipe 188.
Chocolate biscuits	See Birthday cake, Recipe 292.

200 Points to remember when using chocolate decoration

Overheating of any type of chocolate ruins both the consistency and the glaze.
For the very best results buy genuine chocolate couverture. Plain chocolate is better than milk for decorating.

If you are using hard chocolate, it will become very hard when set, so if you wish to keep it softer blend with a little butter icing. This is suitable for a filling. Put in a few drops of oil or warm water to make suitable for a coating.

Cooked and Heated Icings

201

In this section there is the Seven-minute icing, see Recipe 210, and a variation on Fudge icing, Recipe 231, where the ingredients are heated together, and icings where the sugar syrup is cooked to a temperature high enough to alter its state before adding other ingredients.

202 The purpose of cooked icings

By heating the sugar with other ingredients, you alter its flavour, for example you can produce fudge or fondant which are both very suitable for an icing.

203 Advantages of cooked icings

The advantages of the icings vary with the type of icing. For example, American frosting is advantageous to many people because while it looks like a royal icing, it never becomes hard and brittle. It may seem hard on the outside, but the moment you cut through the crispy coating you will find that it is soft and it will remain soft for a considerable period.
Fudge icing has the advantage that it is firm enough to use on a cake without marzipan.
The other advantages of this type of icing are mentioned under the particular headings.

204 Disadvantages of cooked icings

The chief disadvantage is that the mixture must be cooked to exactly the right temperature, otherwise it does not produce the desired result. Care must be taken, therefore, to test sufficiently early to avoid over-boiling. These icings are not suitable for piping.

205 Types of cake to decorate with cooked icings

The type of cake to be decorated varies according to the icing you choose to make.

American frosting	is suitable for either a very light sponge or to take the place of royal icing on rich cakes.
Fondant icing	is a little hard for a sponge but admirable as a coating on rich cakes.
Fudge icing	is generally used with a fairly plain sponge because it is rather sweet.
Brown sugar or honey frostings	are generally used with a fairly plain sponge because, like fudge, they are rather sweet.
Marshmallow icing	should be put on to a rather fragile type of cake, because it is soft and delicate.
Caramel icing	is the most difficult of all, and is generally put on either biscuit-type or soft delicate cakes.

206 To make American frosting

6 oz. loaf or granulated sugar
¼ pint water
1 egg white
pinch cream of tartar

1 Put the sugar and water into a saucepan and heat, stirring until the sugar has dissolved.
2 Boil steadily until mixture reaches soft ball stage, i.e. when a little is dropped into cold water, it forms a soft, pliable ball (238°F.).
3 Beat until the syrup turns cloudy, then pour on to the STIFFLY BEATEN egg white.
4 Beat in cream of tartar till mixture thickens.

207 Amounts of American frosting to use

For a thin layer on top of a 6-inch cake	USE 4 oz. sugar, etc.
For a thick layer on top of a 6-inch cake	USE 6 oz. sugar, etc.
For a thin layer on top of a 7-inch cake	USE 6 oz. sugar, etc.
For a thick layer on top of a 7-inch cake	USE 9 oz. sugar, etc.
For a thin layer on top of a 8-inch cake	USE 8 oz. sugar, etc.
For a thick layer on top of a 8-inch cake	USE 12 oz. sugar, etc.
For a thin layer on top of a 9-inch cake	USE 10 oz. sugar, etc.
For a thick layer on top of a 9-inch cake	USE 15 oz. sugar, etc.

If used as a filling, then allow exactly the same amount of frosting as for the thin top layer. If coating the sides of a shallow cake, allow exactly the same amount as for a thin top layer. If coating the sides of a deep cake, allow same quantity as for the thick top layer.

208 To use American frosting

Picture 1
This shows the sugar being put into the water. In this case a large cake is being decorated, so that a whole pound of sugar is needed.

Picture 2
Testing the heat of the syrup with a sugar thermometer. In order to make sure this registers correctly, stir it round in the hot syrup and do not lift right out of the mixture to read.

Picture 3
Testing the syrup in cold water.

Picture 4
Pouring the frosting on to the cake. The syrup has been cooled slightly and poured over the whisked egg white, whisking all the time, then beaten further until the mixture becomes thick and fluffy.

Picture 5
The icing being spread over the cake.

1 Adding the sugar to the water

2 Heating the sugar and water to 238°F.

3 Testing the syrup

4 Pouring the frosting over the cake

5 The frosting spread over the cake

209 Chocolate surprise cake

3 eggs
3 oz. castor sugar
3 oz. flour
1 tablespoon cocoa
1 oz. butter (melted and
  slightly cooled)
American frosting:
1 lb. loaf sugar
¼ pint water
2 egg whites
apricot jam

Whisk the eggs and sugar until thick, light and fluffy. Carefully fold in the sieved flour and cocoa, and finally add the melted butter. Turn the mixture into three 6-inch or two 7-inch greased and lined sandwich tins and bake in a moderately hot oven (400°F. — Gas Mark 5) for 10—15 minutes.
Cool on a wire tray. Put the sugar and water into a saucepan and heat gently until the sugar has dissolved. Boil for approximately 3 minutes until a little of the mixture, when dropped into cold water, forms a soft ball. Remove from the heat and cool slightly. Whisk the egg whites until they are quite stiff. Pour the syrup over the egg whites, whisking all the time. Continue to whisk until the mixture is thick and fluffy. Sandwich the cakes together with approximately half the icing, then spread the remainder over top and around sides of cake. Use the back of a teaspoon to pull into peaks. Add spoonfuls of apricot jam as decoration.
Illustrated in colour plate 9.

210 Flavourings and variations on frosting

Almond
Add 1 teaspoon almond essence to the mixture.

Chocolate
Stir in ½ oz. sieved cocoa when the icing reaches 238°F.

Coconut
Boil icing until it reaches 238°F.; add 3 oz. desiccated or freshly shredded coconut, stir well, then continue.

Coffee
Use 4 tablespoons strong coffee and 4 tablespoons of water.

Jam or jelly
Whisk 1 egg white until very stiff, then gradually beat in 2 tablespoons sieved jam or jelly. If possible this should be melted, allowed to cool, but NOT set, before being added. This gives a soft, marshmallow type of frosting, which is excellent for sponge cakes, or cakes for children. If the jam or jelly is not melted, you get a slightly mottled effect, but this does not spoil the flavour of the frosting. Continue as before.

Lemon
Use two tablespoons lemon juice and six tablespoons of water to give ¼ pint. Also add ½ teaspoon very finely grated lemon rind, if wished.

Orange
Use 4 tablespoons fresh orange juice and 4 tablespoons of water and add ½—1 teaspoon very finely grated orange rind.

Pineapple
Use either 1 teaspoon pineapple essence in the icing or 4 tablespoons pineapple juice and 4 tablespoons of water.

Seven-minute
Put 1 egg white, 3 dessertspoons cold water, 7 oz. granulated sugar and ¼ teaspoon cream of tartar into a double saucepan or a basin that fits over a small saucepan. Whisk until well mixed. Place over rapidly boiling water. Beat hard and cook for seven minutes until frosting stands up in peaks, then add the vanilla essence.

211 Walnut cake with American frosting

6 oz. margarine or butter
6 oz. castor sugar
3 eggs
6 oz. flour (with plain flour
  use 1¼ level teaspoons
  baking powder)
3 oz. very finely chopped
  walnuts
small amount of milk
Filling and topping (next recipe)

Cream margarine and sugar till soft and light. Gradually beat in the eggs. Fold in the flour mixed with the walnuts. Gradually add enough milk to give a soft consistency. Divide the mixture between two 8-inch sandwich tins which should be lined at the base with greased greaseproof paper and greased and floured on the sides. Bake for approximately 30 minutes just above centre of a moderate oven (375°F. — Gas Mark 4), lowering the heat to 350°F. — Gas Mark 3 after 20 — minutes if browning too much. If preferred, bake in a 7-inch cake tin, again lining as above, and bake in the centre of a very moderate oven (350°F. — Gas Mark 3) for just over an hour.
When the cake is cold, the sandwich cake can either be filled through the centre with vanilla butter icing to which is added a few chopped walnuts OR with frosting.
To make a richer cake, each half of the sandwich can be split through the middle giving three layers of filling. In the same way the 7-inch cake can be split throught the centre or in such a way as to give three layers of filling.

Frosting (Recipe 206)
For top and sides only of 7-inch cake
For top, sides and 1 layer of 7-inch cake
For top, sides and 3 layers of 7-inch cake

Butter icing, if used instead of frosting, for filling a 7-inch cake (Recipe 100)
For filling 3 layers of 7-inch cake

USE 15 oz. sugar
USE 1 lb. 5 oz. sugar
USE 1 lb. 11 oz. — 2 lb. sugar, depending on thickness of layers
USE 2 oz. butter, ½ oz. chopped walnuts, 2½ oz. icing sugar
USE 6 oz. butter, 3 oz. chopped walnuts, 7½ oz. icing sugar

Frosting 8-inch cake
Because this cake will be more shallow than the 7-inch cake, you should find when you coat the sides and top that you can manage with the same amount as for the 7-inch cake. If, however, you intend to fill the cake with butter icing, you need to allow just a little more of it.

Butter icing to fill 1 layer of 8-inch cake

For filling 3 layers of 8-inch cake

USE 2½—3 oz. butter, ¾—1 oz. chopped walnuts, 3—3½ oz. icing sugar
USE 7½—9 oz. butter, 2¼—3 oz. chopped walnuts, 9—10½ oz. icing sugar

212 Mosaic cake with frosting

8 oz. margarine or butter
8 oz. castor sugar
4 eggs
5 oz. flour (with plain flour
use 2 level teaspoons baking
powder — with self-raising
flour add ¾ teaspoon baking
powder)
1 packet raspberry
blancmange powder
1 packet chocolate
blancmange powder
1 packet banana blancmange
powder
American frosting (Recipe 206)
made with 12 oz. sugar, etc.
To decorate:
chocolate drops

Cream the margarine and sugar until soft and light. Gradually beat in the eggs and fold in the sieved flour and baking powder. Divide the mixture into three parts. Into one, blend the chocolate blancmange and a few drops of water or milk. Into the second blend the raspberry blancmange and a few drops of water or milk. Into the third, blend the banana blancmange and a few drops of water or milk.

Grease and flour an 8-inch cake tin and put in spoonfuls of the three different flavoured mixtures. Bake for approximately 1 hour to 1 hour 10 minutes in a very moderate oven (350°F. — Gas Mark 3). Turn out and cool. Make the American frosting. Beat until thick and spread thinly over the top and sides of the cake. Decorate with chocolate buttons.

A slice of Mosaic cake with frosting

213 Devil's food cake

3 oz. plain chocolate
¼ pint milk
8 oz. flour
½ teaspoon baking powder
4 oz. butter
8 oz. castor sugar
2 eggs
3—4 drops vanilla essence
*vanilla or chocolate butter
cream,*★ (Recipe 100) made
with 4 oz. butter, etc.
white or chocolate frosting★
(Recipe 206), made with
1 lb. sugar
★*Or use all frosting made with
1½ lb. sugar, etc.*

Dissolve the chocolate in milk. Sieve dry ingredients. Cream fat, beat in sugar and eggs, one at a time. Stir in dry ingredients alternately with the chocolate and milk. Add vanilla essence and divide the mixture between two greased 8-inch sandwich tins. Bake in the centre of a moderately hot oven (400°F. — Gas Mark 5) for 20—30 minutes. When cool, sandwich together with the butter cream and ice with the frosting, or use frosting for both filling and covering the cake. A little grated chocolate, see Recipe 188, or chocolate vermicelli may be sprinkled on top of white frosting to give a contrasting colour.

Devil's food cake

20mins @ 180 enough. 25-too much.

214 Angel cake

1½ oz. flour (with plain flour
you can use ¼ teaspoon
baking powder, but no
more)
3 oz. castor sugar
3 egg whites
¼ teaspoon cream of tartar
½ teaspoon vanilla essence
For the 7-minute frosting:
1 large egg white
4 oz. castor sugar
pinch of cream of tartar
2 tablespoons water
To decorate:
tiny pieces of angelica
sugar flowers

Sieve the flour and sugar together twice. Whisk the egg whites and cream of tartar until very stiff. Use a metal spoon and fold in carefully the sugar, flour and flavouring. Place in an ungreased angel cake tin, 6 inches × 3 inches deep and bake for 40 minutes in the centre of a cool oven (300°F. — Gas Mark 2) covering the top with greaseproof paper after about 25 minutes. When cooked, invert tin over cake rack and allow to drop out when ready.

Put all the icing ingredients in a bowl and place over a saucepan of boiling water. Whisk with a rotary beater until the mixture holds its shape — about 7 minutes. Remove from heat and continue whisking until the mixture is thick enough to spread — about 3 minutes. Spread over the cake and finish with a flower decoration as illustrated.

Angel cake

215 Angel cake tins

Angel cake tins, or ring tins as they are sometimes called, may be difficult to obtain.

Savarin tins can be used instead, but you can fashion your own angel cake tin as follows: Use an ordinary cake tin and inside this place a small tin, such as a cocoa tin or milk tin. This should be weighted in some way so that it does not move about. The weights from your scales are ideal for this, or alternatively you can use small, clean pebbles.

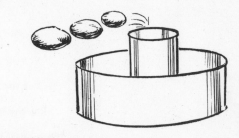

To make your own angel cake tin

216 The purpose of fondant icing

This is a good substitute for marzipan under royal icing.

It can take the place of royal icing for coating a cake.

The main purpose of fondant icing is to provide a covering or base on most types of cakes. It can take the place of marzipan and many people who dislike marzipan would be well advised to put a layer of fondant icing under their royal icing.

217 Advantages of fondant icing

Because this icing has been cooked, it keeps very well and it can therefore be made in bulk and stored to be reheated to make more pliable.

As the recipes show, it can either be spread when very soft or worked and kneaded till it can be cut like marzipan.

218 Disadvantage of fondant icing

It hardens rather quickly and is difficult to handle. This is easily overcome if rewarmed.

219 To make fondant icing

6 oz. loaf or granulated sugar
4 tablespoons water
pinch cream of tartar
1 dessertspoon warm water

1 Put the sugar and 4 tablespoon water into a saucepan.
2 Stir until the sugar has dissolved.
3 Add the cream of tartar.
4 Boil until the mixture reaches 237−238°F., i.e. forms a soft ball when a little is dropped into cold water.
5 Beat until the mixture starts to turn cloudy.
6 Add the warm water.
7 It can then be spread on the cake or put through the centre as a filling.
8 If you wish to use it instead of marzipan, turn on to a sugared board and knead well, then roll out like marzipan.

Boiling the fondant icing mixture to 238°F.

220 Types of cake suitable for fondant icing

Although fondant icing makes a very good coating for a firm cake, it can be used with success for sponges. It is rather sweet and solid for a very delicate sponge, such as the fatless sponge, Recipe 130. It is perfectly all right with a Victoria sandwich, particularly if the cake has been allowed a few hours to settle and become firm.

221 To coat small cakes with fondant icing

With the fondant at the right temperature, blend with just enough warm water or warm fruit juice or diluted coffee to give a pouring consistency. It can then be spooned over the cakes as shown in the picture. So that none of the fondant is wasted, put another tray or a dish underneath the cooling tray. You can take the fondant from this, reheat gently over hot water and use again.

Coating small cakes with fondant icing

222 Amounts of fondant icing to use

For the top of a 6-inch cake	USE 4 oz. sugar, etc.
For the top and sides of a 6-inch cake	USE 8−12 oz. sugar, etc.
For the top of a 7−8-inch cake	USE 6 oz. sugar, etc.
For the top and sides of a 7−8-inch cake	USE 9−18 oz. sugar, etc.
For the top of a 8−9-inch cake	USE 9 oz. sugar, etc.
For the top and sides of a 8−9-inch cake	USE 1 lb. 2 oz. − 1 lb. 10 oz. sugar, etc.
For the top of a 9−10-inch cake	USE 12 oz. sugar, etc.
For the top and sides of a 9−10-inch cake	USE 1½ lb.−2¼ lb. sugar, etc.

When spreading the top and sides, use twice as much as for the top; when kneading out the top and sides, use three times as much as for the top.

223 Flavourings for fondant icing

1 Add few drops of vanilla essence to water.
2 For fruit flavoured fondant, use either 4 tablespoons fresh or canned fruit juice. If using sweetened juice, be sparing with sugar.
3 Use 4 tablespoons coffee or diluted instant coffee or coffee essence for coffee fondant.

224 The purpose of fudge icing

This is a particularly delicious icing to put on to sponge cakes since you can incorporate quite definite flavours into the icing.

Use as topping, filling or complete coating (be sure to get whole cake covered while icing is pliable enough to spread).

225 Advantage of fudge icing

Its delicious soft, creamy texture makes it an outstanding icing, which is generally popular.

226 Disadvantages of fudge icing

It very easily over-cooks; test frequently. Do not make this icing before it is required.

Work quickly as, once cool, it sets, losing its creamy texture. Unsuitable for piping.

227 To make fudge icing

8 oz. granulated sugar
3 tablespoons water
1 oz. butter or margarine flavouring
1 small can condensed milk, full cream if possible

1 Put the sugar and water into a saucepan with the butter.
2 Stir over a gentle heat until sugar dissolves.
3 Add the flavouring and condensed milk.

4 Boil steadily, stirring from time to time till the mixture reaches 238°F. — i.e. forms a soft ball when a little is dropped in cold water.
5 Beat until cloudy.

228 Flavourings for fudge icing

1 Add ½—1 teaspoon vanilla, almond or rum flavouring.
2 Add a little greated lemon or orange rind. Fruit juice may make milk curdle.

3 At the end of the cooking time, ½ oz. cocoa or 1 oz. chocolate can be beaten in.
4 Strong coffee can be used in place of water.

229 Amounts of fudge icing to use

For a moderately thick layer through centre and on top of 6—7-inch cake — USE 8 oz. sugar, etc.
For centre, top and sides of 6—7-inch cake — USE 1 lb. sugar, etc.
For very thin layer through centre and on top of 7—8-inch cake — USE 8 oz. sugar, etc.
For a generous layer through centre and on top of 7—8-inch cake — USE 12 oz. sugar, etc.
For centre, top and sides of 7—8-inch cake — USE 1—1½ lb. sugar, etc.
For layer through centre and on top of 8—9-inch cake — USE 12 oz. — 1 lb. sugar, etc.
For centre, top and sides of 8—9-inch cake — USE 1½—2 lb. sugar, etc.
For layer through centre and on top of 9—10-inch cake — USE 1—1¼ lb. sugar, etc.
For centre, top and sides of 9—10-inch cake — USE 2—2½ lb. sugar, etc.

230 Types of cakes suitable for fudge icing

Excellent on sponge cakes and fruit flavoured cakes, it is rarely used on rich fruit cakes.

231 Mocha fudge cake

4 oz. self-raising flour
1 level teaspoon baking powder
1 heaped tablespoon cocoa
4 oz. softened margarine
4 oz. castor sugar
2 eggs
1 tablespoon coffee essence
For the icing:
4 oz. margarine
3 oz. granulated sugar
4 tablespoons milk
1 tablespoon coffee essence
8 oz. icing sugar
3 level dessertspoons cocoa
For the filling and decoration:
¼ pint thick cream
mimosa balls
angelica
2 oz. chocolate

Sieve together flour, baking powder and cocoa. Place all the ingredients in a bowl and beat together until well mixed. Place in two 7-inch sandwich tins, previously lined with grease-proof paper and brushed with melted margarine. Bake on the middle shelf of a very moderate oven (350°F. — Gas Mark 3) for 25—35 minutes. Turn out; cool on a wire tray. To make the icing melt the margarine in a saucepan, add sugar, dissolve and then bring to the boil. Add milk and coffee essence. Stir till bubbling, remove from heat; cool. Sieve icing sugar and cocoa into a bowl; add liquid. Beat well; leave covered till of coating consistency. Sandwich cakes together with whipped cream; pour icing over. Decorate with mimosa balls, angelica and shredded chocolate. Leave to set. *Note:* As seen here, you can cook sugar, margarine and milk together, adding icing sugar after. This gives easily controlled icing with does not harden so quickly.

Mocha fudge cake

232 Brown sugar or butterscotch frosting

This is rather similar to the American frosting but it needs more cooking to reach the correct temperature. It has a delicious flavour. Proportions vary slightly, as will be seen from the basic butterscotch frosting and the frosting with the chocolate wonder cake.

The first one gives a rather more brittle icing.

The second a rather soft icing which needs an appreciable amount of beating to stiffen. This is basically a frosting, but because the brown sugar gives a slightly different flavour, it is generally considered a separate icing.

For advantages, disadvantages and types of cake for which suitable, see Recipes 203-5.

233 Amounts of butterscotch frosting to use

Use directions for American frosting (Recipe 207) or individual recipe where this differs.

234 Butterscotch frosting

6 oz. brown sugar
4 tablespoons water
1 egg white
pinch cream of tartar

1 Put the sugar and water into a saucepan and stir until the sugar has dissolved.
2 Boil steadily until mixture reaches soft ball stage, 238°F.

3 Beat until the syrup turns cloudy.
4 Pour on to the stiffly beaten egg white.
5 Add the cream of tartar.
6 Continue beating until the mixture thickens.

235 Chocolate wonder cake

8 oz. plain flour*
8 oz. castor sugar
2 oz. cocoa
¼ level teaspoon bicarbonate of soda
½ level teaspoon salt
1 level teaspoon baking powder
12 tablespoons sour milk
6 tablespoons corn oil
½ teaspoon vanilla essence
For the icing:
2 egg whites
10 oz. soft brown sugar
4 tablespoons water
To decorate:
1—2 oz. grated chocolate (Recipe 188)
*Better than self-raising flour.

Grease two 8-inch sandwich tins and line the bottoms with greaseproof paper. Sift all of the dry ingredients together into a mixing bowl. Whisk together the milk, corn oil and essence and add to the dry ingredients. Beat well to form a smooth slack mixture, and turn into the prepared tins.
Bake about 20 minutes in a moderately hot oven (400°F. — Gas Mark 5). Turn out and leave to cool.
To make the icing, mix the egg whites, sugar and water together and beat over hot water until the icing becomes fluffy and stands in peaks. This will take about 12—15 minutes as brown sugar is more difficult to use than white. Fill and ice the cake. Sprinkle the top with grated chocolate.

Chocolate wonder cake

236 Chocolate cream frosting

4 oz. plain chocolate
2 oz. butter or margarine
12 oz. sifted icing sugar
4 tablespoons milk
1 teaspoon vanilla essence
pinch salt

Melt chocolate and butter in double pan or in small mixing bowl over hot water. Remove from heat. With electric mixer, or a rotary whisk, blend in sugar, milk, vanilla essence and salt. The frosting will be slightly thin, so place bowl in cold water and beat until it thickens to spreading consistency. This makes enough to fill and coat the top and sides of a 9-inch cake.

237 Honey icings

There are a number of slight variations of heated recipes using honey, all of which are very delicious. Honey gives a sweet but not over-sweet flavour to the cake decoration.

238 Chocolate honey cake

3 oz. plain chocolate
8 level tablespoons honey
6 oz. plain flour
1 level teaspoon bicarbonate of soda
¾ teaspoon salt
4 oz. butter
3 oz. castor sugar
1 teaspoon vanilla essence
2 eggs
scant ¼ pint water
For the chocolate honey icing:
6 oz. plain chocolate
4 level tablespoons honey
8 oz. icing sugar
2 tablespoons warm water

Put chocolate and honey in small basin over pan of hot water. Stir until chocolate has melted, beat well and leave to cool. Sieve flour and bicarbonate of soda and salt together three times. Cream butter, beat in sugar and continue beating until light and fluffy. Beat in chocolate mixture, then eggs one at a time. Add vanilla essence, stir in flour a little at a time alternately with water. Beat well and pour mixture into two greased and lined 8-inch sandwich tins. Bake in a very moderate oven (350°F. — Gas Mark 3) for 45—50 minutes. Cool slightly before turning out of tins. To make icing, place chocolate and honey in small basin over pan of hot water. Stir until chocolate has melted, remove from pan and allow to cool slightly. Beat in half the sugar, stir in water and remaining sugar and beat well. Spread one cake with a little of the icing and place second cake on top. Coat top and sides with icing, swirling with a palette knife.

Chocolate honey cake

11   Chocolate and raspberry nut cakes

12 Christmas cake

American frosting (Recipe 206)
made with 3 egg whites

239 Beehive cake

Use the cake recipe for Chocolate honey cake in Recipe 238, but instead of baking the mixture in two 8-inch sandwich tins, bake a little more than half the mixture in a deep 8-inch sandwich or cake tin, and the remainder in a 6—7-inch tin.

Or you can use three tins — a shallow 8-inch, a shallow 7-inch and a shallow 5—6-inch, allowing just a little longer cooking time for the deep cakes and rather less time for the smaller cakes.

Sandwich the cakes together with a little American frosting and coat with the rest of the frosting to look like a beehive.

Tiny ornamental bees can be put on top.

Beehive cake

240 Bombe royale

4 oz. margarine
4 oz. castor sugar
2 eggs
4 oz. flour (with plain flour use
   1 teaspoon baking powder)
For the sweet pastry:
4 oz. flour (preferably plain)
pinch salt
2½ oz. margarine
1 oz. castor sugar
2 egg yolks
For the filling:
4 oz. crystallized pineapple
2 oz. crystallized ginger *or*
   other fruits to choice
2 tablespoons lemon juice
1 tablespoon honey
For the icing:
3½ oz. castor sugar
2 tablespoons water
2 tablespoons honey
2 egg whites
For the coating:
little apricot jam
To decorate:
crystallized violets and roses

Cream together the margarine and sugar until light and fluffy. Add the eggs gradually to the creamed mixture, beating thoroughly. Sieve together the flour and baking powder and fold carefully into the creamed mixture. Bake in two greased and floured 7-inch tins in the centre of a moderate oven (375°F. — Gas Mark 4) for approximately 25 minutes.

For the sweet pastry, sieve together the flour and salt. Rub the margarine into the flour until the mixture resembles fine breadcrumbs. Add the sugar. Add egg yolks one at a time, adding second yolk only if necessary to make up to a stiff dough. Knead lightly and roll out into an 8-inch circle. Trim edges, prick and bake on a baking sheet in a moderately hot oven (400°F. — Gas Mark 5) for 20—25 minutes. Cut the crystallized fruit into small pieces. Mix the lemon juice and honey together and soak fruits in this mixture for 1 hour.

Make the icing by boiling the castor sugar, water and honey together until it reaches 242°F. or for approximately 3 minutes, when mixture forms a soft ball in cold water. Beat the egg whites until they are stiff. Gradually pour boiling syrup on to egg whites, beating all the time. Continue to beat for a further 2 minutes after the addition of all the syrup. Spread a tablespoon of the icing on to the cold pastry. Cut one of the cakes in two and spread the cut sides with the apricot jam. Place a third of the crystallized fruit filling on the cake and sandwich together. Place this on to the pastry base.

With a 4½-inch cutter, cut the centre from the remaining cake. Spread a thin layer of icing on the underside of the large outer circle and place on top of the first cake. Fill the centre with the remaining filling and liquor. Place the small cake circle on top of the filling.

Cover completely with icing, making decorative swirling effect with palette knife. Leave ¼ inch of pastry as a border. Scatter the crystallized violets and roses over the icing.

Bombe royale

241 Marshmallow icing

This is a heated icing: it simply means melting the marshmallows, but care must be taken not to over-heat or the delicate texture is lost. This is particularly suitable for sponge cakes.

242 To make marshmallow icing

Allow approximately 4 oz. marshmallows for a good topping on an 8-inch cake. Melt until slightly fluffy. Cool a little and spread over cake. For a more elaborate topping, see Recipe 243.

243 Mallow marble cake

6 oz. butter or margarine
6 oz. castor sugar
1 teaspoon vanilla essence
3 eggs
5 oz. self-raising flour
few drops cochineal
½ oz. cocoa powder
½ oz. cornflour
raspberry jam
For the marshmallow frosting:
30 pink 'recipe size' marshmallows *or* 20 dessert marshmallows
1 tablespoon milk
2 egg whites
1 oz. castor sugar

Cream margarine, sugar and vanilla essence together till light and fluffy. Beat in eggs singly; divide mixture between three bowls.
To first bowl add 2 oz. sifted flour; fold in. To second bowl add 2 oz. sifted flour and few drops of red colouring; fold in well. To third bowl add remaining 1 oz. flour, cocoa powder and cornflour, sifted together; mix in well.
Drop alternate spoonfuls of the mixtures into a greased and lined 7-inch cake tin. Bake in the centre of a moderate oven (375°F. — Gas Mark 4) for 1—1¼ hours, until well risen and firm. Cool on a wire tray.
Cut into two layers and fill with raspberry jam. Melt the marshmallows slowly in the milk, then remove from the heat and leave to cool. Whisk egg whites until stiff, then add sugar and re-whisk until mixture is shiny and stands in firm peaks. Fold into the marshmallow mixture, then leave to stand for about 7—10 minutes before using. For a deeper pink, add a few drops of red colouring. Cover the top and sides of the cake with the frosting and leave in a cool place until ready to serve.
If you find the frosting clings to the knife when you slice the cake, dip knife into hot water.

Mallow marble cake

244 The purpose of caramel icing

The main purpose of caramel icing is to give a crisp hard topping on a cake which, as one would imagine, makes a very pleasant contrast to the texture of a soft cake.

245 Advantages of caramel icing

The chief advantage is a dramatic-looking topping to the cake and a very good flavour.

246 Disadvantages of caramel icing

The caramel is difficult to make in that it must be exactly the right temperature so that it does not harden too much in the pan, or have a slightly burnt flavour.
It must be poured rapidly over the cake when it has reached just the right stage for pouring, without dropping down the sides.
It must be marked in pieces before quite cold, otherwise it will be impossible to cut the icing into slices.
The caramel butter icing is, of course, much easier to control.

247 To make caramel icing

8 oz. sugar*
8 tablespoons water
**Use granulated or loaf sugar preferably, although castor can be used. Brown sugar must not be used. You can, if you wish, use all golden syrup, in which case use 8 oz. golden syrup and no water*

1 Put the sugar and water (or syrup) into a strong saucepan.
2 Heat gently, stirring well until the sugar is dissolved. This makes certain that the sugar does not become dry and granular. There is no need to stir with golden syrup.
3 Boil steadily until a pale golden brown. Do not over-brown, for the caramel continues cooking for a while in the hot pan.
4 Leave for a few moments until of a slightly sticky consistency, then pour over the cake.
5 Test to see if the icing is of the right consistency for cutting and the moment you can mark the portions, do so.

248 Amounts of caramel icing to use

For the top of a 6-inch cake	USE 4 oz. sugar
For the top of a 7-inch cake	USE 5 oz. sugar
For the top of an 8-inch cake	USE 6 oz. sugar
For the top of a 9-inch cake	USE 7 oz. sugar
For the top of a 10-inch cake	USE 8 oz. sugar

For caramel butter icing, see Recipe 103. The amounts to use are the same as butter icing.

249 Types of cake suitable for caramel icing

This is generally put on top of the Hungarian donbroz type of cake. It can also be used on a biscuity cake like a shortbread or for a firm sponge as the Caramel gâteau, Recipe 250.

For the sponge:
4 oz. margarine
4 oz. castor sugar
2 eggs
8 oz. flour
1 teaspoon baking powder
2 teaspoons soluble coffee powder
3 tablespoons milk
For the mocha butter cream:
2 level teaspoons soluble coffee powder
4 oz. sieved icing sugar
2 oz. butter
1 tablespoon chocolate powder
For the caramel:
8 oz. loaf sugar
8 tablespoons water

4 eggs
5 oz. castor sugar
4 oz. flour (with plain flour use ½ level teaspoon baking powder)
1 oz. melted butter
chocolate butter cream (Recipe 100) made with 1—1½ lb. butter
For the caramel:
6 oz. granulated or loaf sugar
6 tablespoons water

250   Caramel gâteau

Cream the margarine and sugar until light and fluffy then beat in the eggs one at a time. Fold in the sifted flour, baking powder and coffee powder alternately with the milk. Pour into two greased and floured 10-inch sandwich tins and spread evenly. Bake in a moderately hot oven (400°F. — Gas Mark 5) for 35—40 minutes until firm. Cool.
Beat all the ingredients for the mocha butter cream together. Cut the two sandwiches across in half. Sandwich three of the pieces together with the mocha cream, and spread over the top and sides. Make the caramel as in Recipe 247; pour over remaining cake layer. Mark this in sixteen pieces as it cools. Neaten edges. Place on top of cake; decorate with rosettes of mocha butter cream. Imitation berries and leaves may be added.

Caramel gâteau

251   Donbros or donbroz cake

Make the sponge by the method under Recipe 130, adding the melted and cooled butter last of all. Bake in two 8-inch sandwich tins for time given in that recipe. When the cake is cool, split each through the centre, giving you four layers. Put the top layer on to a flat surface and coat with the caramel icing, leaving a little over. Let the icing cool for just a few moments, then mark in slices. You will find you may have to make the markings once or twice as the caramel begins to harden. In fact it hardens very quickly on the top of this cold cake.
Sandwich the three remaining layers with the chocolate butter icing. Coat the sides with the remaining chocolate butter icing and roll in crushed caramel; spread some butter icing on the upper layer and carefully lift caramel topping into position.
To produce the crushed caramel, pour all the remaining caramel from the pan on to a flat baking tray. Allow to set and then crush with a rolling pin.
If you have any chocolate butter icing left, a narrow border can be piped round the cake.
Note: The caramel icing should be made as in Recipe 247, but be very careful that you get exactly the right temperature so that it is a golden colour. Pour the icing into the centre of the cake, being satisfied you have only a thin layer, and spread from the centre quickly with a knife dipped in very hot water.

252   Points to remember with cooked and heated icings

The greatest care must be taken in the preparation of the icing, for if it reaches too high a temperature it is impossible to turn it back again to the right consistency. It is equally important to boil to the right heat, since if the icing is under-cooked, it does not set in the proper manner.
Take care when handling the icing to keep small children out of the way, as it is very hot, and could cause very unwelcome accidents if spilt on people.
Work fairly fast, as in most cases the icing sets quickly. In some cases, such as the fondant icing, it is possible to re-heat, but re-heating fudge icing and American frosting is not possible.

Marzipan or Almond Paste

253   The purpose of marzipan or almond paste

Apart from decoration (see Recipes 320—30), its main use is as a base for royal or other icings.

254   Advantages of marzipan or almond paste

Marzipan or almond paste gives an excellent base for icing, and so produces a truly professional-looking finish to a cake. It also gives the cake an additional and contrasting flavour. If the cake is a bad shape, you can camouflage this by moulding the marzipan cleverly.

255   Disadvantages of marzipan or almond paste

Marzipan is an expensive form of icing, that is why there are several recipes given some of which are cheaper than others.
Marzipan or almond paste can discolour icing unless correctly blended and handled. Note these points very carefully.

256 Marzipan or almond paste 1

4 oz. ground almonds
2 oz. castor sugar
2 oz. icing sugar
few drops almond essence
egg yolk to mix

1 Mix all the ingredients together, adding enough egg yolk to make a firm mixture.

2 Knead thoroughly.
3 Do not over-handle.

257 Marzipan or almond paste 2, cooked

8 oz. granulated or loaf sugar
4 tablespoons water
pinch cream of tartar
6 oz. ground almonds
few drops almond essence
1 egg white
2 tablespoons icing sugar

1 Put the sugar and water in a strong saucepan, and stir until the sugar dissolves.
2 Add the cream of tartar.
3 Boil steadily until the mixture reaches 240°F. or forms a soft ball when a little is dropped into cold water.

4 Remove from the heat and beat for a minute or two until the mixture becomes cloudy.
5 Add the ground almonds, almond essence and the lightly whisked egg white.
6 Stir over the heat for about 2 minutes.
7 When cool, knead, with the icing sugar.

258 Marzipan or almond paste 3, economical

6 oz. granulated sugar
¼ pint water
4 oz. butter or margarine
4 oz. finest semolina
2 oz. ground almonds
½ teaspoon almond essence
½ teaspoon vanilla essence

1 Boil the sugar and water together until thick and syrupy but remove from the heat before it changes colour.
2 Melt the butter or margarine.
3 Stir in the semolina and brown slightly.

4 Add ground almonds and essence.
5 Add this mixture to the syrup.
6 Stir over low heat until thick, and cook gently for 3 minutes.
7 Leave to cool.

259 Marzipan or almond paste 4, with condensed milk

12 oz. ground almonds
4 oz. castor sugar
4 oz. icing sugar
¼ teaspoon vanilla essence
2—3 drops almond essence
1 teaspoon lemon juice
5 tablespoons condensed milk

1 Sieve together the ground almonds and icing and castor sugar.
2 Add the flavourings and then the condensed milk, carefully.

3 Mix thoroughly with a wooden spoon.
4 Press together with the hands into a ball and knead well.
5 Roll out and use as required.

260 Approximate amounts of marzipan to use

For the top of a 7-inch cake — USE 4 oz. ground almonds, 2 oz. castor sugar, 2 oz. icing sugar, 1 egg yolk, few drops almond essence

For the top and sides of a 7-inch cake — USE 8 oz. ground almonds, 4 oz. castor sugar, 4 oz. icing sugar, 2 egg yolks, few drops almond essence

For the top of an 8-inch square or 9-inch round cake — USE 6 oz. ground almonds, 3 oz. castor sugar, 3 oz. icing sugar, 1½ egg yolks, few drops almond essence

For the top and sides of an 8-inch square or 9-inch round cake — USE 12 oz. ground almonds, 6 oz. castor sugar, 6 oz. icing sugar, 3 egg yolks, few drops almond essence

For the top of a 9-inch square or 10-inch round cake — USE 8 oz. ground almonds, 4 oz. castor sugar, 4 oz. icing sugar, 2 egg yolks, few drops almond essence

For the top and sides of a 9-inch square or 10-inch round cake — USE 1 lb. ground almonds, 8 oz. castor sugar, 8 oz. icing sugar, 4 egg yolks, few drops almond essence

The amounts of marzipan referred to in this chart are needed if you use Recipe 256, but for Recipes 257—9 you can still work out the amounts for various sized cakes.
For example, marzipan made with 4 oz. ground almonds has 2 oz. castor sugar, 2 oz. icing sugar, 1 egg yolk, therefore its total weight is 8 oz. This means, if substituting one of the other recipes, use ingredients to make 8 oz. of finished marzipan.

261 To use marzipan for decoration

This Simnel cake illustrates how marzipan can be used for a simple lattice design. The cake is filled and covered with marzipan. The extra trimmings of marzipan, cut into strips, can then be used for the lattice design. For this Simnel cake, the marzipan is then gently browned under the grill or in the oven and the final decoration given by adding seedless raisins. To plump the raisins, put into cold water, bring to the boil, drain and dry. See Recipe 323 for Simnel cake.
For more elaborate uses of marzipan in decoration, see Recipe 320. In Recipe 328 you will find instructions for moulding marzipan, but remember that it is ideal if rolled and cut into simple strips and shapes.

Simnel cake with lattice design

262 To cover a cake with marzipan or almond paste

Brush away the loose crumbs from the cake. Prepare either sieved warm apricot jam or egg white for brushing on so that the marzipan adheres well.

There are three ways to apply the marzipan:
1 Put top on first, then side strip.
2 Put side strip on first, then top.
3 Roll out icing to a round large enough to cover top and sides, and mould to cake.

Method 1
Picture 1
This shows the top of the cake being spread with sieved apricot jam.

Picture 2
Roll out the marzipan on a sugared board or table, using just under half the quantity for the top of the cake.

Picture 3
Lay the cake on top of this marzipan and check for size. Either press the cake to the marzipan, or lift the cake the right way up again, and press the top marzipan to this.

Picture 4
Roll out the remainder of the marzipan to a strip exactly the depth of the cake, and about ⅛-inch longer than the circumference. Either brush the sides of the cake or the strip with apricot jam or egg white, then roll the cake along the strip rather like a hoop.

Neaten the sides by rolling a jam jar or rolling pin, held upright, round the sides of the cake, and you can roll the top of the cake with a rolling pin.

Method 2
Cut the marzipan out in exactly the same way as method 1, but put the side strip round first, making this about ½—1-inch deeper than the cake. Then fold the extra marzipan over the top. Finally put on the top round.

Method 3
Roll out the whole of the marzipan to a round large enough to cover top and sides. Brush the top and sides with apricot jam or egg white, then lay the marzipan over this and press firmly. Tidy the sides as suggested above.

Note: If you are fairly practised in handling marzipan, you will be able to put the icing on straight away. If you have had to knead the marzipan a fair amount to make it pliable, it is better to let this dry out for 48 hours.

1 Spreading the cake with jam

2 Rolling out marzipan for top cake

3 Covering the top of the cake with marzipan

4 Covering sides of cake with marzipan

Royal Icing

263 The purpose of royal icing

The purpose of royal icing is firstly to give a good coating over the cake. Secondly to be used for piping; it is perfect for this purpose. Thirdly, to use on a rich cake that will keep. It is not suitable for a filling, it is far too hard for this.

264   Advantages of royal icing

The advantage of royal icing is that it can be used for perfect piping. It is soft enough to handle, yet hardens and becomes brittle. With practice you can achieve perfect results.

265   Disadvantages of royal icing

To many people the disadvantage of royal icing is the fact that it is rather hard.

In Recipe 270 you will find hints on adjusting the texture to personal requirements.

266   Types of cakes suitable for coating with royal icing

Any cake can be coated with royal icing, although it would not be a wise choice to put it over a very light sponge.

You must exert a certain pressure in cutting through the icing, and in doing this you may break the slices of a sponge cake.

267   Royal icing

1 egg white
8 oz. sieved icing sugar
1 dessertspoon lemon juice

1 Whisk the egg white lightly.
2 Stir in the icing sugar and lemon juice.

3 Beat well until the icing is very white and has a smooth texture.

268   Approximate amounts of royal icing to use

For the top of a 7-inch cake

USE 1 egg white
8 oz. sieved icing sugar
1 dessertspoon lemon juice

For the top and sides of a 7-inch cake

USE 2½ egg whites
1¼ lb. sieved icing sugar
1¼ tablespoons lemon juice

For the top of an 8-inch square or 9-inch round cake

USE 1½ egg whites
12 oz. sieved icing sugar
1½ dessertspoons lemon juice

For the top and sides of an 8-inch square or 9-inch round cake

USE 4 egg whites
2 lb. sieved icing sugar
2 tablespoon lemon juice

For the top of a 9-inch square or 10-inch round cake

USE 2 egg whites
1 lb. sieved icing sugar
2 dessertspoons lemon juice

For the top and sides of a 9-inch square or 10-inch round cake

USE 5 egg whites
2½ lb. sieved icing sugar
2½ tablespoons lemon juice

These amounts allow for one *good* layer of icing, and piping. When you are icing a very special cake, it is far better to have two coats rather than one. The first can be fairly thin, but two coats will give a very much better surface on which to work for piping. In order to calculate the amount of icing needed to include a second coat, use half as much again, i.e. using 2 lb. of icing sugar, add a further 1 lb., with the other ingredients in proportion.

269   To flavour royal icing

The lemon juice added to royal icing provides a little flavour, but various essences can be added to match the colouring, i.e. a few drops of orange essence if you are tinting the icing orange; raspberry essence if you are tinting it pink.
A very small amount of very strong coffee could be incorporated.
It must be realized that if you add too much fresh fruit juice to a royal icing you are destroying the basic proportion of the icing, and in this case essences are much better to use.

Adding lemon juice to the royal icing

270   To prevent royal icing hardening

If you wish royal icing to remain rather softer, you can use part egg white and part water. One egg white and approximately one tablespoon of water to 1 lb. icing sugar will give a coating icing that hardens, but never becomes as hard as if all egg white was used. This is less good for piping. You do not get the sharpness that true royal icing produces.

The addition of glycerine is another way to soften royal icing. Allow up to one teaspoon of glycerine to each 8 oz. sieved icing sugar. If you are using royal icing for wedding cakes, where you wish to support the weight of pillars, you must not omit any egg white or put in glycerine. The softer texture would not support the weight of pillars or tiers.

Although the basic recipe for royal icing varies little, except that you may need slightly less icing sugar if the egg whites are very small, or a little more if they are large, it is the amount of beating given to royal icing that produces the very shiny white appearance and its correct consistency.

This means that for coating a cake, where you wish an icing that will spread easily, you should not beat quite as much as for piping. If you are making the full quantity of royal icing to coat and pipe at one time, take out the amount needed for coating, cover the rest, as instructed under Recipe 285 with a damp cloth, then beat very well before using the mixture for piping.

For a perfect *coating* consistency royal icing should hold its shape very well when the spoon, or beater of an electric mixer, is lifted from it. Place the cake on its board before beginning to ice.

In order to be absolutely certain that no oil from the marzipan seeps through to the icing and spoils the colour, brush the marzipan with a very little egg white and allow it to dry for a short time before icing.

Picture 1

1 Place almost half the icing on top of the cake, and smooth round with palette knife or spatula, working the icing to remove bubbles.

Picture 2

2 Either use the palette knife in a slightly dragging movement or hold it at both ends at an angle to pull surplus icing towards you. This is much easier if the blade of the knife is sufficiently long to sweep across the whole width of the cake. If it is too short, you have to keep repeating the process and this means uneven spreading.

If you are not satisfied that it is perfectly even then place the palette knife or spatula halfway across the cake. Keep it absolutely flat so the blade of the knife is touching the icing. Press down lightly. Turn the cake so that the knife moves round in a full circle. This should give a perfectly smooth look. If you are only icing the top of the cake, put the surplus back into the bowl.

Picture 3

3 Spread the remaining icing round the sides. (You may prefer to put *all* the icing over the cake before flattening.)

Picture 4

4 Smooth the icing with a clean knife, holding it to the side of the cake with one hand and turning the cake completely and smoothly round with the other.

5 In coating, as in piping, a turntable or substitute turntable helps enormously.

6 If you are putting two coats of icing on to the cake, always allow the first coat to dry before the second is applied and keep the icing for the second coat the right consistency by covering bowl with paper or damp cloth.

1 Spreading royal icing on top of the cake

2 Smoothing royal icing on top of the cake

3 Spreading royal icing round sides of cake

4 Smoothing royal icing round sides of cake

Tools for Perfect Icing

The picture below shows some of the tools that are necessary for perfect icing. *Back row (left to right):*

1 Cake boards and cards. These support the cake and give a professional look. They are purchased from a stationer and cost from 10½d for the 7-inch round cake boards to 4s 3d for a more elaborately decorated 16-inch square board.

2 A turntable. This is necessary if you are icing cakes regularly. The cake on its board is placed on the top of a turntable. As you coat the sides of the cake or, when ready, pipe the sides, you can slowly revolve the turntable with one hand, while spreading or piping with the other. Costs of turntables vary from 4s 6d (approximately) for a small metal one to 11s 9d for a plastic one, or 14s 11d for a chromium one. You can also obtain more expensive ones at about £3 which are suitable for all cake sizes, and can also be tilted. If you do not wish the expense of a turntable, the same effect can be achieved by putting the cake board on to an upturned basin or cake tin. The problem may well be that with a large and heavy cake this gives rather inadequate support, so do test that it is absolutely safe before you attempt to turn it.

3 A basin and wooden spoon for beating icing.

4 Scales to ensure correct weights.

Front row *(left to right):*

1 Plastic, cotton or nylon icing bags. Many people prefer these to paper, which is inclined to split. As you will see, a special nozzle is essential on the base of these bags to hold the small icing pipes in position. Nylon icing bags cost approximately 3s 6d to 5s depending on size. Cotton bags cost from 1s 6d. The screws are 1s 3d each.

2 Writing pipes are fully described in Recipe 87 and these cost 1s 3d each.

Instead of a bag, however, many people will prefer to use a syringe and the one shown under Recipe 277 costs 3s 9d.

The syringe under Recipe 133 would cost approximately the same.

3 Next to the pipes is a palette knife. This is essential for a really smooth coating. Try to purchase one with a long blade if you are working on a very large cake, i.e. if the diameter of the cake is 12 inches, you should have a palette knife of the same length.

A palette knife would cost from 3s.

If you cannot get a long palette knife, a long metal ruler from a stationer or a long icing ruler (costing about 2s 9d) could be used.

4 The flat wooden spatula is very good for spreading the icing over the cake initially. This costs approximately the same as wooden spoons, i.e. 2s, 2s 6d.

5 The small plastic utensil is for separating the white from the yolk of the egg for royal icing. This is not essential.

6 At the bottom right-hand corner of the picture there is a set of icing rings. The purpose of these rings is to enable a perfectly symmetric design to be planned on the top of the cake, as illustrated under Recipe 284. When the icing on the cake is set, lay a ring of the required size on top and with a fine needle mark out at regular intervals. A set of these rings costs about 2s 6d.

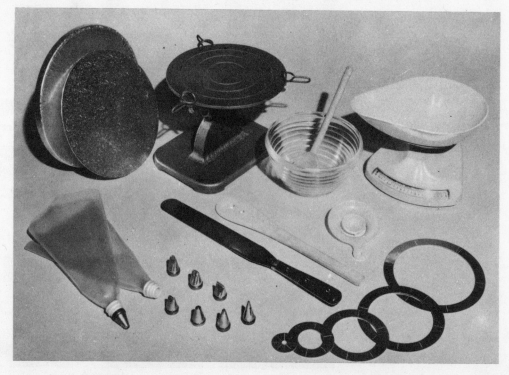

Tools for perfect icing

13 Crinoline lady

14 Slice of a child's birthday cake

15 Danish biscuit layer cake

16   Chocolate birthday cake

273 Utensils required for coating evenly

1 A turntable or substitute turntable. It not only gives greater freedom of movement but raises the cake to a better level for working.
2 A spatula for spreading the icing initially.
3 A firm palette knife. It must be rigid to get a flat surface. A metal ruler will do instead.

4 A jug of hot water is very helpful if the icing is a little stiff. Dip the palette knife or the utensil being used into the hot water, pat fairly dry, and use while warm.
5 Damp cloth or damp paper to keep over the icing until you are ready to use it.

274 Preparations for piping

1 The most important preparation for piping is to see that groundwork on the cake is dry. Always leave cake for some hours to harden.
2 Make sure that the icing is exactly the right consistency to hold its shape.
3 Work out the design you intend to pipe.

4 Choose the pipes you intend to use and decide whether you are using a paper, nylon or cloth bag or an icing syringe. If you do very little piping and decorating, a greaseproof paper bag is economical and many people find it gives them the greatest control over the pipe.

275 To make a paper bag for piping

1 The bag can be made from a square piece of greaseproof paper folded to give a triangle. This gives a firm bag holding large amounts of icing. You can make a square, cut across into a triangle and work with a single thickness.
Picture 1
2 With the triangle of either double or single thickness take hold of the top right-hand corner so that the hand lies on the main part of the paper, and the point is folded between the thumb and forefinger.

Picture 2
3 Roll the hand over and bring the point of the paper to centre of long bottom edge.
Picture 3
4 Continue rolling the hand over until the point on the left edge is almost reached. Bring this point up to meet the other points, so making the sharply pointed cone.
Picture 4
5 Secure the points together by folding in.
6 Snip tiny bit from end of cone; insert pipe.

1 The first position for holding the triangle

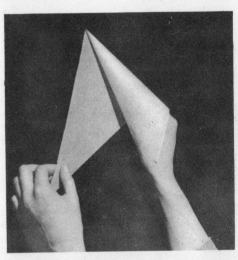

2 Rolling the triangle over

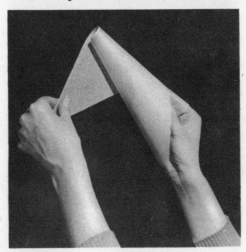

3 Bringing the points together

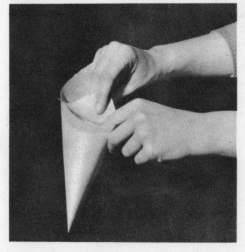

4 Securing the points

276 To use a piping bag

The instructions in Recipe 275 show how to make a paper bag; you may decide that you prefer to use a nylon, hypalon (plastic) or cotton bag. The procedure varies a little.

With nylon, hypalon or cotton bag

1 Make sure supporting screw for pipe is firmly in position, if bag is fitted with one.
2 Screw the pipe you require on to this or slip the pipe in.
3 Half fill the bag with icing and screw round firmly at the top so on can escape.

With greaseproof paper bag

1 When the bag has been made and the base has been snipped off, drop the icing pipe into the base of the bag. If the pipe does not protrude sufficiently from the hole at the bottom, you will have to remove this from the greaseproof paper bag, snip a little more of the paper away, and then replace the pipe. Do not let more than half the depth of the pipe protrude from the bag or some of the icing will ooze out at the base of the paper.
Picture 1
2 Half-fill bag with icing; fold over the top.
Picture 2
3 To make sure that you have perfect control over the icing in the bag, press down firmly with one hand using the finger of the other to guide the flow of icing.

If filling a large cloth bag with icing, you obviate wastage if the material is folded back so that you can put the icing to the base.

1 The piping bag half filled

2 The position for holding the piping bag

A cloth icing bag folded back ready to fill

277 Advantages and disadvantages of a syringe

A syringe has the great advantage that should you wish to do a little piping with one pipe and then change to another, all you need to do is unscrew the first pipe from the bottom of the syringe, replace it with your second choice of pipe and you are ready to proceed.

Another advantage is that the softer butter icing will never become overheated and sticky in a syringe. The disadvantage many people find with a syringe is that they do not have the perfect control obtainable with a bag. This will be overcome with practice.

278 To use a syringe

Picture 1
1 Remove the plunger from the syringe.
2 Put in the icing, making certain it is exactly the right consistency. Never fill the syringe more than half way with icing.
3 Replace the plunger and press down gently.
4 As soon as a little icing appears at the bottom opening, screw the selected pipe in position.
Picture 2
5 Insert the thumb of your right hand into the ring at the very top of the plunger and two of your fingers, generally the index and third finger, into the two slots at the top of the body of the syringe. Left-handed people may prefer to use their left hand.
6 Press down firmly, carefully and slowly with your thumb. You will then find that you are ejecting the icing. It is essential that the syringe is supported with your other hand.

When you are doing a continual piping line round the sides of a cake, and turning the turntable simultaneously, you will, of course, have to release your support on the syringe for just a moment.

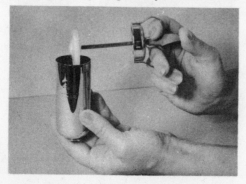

1 Replacing the plunger in the syringe

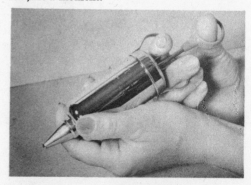

2 The position for holding the syringe

The following pictures show the great diversity of shapes
that are made by the various numbered pipes.

Pipe No.	Description	Use
1	Fine writer	Writing, see Recipe 87. Also used to give very fine wavy lines. Just move the pipe quickly backwards and forwards.
2	Medium writer	Writing and any designs as shown based on a line or on a dot. To make the dot see Recipe 282.
3	Thick writer	As Nos. 1 and 2 but a coarser pipe.
4	Small border	For a flowing border design.
5	Rope	For a fluted border design.
6	Fine 6-star	Fluted border design. Also for an upright star.
7	Large 6-star	As No. 6 but larger.
8	8-star	As Nos. 6 and 7.
9	Fancy band	For a band. Can give a raised band by going back a little.
10	Large leaf	For a leaf design.
11	Large petal	To make individual petals of a flat flower.
12	Shell	To form small shells or a long ribbed design.
13	5-star	Upright stars; petals; flattish border.
14	10-star	Flattish design; many pointed stars; ribbed design.
15	Dahlia	For making large flat petals.
16	Double thread	Making a double thread design.
17	Small leaf	For tiny leaves of fairly irregular shape.
18	Large rose	For moulding petals of a rose.
19	4-star	For an upright star shape or a flattish design.
20	Fine rope	Very fine border design or rosettes.
21	12-star	Excellent for a shell border design or star shape.
22	Border	A rope border design.

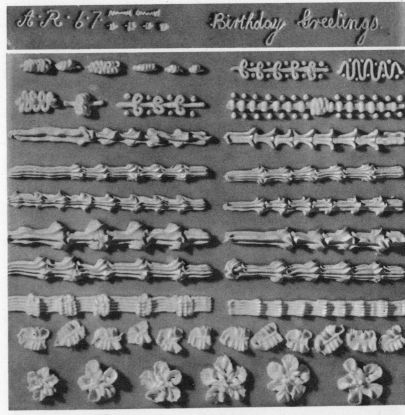

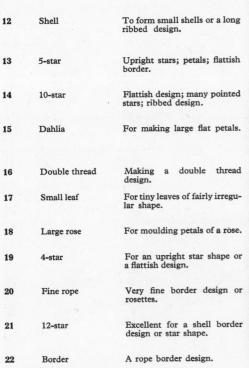

Pipe No.	Description	Use
23	Wide raised band	Raised wide border design.
24	Frilled ribbon	Ideal for giving the effect of ribbon if you go back on the straight part.
25	Fluted upright band	Not a particularly useful pipe. Could be used for a straight upright band.
26	Grape	Gives a better dot for grapes than the writing pipes.
27	Fancy star	To make a twisted border design or an upright star or shell shape.
28	Forget-me-not	Excellent pipe for tiny flowers.
29	Wide ribbon	Gives the flow in a ribbon border design.
30	Narrow ribbon	Same as No. 29 only narrower.
31	Clematis	Makes any flat 5-petalled flower which can be built up to be larger than No. 28.
32	3-thread	Draws three threads simultaneously for borders or freehand designs.
33	Scroll	Excellent flow for rather severe scrolls.

Pipe No.	Description	Use
34	Wide ribbed band	A ribbon design similar to No. 29, but ribbed.
35	Narrow ribbed band	Similar to No. 30, but ribbed.
36	Small rose	A finer pipe than No. 18 for tiny rose petals.
37	Fine fancy band	This will give a very fine flowing design.
38	Narrow raised band	Not suitable for flat bands. Gives a thick result.
39	Fluted ribbon	Another ribbon like Nos. 34 and 35 but more fluted.
40	Fluted frilled ribbon	A less neat ribbon design.
41	Sweet pea or pansy petal	For making delicate petals for flowers.
42	Small petal	Similar to No. 41, but smaller.
		The last picture shows a combination of a No. 8 and a No. 2 pipe.

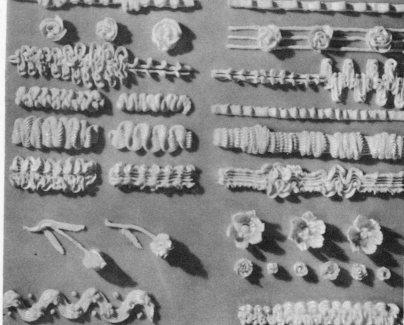

NOTE: In order that the pipes may be identified in many of the recipes in this book, the actual number is given. Please do not imagine you must use this pipe. Any that will give a fairly similar effect can be substituted.

280 Larger-sized pipes

In addition to the icing pipes mentioned in the previous section there are many occasions when a larger pipe is used.

(**a**) For a border design in cream.

(**b**) For piping meringues.

1	5-star	$\frac{1}{2}$-inch diameter.
2	12-star	$\frac{5}{8}$-inch diameter.
3	6-star	$\frac{3}{8}$-inch diameter.
4	7-star	$\frac{3}{8}$-inch diameter.
5	8-star	$\frac{3}{8}$-inch diameter.
6	8-star	$\frac{1}{2}$-inch diameter.
7	10-star	$\frac{5}{8}$-inch diameter.
8	plain	$\frac{1}{16}$-inch diameter.
9	plain	$\frac{1}{8}$-inch diameter.
10	plain	$\frac{1}{4}$-inch diameter.
11	plain	$\frac{3}{8}$-inch diameter.
12	plain	$\frac{1}{2}$-inch diameter.

(**c**) For piping choux pastry.

These larger pipes are called potato or meringue roses or are sometimes just given by their measurement. They cost approximately 1s to 1s 6 d.

13	plain	$\frac{5}{8}$-inch diameter.
14	plain	$\frac{3}{4}$-inch diameter.
15		
16	4-star curved	$\frac{1}{4}$-inch diameter.
17	5-star curved	$\frac{1}{4}$-inch diameter.
18	7-star curved	$\frac{3}{8}$-inch diameter.
19	6-star curved	$\frac{3}{8}$-inch diameter.
20	12-star curved	$\frac{3}{8}$-inch diameter.
21	8-star curved	$\frac{3}{8}$-inch diameter.
22	8-star curved	$\frac{5}{8}$-inch diameter.
23	10-star curved	$\frac{5}{8}$-inch diameter.

These large pipes could be inserted into a paper bag, but generally speaking it is better to use a nylon, plastic or cotton bag, see Recipe 272.

Because the pipes are so much bigger, they fit into the base of the bag without the screw. Occasionally you may find that the pipe is too big to be pushed through the hole at the bottom of the bag, in which case this must be loosened a little.

If dealing with a large quantity of choux pastry, cream or meringue, there are 16-inch, 18-inch and 20-inch bags available. These cost from 5s to 8s.

281 First investments with pipes

Undoubtedly few people will to purchase the complete set of pipes.

The most useful pipes for a beginner would be: A No. 2 writing pipe.

A No. 6, 7 or 8 star which could be used for upright stars.

Maybe a ribbon pipe and No. 34 is one of the best to use.

To Use Pipes

282

Before piping on to a cake for the very first time, it is a good idea to practise either on a board or a less important cake. The pictures below give an idea of learning to control the basic pipes.

Pictures 1, 2 and 3

These show a No. 2 writing pipe in use. You will see the pipe is held suspended at only a small distance from the surface.

Picture 1

The idea here is to have a long unbroken sweep and this is made possible with a steady control over the flow of icing.

Picture 2

This shows the control necessary to produce a series of parallel lines of matching length. Draw the first line and, when the required length is reached, pull up the pipe sharply.

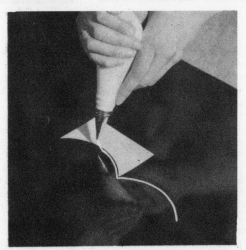

1 Piping a long unbroken line

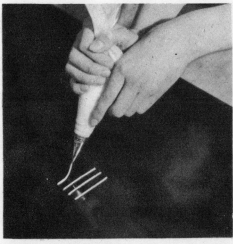

2 Piping parallel lines

Picture 3

To make dots from the same pipe, simply hold it upright, press down and lift quickly.

Picture 4

Making stars is not difficult.

The basic star is made with a No. 7 pipe. This means pressing down once and lifting the pipe fairly sharply after exerting the pressure. The larger rosettes are made by a circular movement indicated by the arrow. When rosette is large enough, lift the pipe.

Picture 5

This shows the same No. 7 star pipe used this time in a border design. The first star shows the flow rather than the upright result. This is achieved by holding the pipe at an angle as when writing.

For the continuous shell pattern, hold the pipe just clear of the surface. Squeeze out enough for your first shell, raise slightly (this means you do not break the flow of icing), lower again for the second shell, lift again. This gives the unbroken border design.

Picture 6

This shows how this simple work can create an effective design for the top of a cake.

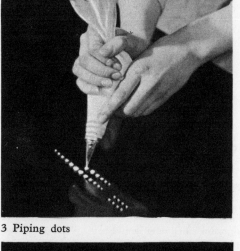

3 Piping dots

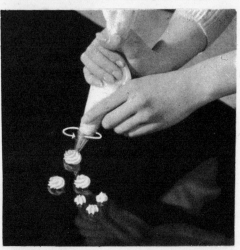

4 Piping stars and large rosettes

5 Continuous piped shell design for a border

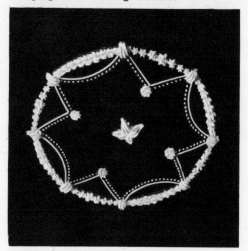

6 A design for the top of a cake

283 More elaborate designs with piping

Having gained control of the pipes, you can then begin to build up more elaborate designs.

Basket work. This is a very effective design round the side of a cake. To make it you need: for coarser work pipe No. 34; for finer work pipe No. 35.

Sketch 1 shows straight lines drawn down the sides of the cake. Space these at intervals of about 1 inch.

Sketch 2 Next draw the lines across the cake, spacing these at about ¼-inch intervals.

When the cake has been completely covered like this, you then have the effect of *basket work*.

Sketch 3 By making short vertical lines over the horizontal lines halfway between the vertical ones, and short horizontal lines between the vertical lines, the icing looks as if it is threaded.

Lattice work. To make this you need pipe No. 1, 2 or 3.

This is a favourite type of icing, particularly put over icing nails or patty tins, see Recipe 288. Success depends on piping extremely straight lines.

Sketch 1 shows the basis for the lattice work. Lines are drawn down very carefully.

Sketch 2 shows a square lattice made by drawing lines in the opposite direction.

Sketch 3 shows both lines drawn diagonally

Sketch 4 shows the first lines drawn straight down, the second lines drawn diagonally to give a diamond lattice.

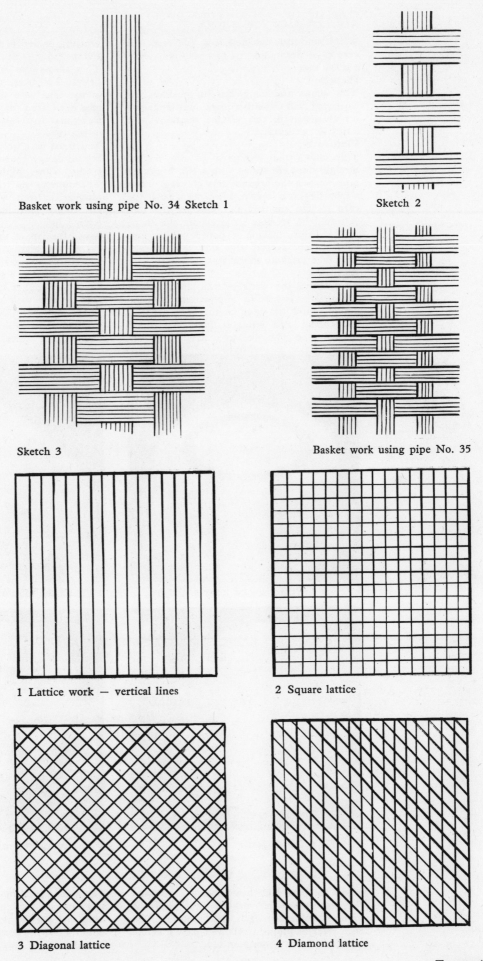

Basket work using pipe No. 34 Sketch 1

Sketch 2

Sketch 3

Basket work using pipe No. 35

1 Lattice work — vertical lines

2 Square lattice

3 Diagonal lattice

4 Diamond lattice

284 To plan the design

When you have decided how you wish the cake to be decorated, the first step is to mark out the cake.

Picture 1

This shows the icing ring in position. As suggested, you can either prick out the spacing or, as shown in this picture, mark it with a tiny dot of icing.

Picture 2

This shows the beginning of the design. Straight lines are drawn with a No. 2 writing pipe between the original dots of icing. Then a loop design is drawn down the side of the cake to join the straight lines on the top. It would be sensible to prick out the shape of the loops, making a paper pattern and holding this against the side of the cake first, then pricking round this.

Picture 3

This shows the shell pattern described in Recipe 319. Use a No. 7 pipe, and pipe the design round the edge of the cake between the curved and straight lines. A No. 2 writing pipe was also used for piping the

greeting on top of the cake and for the dots.

Picture 4

This shows the completed cake. The shell design has been repeated round the base of the cake with the No. 7 pipe, which has also been used for the very tiny stars placed at regular intervals round the top and sides of the cake.

You must be absolutely certain that the shell border design round the top edge of the cake is dry before piping the stars in position. The flowers on this particular cake were purchased from a good-class confectioner, but could be made from the directions in Recipe 286.

Note: Instead of these metal rings, you can use a cake marker, see sketch on left. This will enable you to mark out even spacing and, if wished, act as a stencil for a simple design. Place the marker in the centre of the cake, hold secure with a pin through the hole. Then move the 'blades' out to give an even spacing. Prick with a pin or mark with tiny dots of icing as described with the rings.

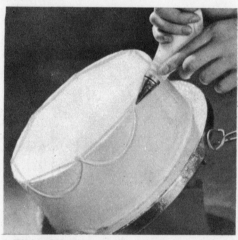

A cake marker for even spacing

1 Using an icing ring to mark a design

2 Piping the loop design

3 Piping the shell pattern

4 The completed cake

285 To keep icing pliable for piping

Stress has been laid throughout this book on the importance of making sure that the groundwork is dry. It is also important that each layer of piping is allowed to dry before additional work is done on top.

There is no need to continually make up fresh amounts of royal icing. Simply cover the royal icing with a damp cloth and it keeps in perfect condition to use some hours later or even the next day.

17 21st birthday cake

18 Detail of 21st birthday
cake

19 Christmas record gâteaux

286　To make flowers with icing

Here are roses made with the No. 18 pipe.

Piped roses made with an icing syringe

In order to build up the petals of a raised flower, it is useful to work with an icing nail.

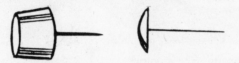 

1 Icing nails

1 Secure tiny pieces of waxed or greased greaseproof paper on the icing nail.
2 Make a small cone shape of icing with a writing pipe No. 2.
Make a slight ribbon band round this with the writing pipe. This gives the heart of the rose.
Change to the No. 18 pipe, or No. 36 for tiny flowers, and gradually build up the shape of the petals as the sketches show.
If you cannot obtain an icing nail, then you

can work on to a slightly greased wooden cocktail stick. The idea of the nail or the stick is that you can turn it as you pipe, so getting the flow of icing to give a real petal shape.
3 Flat petals for other flowers are made with petal pipes No. 11 or 42 and the sketches show how these are built up.
When the flowers are hardened and set, lift the paper off the icing nail and peel away from the icing or gently pull the cocktail stick away from the icing.

2 Building up the petals of a raised flower

3 To pipe a flat five-petal flower

287　To make leaves with icing

If these are to be fairly flat on the cake, they can be piped directly over the well-dried groundwork using a No. 10 or 17 pipe. If you

want a slightly raised effect as in the pictures on next page, pipe the leaf on to paper on icing nail, lift off and secure as with flowers.

288　Raised trellis work

For this you need the net nails as shown to the right. They are priced from 1s to 1s 6d.
To make the raised trellis work pipe along the lines of icing over net nails. Allow to harden, lift off the nail when ready. If net nails are not available, then use upturned patty tins.
The raised trellis work is put on to the cake and secured with a little icing.

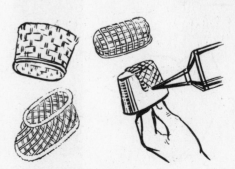

Raised trellis work

289 To use flowers in decoration

Picture 1.

This shows leaves and flowers in position on a birthday cake. A large number of roses like this look more attractive in a very pale colour. The interesting point about this cake is the use that has been made of a writing pipe to give a scroll design. The writing pipe shown here in use for the greetings, has been inserted into the screw at the base of a hypalon (plastic) bag.

Picture 2

This shows a variation on the flower theme. The roses have been built up to form almost a bouquet at one side of the cake and are being secured with icing from the writing pipe.

The scroll design has been used over the top as well as the sides of the cake.

The frontispiece illustrates a birthday cake beautifully decorated with flowers.

1 Using a writing pipe to write greetings

2 Securing roses with icing from writing pipe

290 Flooded edging to a cake

This shows a cake that is most professional in its simplicity. The writing has been raised to give this shadowy effect.

The greeting was first piped in the basic colour on the dry groundwork of the cake. This was allowed to dry and then repeated in a different colour so lifting the words high.

The edge of the cake has been outlined in a line-and-dot design, the edging just with dots. The edging has been achieved by flooding. To get this effect mark out, first with a pencil, then with icing and a writing pipe No. 1, 2 or 3, the inner line, which will be exactly the same size and shape as the outer edge at the top of the cake. Do this on a flat board covered with waxed paper. Then draw round this the design for the edging. Carefully flood, not too thickly, between these lines with icing and allow to dry completely.

Spread a little soft royal icing on the top edges of the cake to secure the flooded edging, which must be lifted from the waxed paper with great care and put into place. In this way you have the edge projecting from the cake.

A similar flooding effect has been made at the base. The cake board is iced, then a design similar to the edging is piped round the bottom edge of the cake and on the board. The outer part of the board is finished with a scroll design.

The flowers and figures on the side of this cake have been painted with culinary colourings. This is a delightful way to decorate a cake for someone who is extremely good at painting. If the technique given for flooding seems too difficult, and you still wish to have the edging projecting round the cake, you can use either the Australian type of fondant icing or the satin icing. Cut out your edging and secure it to the cake with a little royal icing.

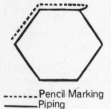

------ Pencil Marking
——— Piping

To make flooded edging for cake

Cake decorated with a flooded edge

Birthday Cakes

291 Choice of cake

The choice of cake used depends very much on the age of the children, the number of portions you need and the time you have available to make and decorate the cake.

Illustrated in *colour plate 14* is a portion of a birthday cake which would be very suitable for younger children who do not like rich fruit cake or for whom it is not really very good. This is a Victoria sandwich, Recipe 1 or 2, filled with chocolate and raspberry butter icing and decorated with white butter icing and simple piping. Richer cakes can be chosen for older children and adults — one of them is illustrated below. It is not too rich, but it is a very good cake.

To put candles on birthday cakes

You must have proper candle holders since these will catch the wax from the tiny candles. Work out the position of the candles when you plan the design, for you can easily make a cake look cluttered up if too many candles are used. Press the candle holders into the icing before it is completely set. If you do this when the icing is set and hard it will crack.

Pipe the cake and, when it is completed, and the piping dry, put candles in the holders.

292 Chocolate birthday cake

4 eggs
4 oz. castor sugar
little vanilla essence
4 oz. flour (with plain flour use 1¼ teaspoons baking powder)
1½ tablespoons cocoa
vanilla butter icing, (Recipe 100), made with 4 oz. butter, 6 oz. icing sugar, few drops vanilla essence
2 packets milk chocolate finger biscuits
ribbon
glacé icing, (Recipe 53), made with 6 oz. icing sugar, 1½ tablespoons water, few drops colouring
6 chocolate buttons
candles
candle holders

This cake is ideal for young children.

Place the eggs, sugar and vanilla essence in a bowl and whisk until thick, light and fluffy. Carefully fold in the sieved flour and cocoa. Turn into three 9-inch straight-sided sandwich tins. Bake in a moderately hot oven (400°F. — Gas Mark 5) for about 20 minutes. Cool before decorating. Sandwich the layers together with butter icing and spread a thin layer around the sides of the cake. Place on a plate or board. Press the finger biscuits round as illustrated and tie the ribbon round.

Make the glacé icing to a thick coating consistency and turn on to the top of the cake. Spread evenly and allow to set.

Cut the buttons in half and place on top of the cake to form the birthday age. Add the candles.

Illustrated below and in colour plate 16.

Chocolate birthday cake

2 oz. glacé cherries
2 oz. almonds
8 oz. currants
5 oz. sultanas
3 oz. stoned raisins
2 oz. cut mixed peel
finely grated rind 1 lemon
3 dessertspoons brandy,
   optional
6 oz. plain flour
¾ teaspoon mixed spice
¼ teaspoon nutmeg
1½ oz. ground almonds
5 oz. margarine
5 oz. soft brown sugar
1 tablespoon black treacle,
   optional
3 eggs
little sieved apricot jam
almond paste (Recipe 256)
   made with 8 oz. ground
   almonds for a thin layer
   or 12 oz. ground almonds
   for a thicker layer
royal icing (Recipe 267) made
   with 1¼—1½ lb. icing sugar

293 Traditional birthday cake

Chop the cherries, skin the almonds. Chop the almonds finely and mix with the fruit, peel and grated lemon rind; pour over the brandy, if used. Sieve flour, mixed spice and nutmeg and add the ground almonds. Cream margarine and sugar together until light and fluffy. Beat in the treacle, if used. Add eggs one at a time, beating each in thoroughly and adding a little sieved flour with every egg after the first. Fold in remaining flour mixture and fruit, half of each at a time. Place in a greased and lined 7-inch round cake tin. Protect the outside of tin with layers of brown paper or newspaper. Smooth top of mixture with a knife. Bake in the centre of a very slow oven (275°F. — Gas Mark 1) for 3 hours. Test, then allow to cool in tin. Store in an airtight tin until ready to decorate. Brush with sieved apricot jam and coat cake with almond paste, see Recipe 256. Make the royal icing, Recipe 267. Place the cake on an 8-inch round silver cake board. Ice the top and then the sides of the cake, leaving about a quarter for decorating. Leave the icing to dry thoroughly before piping.

To decorate

Start with the greeting. Use a writing pipe, No. 1 or 2. If you are uncertain about writing neatly, sketch this with a fine needle or pin. Pipe the greeting. Using the same pipe make the lines with the same movement as the writing. To make the dots hold the pipe upright and give sharp presses on the bag or syringe, varying the amount of icing that comes out to determine the size of the dots. For the petals, hold the pipe slightly at an angle so that you get an elongated dot.

For the edging of the top and the base of the cake, use a No. 5 rope pipe, although a similar effect could be obtained with a 5, 6, 8 or 12 star pipe. Start at the narrowest part of the design. Press out a little icing. Hold the rope or star pipe at much the same angle as when piping the greeting. This makes certain you have an even control. As you move along the first portion, increase the pressure very slightly so that you get a widening flow of icing. Decrease to give the next shape and continue like this, dragging and increasing and decreasing the pressure to give the effect shown. To ice the base, it is easier to start on the widest part of the feather-shaped design. Press out a fairly generous amount of icing, then, as you draw the pipe towards the base of the cake, lessen the pressure so that you obtain a diminishing amount.

There are two ways to achieve the result shown. One is to actually lift the pipe so the icing breaks off at the end of each feather and then start again at the top and bring the next feather down so that it joins the one before. The second way to do it is to loop the design, so that you have a continuous flow of icing.

Feather shaped design in piping

Birthday cake

Christmas Cakes

There are an enormous number of ways in which a Christmas cake may be decorated with piping, some very simple, some much more elaborate and intriguing.

Christmas cake 1

This is an ideal cake for a beginner to decorate, as the amount of piping is very small. The raised border round the edge of the top and the base is made by holding the icing bag or syringe, in which you have inserted a 5-star or rope pipe, in an upright position, placing the pipe close to the cake. Press the bag or syringe gently to give a flow; then lift quickly. Colour and interest are given by looped bows of ribbon or the special type of ribbon sold for wrapping parcels which is very springy and holds its shape. This can be in bright red.

Real or artificial holly leaves can then be placed around. To make sure the bows adhere to the cake, put a little icing under each one.

Christmas cakes 2, 3 and 4

Below are shown three Christmas cakes or decorated cakes ready for a festive occasion.

Cake 2

The cake in the background below is decorated with rough royal icing, see Recipe 267.

Cake 3

The cake with the Christmas greeting is piped in a very simple design. To get the raised greeting, pipe the letters with a No. 1, 2 or 3 writing pipe. Allow this to harden, then pipe again over the letters to make them stand out in high relief.

For the design round the top of the cake use a No. 5, 6, 8, 10 or 12 star pipe and hold the pipe very near the cake against the extreme edge. Press quite firmly to produce a big star that flows on to the top and slightly down the side of the cake. Pull the pipe away sharply and this gives the slightly pointed effect shown.

Christmas cake 1

The little dots on the side are made by the writing pipe being used in exactly the same fashion and the design at the base is made in the same way as the top rim, the pressure exerted on the icing determining the size.

Cake 4

The cake on the left below can be made by using a No. 3 writing pipe or the plain scroll pipe.

Lines are marked on top of the icing and the lattice work created by drawing the pipe across the cake. Tiny dots are then piped on. The scroll design round the top is done with the same movement as for writing, but instead make this attractive pattern.

The very neat lines round the outside of the cake are quite difficult to produce as evenly as shown and it needs a very straight eye and steady hand to continue to pipe lines of icing around a cake.

The scroll design on the bottom edge is done in the same way as the top.

Christmas cakes 2, 3 and 4

295 Christmas cake 1 — economical in fruit

6 oz. margarine
6 oz. soft brown or Barbados sugar
1 oz. ground almonds
4 eggs
8 oz. plain flour
juice 1 lemon
8 oz. currants
8 oz. sultanas
4 oz. chopped glacé cherries
2 oz. mixed peel
rind ½ lemon
1½ level teaspoons mixed spice

Cream the margarine and sugar until light and fluffy. Gradually add ground almonds and beat in well. Add 1 egg and stir lightly; do not over-beat in this type of cake. Repeat using two more eggs and then add a little flour. Add the last eggs as before and the lemon juice. Fold in (do not beat) a little more flour. Add the currants, sultanas, cherries, peel and rind. Fold in the remaining flour sieved with the mixed spice. Transfer the mixture, which should be of a stiff dropping consistency, to the prepared 8-inch tin, see Recipe 297. Smooth and level the mixture in the tin and bake in a very moderate oven (300—325°F. — Gas Mark 2) for 2 hours. Reduce heat to 275°F. (Gas Mark 1) for a further 1—2½ hours. Test carefully, see Recipe 298. Allow to cool in tin. Mature before icing, see Recipe 299.

Cover with almond paste or marzipan (made with 12 oz. ground almonds, etc.), as in Recipe 256, then ice as Recipe 300.

Illustrated in colour plate 12.

296 Christmas cake 2 — rich in fruit

12 oz. plain flour
1 teaspoon cinnamon
1 teaspoon mixed spice
½ teaspoon salt
4 oz. candied peel
2 lb. dried fruit (1 lb. currants, 8 oz. sultanas, 8 oz. raisins)
4 oz. cherries
4 oz. blanched, chopped almonds
finely grated rind 1 lemon
4 eggs
4 tablespoons milk *or* sherry, *or* brandy
8 oz. butter
8 oz. soft brown sugar
1 tablespoon black treacle

Sieve together all the dry ingredients. Mix the peel, fruit, cherries (which should be lightly floured if very sticky), chopped almonds and lemon rind. Whisk the eggs and milk, sherry or brandy together. Cream the butter, sugar and black treacle until soft. Add the flour and egg mixtures alternately to the butter mixture, do not over-beat. Lastly, stir in the fruit mixture. Put into a prepared 8-inch square or 9-inch round tin, see Recipe 297. Tie a double band of brown paper round the outside of the tin, standing well up above the top of it. Bake in the middle of a very moderate oven for 3¼—3½ hours. If using gas, use Gas Mark 3 for 1½ hours, then Gas Mark 2 for the remainder of the time. In an electric oven put the cake in at 300—325°F. for 1½ hours then reduce heat to 275—300°F. for the remaining 1¾—2 hours. Cool in cake tin, then store in airtight tin.

For a very moist cake, prick the cold cake and pour over a little sherry at intervals before icing. For a 6-inch round or 5-inch square cake, use half the quantity of ingredients and bake for approximately 2¼—2½ hours.

For an 8-inch round or 7-inch square cake use two-thirds the quantity and bake for approximately 2½—3 hours.

297 To prepare cake tin for rich fruit cake

To line the base of the tin
1 Place tin on top of two or four thicknesses of greaseproof paper.
2 Trace round the tin.
3 Cut on the inside of the pencilled tracing.
4 Check fitting and trim if necessary.
5 Lightly grease each circle of paper and place on top of each other.

To line the sides of the tin
1 Take a length of two or four thicknesses of greaseproof paper, long enough to circle the tin and overlap 1—2-inches and deep enough to extend 2 inches above the rim of the tin.
2 Lightly grease and put on top of each other.
3 Fold up 1 inch along base; unfold, cut slantwise up to fold marking at ½-inch intervals.

4 Place this length inside the tin, which should also be lightly greased so the paper sticks to the tin. The cut ends will overlap and lie flat on the base of the tin.
5 Press firmly together where the band overlaps and insert the base lining.
Note: For an even more protective base either layers of newspaper or brown paper can be put under the greaseproof paper at stage 5. For protection round the outside of the cake tin, tie a double or treble band of brown paper on the outside so that it stands well above the tin. For a very rich cake that needs prolonged cooking, you can stand the tin in or on another. This is particularly advisable if your oven is inclined to be fierce.

298 To test a rich fruit cake

To test whether a rich fruit cake is adequately cooked, first see if it has shrunk away from the sides of the tin.
Secondly, press firmly on top and if it feels it has seet, bring it out of the oven.

After this, listen carefully and if no humming noise is heard, then the cake is cooked. If even the faintest hum is heard, it means the cake is not adequately cooked and should be put back into the oven.

299 To mature cakes

Rich cakes must be allowed to mature before icing, for their first-class flavour is easily lost. The very rich cake or Christmas cake 2 needs at least three weeks. The economical cake or Christmas cake 1 needs a fortnight.

300 To ice Christmas cakes without piping

As *colour plate 12* shows, a Christmas cake can look most attractive without piping in any way. In fact, many people prefer this particular form of icing because it looks so much like a traditional white, snowy Christmas.

To achieve this effect

1 Coat with a very thin layer of royal icing and allow this to harden.

2 Put on the second layer evenly, covering the cake completely. It is not necessary for this to be absolutely flat.

3 To get the 'picked-up' effect round the sides, sweep up the icing while still soft with a knife, the handle of a teaspoon or a fork as described in Recipe 115 and illustrated here. Because royal icing holds its shape so wonderfully, you can use a slightly different technique.

Pat the icing with a very small knife and pull the knife away from the cake. This pulls up the icing in very definite points.

4 Continue in the same way on the top of the cake, sweeping up at irregular intervals.

5 Place the decorations in position while the icing is still soft.

6 To get the effect of a toboggan run, sweep down the icing with a flat knife.

7 If you wish to build up the hill effect, you can make a small mound of extra marzipan and place this under the first coat of icing.

Decorating a Christmas cake without piping

301 Star Christmas cake

10 oz. currants
7 oz. sultanas
4 oz. raisins
3 oz. glacé cherries
2 oz. whole almonds
3 oz. mixed cut peel
rind 1 lemon
2 tablespoons brandy
7 oz. plain flour
1 level teaspoon mixed spice
½ teaspoon nutmeg
2 oz. ground almonds
5 oz. luxury margarine
6 oz. soft brown sugar
1 tablespoon black treacle
4 eggs
almond paste (Recipe 256) made with 1 lb. 2 oz. ground almonds
royal icing (Recipe 267), made with 1½ lb. icing sugar, etc.

The picture shows a similar type of decoration to Recipe 300 and is completed by tiny stars of shiny paper and artificial holly leaves.

In this case, the top of the cake is smoothed. The cake is made from a one-stage economical recipe. By using a soft luxury margarine you can mix everything together (other margarine can be softened).

Place all the ingredients in a large mixing bowl and beat together until thoroughly mixed. Place in a prepared 7-inch cake tin, Recipe 297; smooth the top with the back of a wet spoon. Bake in the centre of a very slow oven (250−275°F. − Gas Mark ½−1) for approximately 4 hours.

Cool in tin, turn out and when completely cold store in an airtight tin.

This cake improves with keeping.

Cover with almond paste and royal icing, see Recipes 262 and 271.

Star Christmas cake

302 Square cake

The square cake here is made with the rich or Christmas cake 2 mixture, Recipe 296, and the icing is smoothed over the top, sides and the cake board. It is then marked very carefully and evenly with the prongs of a fork. The fork is drawn down the sides and along the cake board. On the top it is drawn across in three distinct lines. In between these lines use short downward and crossways movements of the fork.

To complete the decoration, tinted leaves and holly berries of marzipan, and a candle are placed in one corner.

Square cake

303 Bell cake

The cake illustrated is made with the rich or Christmas cake 2 mixture, Recipe 296, and the marzipan is moulded to give the slightly rounded bell shape on the top of the cake. The icing is allowed to flow quite freely. Holly and ribbons add to the final effect.

Bell cake

Wedding Cakes

304 Very rich wedding cake

6 oz. margarine or butter
6 oz. sugar (preferably brown)
1 teaspoon black treacle or gravy browning
2 eggs
3 dessertspoons brandy, sherry, rum or whisky
6 oz. plain flour
½ teaspoon mixed spice
12 oz. currants
6 oz. raisins
6 oz. sultanas
2 oz. candied peel
2 oz. glacé cherries
2 oz. chopped almonds
1 teaspoon grated lemon rind

Use a 6-inch round or 5-inch square tin at least 3 inches in depth; prepare as Recipe 297. Cream together margarine or butter, sugar and black treacle. Beat eggs well and add brandy. Sieve the dry ingredients together. Mix the fruit, peel, floured cherries, almonds and lemon rind. Add the eggs and flour alternately to the butter mixture, stirring well but not over-beating. Lastly, mix in the fruit. Put into the tin and bake for 2¾—3 hours in the centre of a moderate oven (325—350°F. — Gas Mark 3) for the first hour, and 300°F. — Gas Mark 2 — for the rest of the time.

Allow to cool in the tin. Store with the paper on the cake.

305 To plan the sizes

If you plan a two- or three-tier wedding cake, have the bottom tier at least 2 inches, and preferably 3 inches, bigger than the cake above, to show a good margin of each tier.

306 To make different-sized cakes from Recipe 304

For an 8-inch round or a 7-inch square cake, use double the ingredients and bake for 4½ hours. After 1—1½ hours at moderate (325—350°F. — Gas Mark 3) turn the oven down. If the cake is very pale, it can go down to very moderate (300°F. — Gas Mark 2), but if it is becoming rather brown, turn the oven to slow (275°F. — Gas Mark 1) for the remaining cooking time.

For a 10-inch round or 9-inch square cake, use four times the ingredients and bake for six hours. After 1½—2 hours at moderate (325—350°F. — Gas Mark 3) turn the oven down. If the cake is very pale, it can go down to very moderate (300°F. — Gas Mark 2), but if it is becoming rather brown, turn the oven to slow (275°F. — Gas Mark 1) for the remaining cooking time.

For a 12-inch round or 11-inch square cake, use six times the ingredients and bake for 7½—8 hours. After 1½—2 hours at moderate (325—350°F. — Gas Mark 3) turn the oven down. If the cake is very pale, it can go down to very moderate (300°F. — Gas Mark 2); but if it is becoming rather brown, turn the oven to slow (275°F. — Gas Mark 1) for the remaining cooking time.

Some ovens are rather fierce, and it may be better to start your cooking at a slightly lower temperature than given. Watch the browning of a wedding cake very carefully, especially with large cakes which only just fit into small modern ovens. If at any time the cake appears to be browning too quickly, turn the oven down.

Because ovens vary quite a bit, times given for turning down are only approximate; you must be guided by knowledge of your own oven.

307 Alternative to a very rich wedding cake recipe

A very rich cake must have at least 4—6 weeks to mature. If you wish a slightly less rich cake, use a Christmas cake recipe and let mature as Recipe 299. If you are having more than one tier it is not necessary to cook all the cakes on the same day.

308 To purchase pillars

In order to support the various tiers of a wedding cake, you must have the special pillars. You can buy round pillars for round cakes and oblong ones for a square or rectangular cake. Allow enough pillars to give adequate support to the tiers. You need three of four, though with a square or oblong cake, four are more in keeping with the shape.

You can buy pillars from a good stationer or the stationery section of a large store.

309 To purchase cake boards

Wedding, Christmas, birthday and other decorated cakes which last a long time, or are going to be cut into a large number of portions, are placed not on plates but on cake boards. These are generally covered with a silver paper which sets off the look of the cake.

The cake does not look effective if the board is exactly the same size as or very little bigger than the cake. You need a margin of board round the cake, so always allow for a board that is at least 2 inches bigger than the completed cake.

310 Two-tier square wedding cake

Ingredients for small cake as given for *Star Christmas cake* (Recipe 301)

Ingredients for large cake:
1¼ lb. currants
13 oz. sultanas
7 oz. raisins
5 oz. glacé cherries
5 oz. whole almonds
5 oz. mixed cut peel
finely grated rind 2 lemons
3—4 tablespoons brandy
14 oz. flour
1½ teaspoons mixed spice
¾ level teaspoon nutmeg
4 oz. ground almonds
10 oz. margarine (luxury or softened)
12 oz. soft brown sugar
2 tablespoons black treacle
7 eggs

Prepare one 7-inch and one 10-inch cake tin. Make each cake by the one-stage method given in Recipe 301.

Bake the small cake in the centre of a very slow oven (250—275°F. — Gas Mark ½—1) for approximately 4 hours, and the larger cake at the same temperature for approximately 5 hours. Store until required.

For marzipan you need:
marzipan made with 1 lb. 12 oz. ground almonds etc., for the 10-inch cake
marzipan made with 1 lb. 2 oz. ground almonds, etc., for the 7-inch cake
This gives a generous layer, see Recipe 260. Place cakes on cake boards.

For royal icing you need a minimum of:
royal icing made with 2½ lb. icing sugar for the 10-inch cake
royal icing made with 1½ lb. icing sugar for the 7-inch cake
If you intend to have two generous layers allow total 5—6 lb., see Recipe 268.
Coat the cakes with marzipan and with two coats of royal icing, making sure that the icing is very hard. Allow to dry completely. Work out the design — on these particular cakes it is based largely on trellis work, see Recipe 288. A circle of trellis is formed in the centre of the cake and, when hard, finished by tiny star shapes round the edge.

The corners and sides are filled in with semi-circles of trellis, again outlined by tiny stars. The roses are made on an icing nail, see Recipe 286. The design round the edge of the cakes is made with tiny flowers, using a No. 28 forget-me-not pipe, leaves are made with a sweet pea or fancy petal pipe, and large roses are again placed in position.

The same star design could be used for the edge and base of the cake or, if you do not wish to change the writing pipe, hold this upright, having drawn the trellis work, and make fairly big dots.

The design on the cake board is made by coating the boards with a thin layer of icing. Allow this to dry and then pipe a tracery of lines with a No. 2 writing pipe. Eight feet of ½-inch-wide pink velvet ribbon has been used to edge the boards. Put four square pillars on large cake and position small one carefully.

Two-tier square wedding cake

Ingredients for 6-inch cake:	**8-inch cake:**	**11-inch cake:**
6 oz. currants	10 oz.	1¼ lb.
4 oz. sultanas	7 oz.	13 oz.
2 oz. raisins	4 oz.	7 oz.
1½ oz. glacé cherries	2½ oz.	5 oz.
1½ oz. whole sweet almonds	2½ oz.	5 oz.
1½ oz. mixed cut peel	2½ oz.	5 oz.
grated rind ½ lemon	1 lemon	2 lemons
1 tablespoon brandy	2 tablespoons	4 tablespoons
4 oz. plain flour	7 oz.	14 oz.
½ teaspoon mixed spice	1 teaspoon	1½ teaspoons
1 oz. ground almonds	2 oz.	3½ oz.
3½ oz. margarine	6 oz.	12 oz.
3½ oz. soft brown sugar	6 oz.	12 oz.
½ tablespoon black treacle	1 tablespoon	2 tablespoons
2 eggs	4 eggs	7 eggs

Mix each cake by the method used for the Birthday cake, Recipe 293, and bake in the centre of a slow oven (250—275°F. — Gas Mark ½—1) allowing approximately 3 hours for the 6-inch cake, 4 hours for the 8-inch cake and 5 hours for the 11-inch cake. Store until ready to use.

For marzipan you need:
marzipan made with 10 oz. ground almonds for the 6-inch cake
marzipan made with 1 lb. 2 oz. ground almonds for the 8-inch cake
marzipan made with 2 lb. ground almonds for the 11-inch cake
This gives a generous layer, see Recipe 260. Place cakes on cake boards.

For royal icing you need a minimum of:
royal icing made with 1 lb. 8 oz. icing sugar for the 6-inch cake
royal icing made with 2 lb. 8 oz. icing sugar for the 8-inch cake
royal icing made with 3 lb. 8 oz. icing sugar for the 11-inch cake
This will give you two coats and piping, see Recipe 268.
When you are icing two or three cakes together, you can often cut down slightly on the total amount of icing sugar needed.
A very simple piping design is used on these cakes. The top and sides are left quite flat. The rather wide rope design round the edge of the cakes can be made with a 5, 6, 8, 10 or 12 star or a No. 5 rope pipe. The loops of icing underneath the edge and round the sides of the cake are made with a No. 2 or 3 writing pipe.
The fluted ribbon round the base is a very easy pipe to do. In order to get this particular effect, you draw a line with the ribbon pipe and then go back slightly over the line of piping. In this case you start from left to right, then move back to the left slightly, pipe a small amount of band and move to the right again.
Place silver leaves in position with a little icing. Put three round pillars on each of the two larger cakes, stand one on the other with the small cake on top. Put a small amount of royal icing under a silver vase and place it in position on the top tier. It can then be filled with flowers on the day of the wedding.

Three-tier wedding cake

Fluted ribbon design in piping

312 Wedding cake with simple decorations

12 oz. plain flour
¾ teaspoon salt
1½ level teaspoons cinnamon
2 teaspoons mixed spice
¾ teaspoon ground nutmeg
1½ lb. seedless raisins
1½ lb. sultanas
1 lb. currants
6 oz. candied peel
6 oz. glacé cherries
6 oz. chopped, blanched
  almonds
12 oz. butter
12 oz. soft brown sugar
3 dessertspoons black treacle
3 oz. plain chocolate, melted
9 eggs
8 tablespoons brandy
¾ teaspoon bicarbonate
  of soda
3 dessertspoons warm water
little sieved apricot jam
almond paste (Recipe 256)
  made with 1½ lb. ground
  almonds
royal icing (Recipe 267)
  made with 5 lb. icing sugar,
  etc., softened with glycerine
  (Recipe 270)
To decorate:
4 cake pillars
satin ribbon
silver vase of flowers

Sieve the dry ingredients and prepare the fruit. The raisins can be plumped by covering with cold water, bringing to the boil, leaving to stand for 5 minutes, draining and drying. Mix the fruit and nuts with one third of the dry ingredients. Cream the butter and sugar, add the black treacle and chocolate. Cream the egg yolks and fold them into the butter mixture alternately with another third of the dry ingredients. Add to the fruit mixture. Whisk the egg whites until stiff, fold into the mixture together with the brandy and remaining dry ingredients. Add the bicarbonate of soda dissolved in the warm water. Put the mixture into two prepared cake tins, one 9-inch and one 6-inch, filling both to the same level. Bake in a very moderate oven (300°F. — Gas Mark 2) allowing approximately 3 — 3½ hours for the larger cake and 2½ — 3 hours for the smaller cake, watching carefully to see if the temperature needs turning down, see Recipe 306. Store until required. Coat with the jam. Make the almond paste and cover each cake, see Recipe 261. Allow to dry for at least a week, or cover at once with the icing, see Recipe 261. Make the royal icing and coat each cake with two layers, allowing 24 — 48 hours between each layer for it to harden, Recipe 271. Place each cake on a silver cake board, and pipe a shell design, Recipe 319, round the top and bottom edge of each.
Tie bands of wide satin ribbon round each cake, and place the pillars firmly into position with icing. A silver vase of real flowers put in the centre of the top tier is very attractive; its base can be outlined in a shell design.

Wedding cake with simple decorations

313 To cut a wedding cake

To make it easier for the bride to cut the first slice of wedding cake, it is usual for this to be prepared beforehand.
Cut a large slice out of the cake after you cover with marzipan and icing and insert greaseproof paper or foil. Replace the slice of cake, and decorate in the usual way.
Before the cake is put on to the table, carefully cut through the decorations, remove the cut

slice of cake and tie a piece of silver or white ribbon round it, so that when the bride inserts the knife either side of the wedge, she can pull out the slice with the ribbon.
The wedge can then be cut into tiny fingers about 1 inch wide and served to the guests. Because the portions served at a wedding are so tiny, a great number of portions are obtained from even a small cake.

314 To keep fruit cake moist

When storing a rich fruit cake keep it very well wrapped up in foil, or use an airtight tin, because exposure to the air will dry it.
As suggested in the Christmas cake 2, Recipe 296, it is a good idea, for a moist cake, to prick and pour over a little sherry at intervals.

Use a fine skewer to avoid crumbling; if you prick the top the first time, and the bottom next time, you make sure the whole cake is thoroughly moistened. You can use rum or brandy instead of sherry. This can be done at intervals of about one to two weeks.

315 Temperatures for baking

Throughout this book there are a number of similar cakes, some slightly richer than others. You will find these need different directions for baking. For example with cakes like wedding cake the outside is set in a very moderate oven and then the heat is reduced; with others you cook at a uniform temperature.

Each method has its particular advantage. Method 1 tends to give a more moist cake. Method 2 makes absolutely certain there is no fear of over-cooking and is therefore the better one to follow if you are going to leave the cake unattended or you are a little uncertain about the heat in your oven.

316 Silver wedding cakes

These can be decorated in exactly the same way as an ordinary wedding cake, with the emphasis on silver decorations.

It is quite a good idea to have a very simple written reminder of the original wedding date on top of the cake.

317 Golden wedding cakes

Keep the emphasis on gold. Use golden colouring for the horseshoes and flowers.

Again it is a good idea to have a reminder of the original wedding date on top of the cake.

Christening Cakes

318

The type of cake chosen will very much depend on the average age of the guests at the christening party. If a number of children are present, choose a rather plain type of cake. If you have a number of adults present, a richer cake can be made. Many people like to keep the top tier of their wedding cake for a christening cake. Although the cake will have kept perfectly, the icing is often badly discoloured. It should therefore be broken away from the cake, and the cake re-covered with marzipan and icing.

319 Christening cake

8 oz. currants
6 oz. sultanas
4 oz. raisins
2 oz. chopped glacé cherries
2 oz. chopped walnuts
2 oz. mixed cut peel
rind 1 lemon, finely grated
1 tablespoon brandy
6 oz. margarine
6 oz. soft brown sugar
3 eggs
1 level tablespoon black treacle
8 oz. plain flour
1 rounded teaspoon mixed spice
½ level teaspoon nutmeg
1 oz. ground almonds
To coat and decorate the cake:
marzipan (Recipe 256) made with 10 oz. ground almonds, etc.
royal icing (Recipe 267) made with 1½ lb. sugar, etc.

Prepare a 7-inch round cake tin as Recipe 297, and cover the outside and bottom of the tin with several thicknesses of folded newspaper to prevent the outside of the cake from burning. Mix the fruit together in a large mixing bowl with the cherries, walnuts, peel, lemon rind and brandy (optional). Cream margarine and sugar together until light and fluffy. Beat in the eggs, one at a time, adding a little of the sieved flour with the third egg. Stir in the treacle and fold in the sieved flour, mixed spice, nutmeg and ground almonds. Add the prepared fruit and mix in thoroughly. Bake in a very slow oven (250—275°F. — Gas Mark ½—1) for 4—4½ hours. Leave in the tin for 30 minutes to cool. Remove from tin and cool on a wire tray. Remove the greaseproof paper when the cake is cold. This cake can be stored in an airtight tin. Cover the cake with marzipan and then with royal icing, leaving enough for piping. Tint delicate blue or pink according to sex of baby.

Pipe the name first. The scroll line under the name is made by holding the writing pipe upright to give the first dot, then drawing the line and holding the pipe upright again for dot at other end. The name is raised by a second layer of piping, see Recipe 290.

The design in a case like this will probably need to be pricked out to get even spacing. The top border is made first of all with a double shell or rosette shape. Start at the narrow end of the shell, widen and then narrow off again. Allow the shell to dry and then outline with the same writing pipe as for the top, to give a much more dramatic edge. This pipe is used again to give the looped lines emphasizing the shells. Round the centre of the side flowers are made with a No. 11 or 15 pipe, held with the centre of the pipe flat against the side of the cake. A delicate stalk is made in between with a writing pipe. The shell design round the base is emphasized by a line of icing with the writing pipe.

Shell design in piping

Christening cake

Marzipan for Decoration

320 The uses of marzipan decoration

Marzipan is not only an effective coating, but it is a means of making decorations by itself.

Marzipan is used particularly on Simnel and Battenburg cakes and for moulding flowers.

321 Battenburg cake

4 oz. margarine
4 oz. castor sugar
2 eggs
6 oz. plain flour
½ level teaspoon baking powder
little warm water
1 heaped teaspoon soluble coffee powder
few drops cochineal
marzipan (Recipes 256 or 259) made with 6—8 oz. ground almonds
green colouring
little jam
icing made with 6 oz. icing sugar, little water, pink and green colouring, ¼ teaspoon soluble coffee powder
little coffee butter icing (Recipe 103)

Cream the fat and sugar until light and fluffy, then beat in the eggs. Fold in the flour sieved with the baking powder and a little warm water to make a soft dropping consistency. Mix the soluble coffee powder into one half of the mixture. Add cochineal to other half. Put each half into separate prepared loaf* tins and hollow out slightly in the middle. Bake in a moderate oven (375°F. — Gas Mark 4) for 35—40 minutes until firm. Leave to cool.
Make the marzipan. Heat the jam. Cut each piece of sponge down the middle and trim the edges evenly, to form four strips. Spread two sides of the sponge with jam and press together firmly, alternating the pink and coffee sponge. Roll the marzipan out, on a sugared board, to the length of the sponge strips and to a width four times as great as the depth of the chequered cake. Spread with jam. Place the cake on the middle of the paste and press evenly to the cake with the join down the centre top and the ends open. Turn over.
Mix the sieved icing sugar with a little water to make a soft consistency. Divide between four basins, making one portion a little larger than the others and leaving this white. Colour the other portions green, pink and coffee.
Spread the white portion on top of the cake. While this is still wet, very quickly pipe across in lines of alternate colours. Draw a knife lengthwise down the icing about ¼ inch from the edge. Then draw the knife backwards through the icing in the opposite direction about ¼ inch from the first line. Continue like this across the whole width of the cake, until you have a 'feather' effect.
Pipe coffee butter icing along the side edges.
Illustrated in colour plate 20.
If more convenient, line an ordinary Swiss roll tin with greased greaseproof paper and put the pink mixture at one end of the tin, the coffee at the other end. Bake just above the centre of a moderate oven (375°F. — Gas Mark 4) for approximately 30 minutes. An ordinary Victoria sandwich can be used instead of this recipe, which will give a lighter mixture; Recipes 30 or 59, made with 2 eggs.

322 Simnel cake 1

6 oz. margarine
6 oz. castor sugar
3 eggs
8 oz. plain flour
3 rounded teaspoons mixed spice
1 tablespoon milk
1 oz. almonds
6 oz. currants
4 oz. sultanas
2 oz. glacé cherries, chopped
1 oz. mixed cut peel
almond paste (Recipe 256) made with 1 lb. ground almonds*
To decorate:
1 tablespoon apricot jam
½ beaten egg
red colouring
4 small Easter eggs
1 chick
* This gives generous layers and decoration and could be cut down.

Cream the margarine and sugar together until very light and fluffy. Beat in the eggs, one at a time, adding a little sieved flour if necessary. Fold in the remaining flour sieved with the mixed spice, then add the milk. Blanch the almonds and remove their skins, and chop coarsely. Add the almonds, currants, sultanas, cherries and peel to the mixture and fold in thoroughly. Place half the mixture in a deep lined and greased 7-inch cake tin.
Roll one third of the almond paste into a 7-inch round and place on top of the cake mixture. Put the remaining cake mixture on top and smooth. Bake on the middle shelf of a slow oven (275—300°F. — Gas Mark 1—2) for 2—2½ hours. Remove and allow to cool. Brush the top of the cake with heated apricot jam.
Roll out one third of the remaining almond paste to a 7-inch round and place on top of the cake. Mark the paste with a fork to give a trellis effect.
Roll out some of the remaining almond paste into a long thin strip and twist. Brush the top of the cake with beaten egg and place the twist around the edge to make a border. Make eleven small balls of almond paste and place inside the twist, brush with egg. Place in a moderately hot oven (400°F. — Gas Mark 5) for 5 minutes to lightly brown the almond paste. Remove and cool.
Colour a small piece of almond paste red, roll out and cut into a round with a 2-inch fluted cutter. Place in the centre of the cake. Decorate with the Easter eggs and chick.

Simnel cake 1

2 oz. glacé cherries
2 oz. blanched almonds
¼ pint plus 2 tablespoons
    water
10 oz. margarine
8 oz. currants
8 oz. sultanas
4 oz. chopped mixed peel
finely grated rind 1 orange
finely grated rind 2 lemons
1 large can condensed milk
10 oz. plain flour
pinch salt
¾ teaspoon bicarbonate
    of soda
marzipan (Recipe 259) made
    with 1½ lb. ground almonds*
little jam
glacé icing (Recipe 53) made
    with 4 oz. icing sugar, etc.
*This is a very lavish amount
and could be cut down*

323　Simnel cake 2

Chop the cherries and almonds, put with water, margarine, fruit, peel, rinds and condensed milk into a saucepan. Bring to the boil, stirring all the time. Lower the heat and simmer for 3 minutes. Remove from heat and cool. Sieve flour and salt into a bowl. Add bicarbonate of soda to cooled fruit mixture and stir quickly. Pour into the flour and mix quickly together.

Put half the quantity into an 8-inch lined and greased tin. Spread evenly and place a round of almond paste 1 inch thick on top. Cover with remaining cake mixture and bake in the centre of a slow oven (275—300°F. — Gas Mark 1—2) for 2¾ hours. Cool in the tin. Decorate as in Picture 1.

324　Other ways of decorating simnel cakes

Picture 1
The top of the cake is brushed with jam and covered with a layer of marzipan. A long thin sausage shape which should be brushed with a little jam underneath so that it adheres, is put round the edge. Mark with knife blade. The only other decoration is glacé icing poured into the centre of the marzipan ring, imitation chicks and a real egg shell, washed. In this case the marzipan is *not* glazed.

Picture 2
The top of the cake is brushed with jam and covered with a layer of marzipan, with a small circle cut from the centre. A ring of marzipan balls, brushed with egg white and glazed in the oven or under a moderately hot grill, is placed round the edge. The circle in the centre is filled with glacé icing and the cake completed with toy and marzipan animals. A band of ribbon is tied round.

Picture 3
This shows a cake topped with marzipan and a thin coating of glacé icing. The surplus marzipan is rolled into thin ropes, which are then twisted together to form a border and the nest shape. The marzipan is glazed and browned slightly before the little Easter eggs and small chicks are added.

1 Simnel cake decorated with unglazed marzipan ring and glacé icing

2 Simnel cake decorated with glazed marzipan balls and glacé icing

3 Simnel cake decorated with glazed marzipan twist and glacé icing

6 oz. butter
6 oz. sugar
4 eggs *or* 3 eggs and 2 tablespoons milk *or* madeira
8 oz. flour (with plain flour
  — 1½ level teaspoons baking
  powder)

Madeira cake (Recipe 325)
vanilla butter icing (Recipe
100) made from 10 oz.
butter, etc.
marzipan (Recipe 256) made
  with 2 — 4 oz. ground
  almonds
little colouring

325 Madeira cake

Cream the butter and sugar together until soft
and light. Gradually beat in the eggs, then fold
in the flour and baking powder. Bake in a
7-inch cake tin for approximately 1½ hours in
the centre of a very moderate oven (300 to

350°F. — Gas Mark 2—3).
For a plain Madeira cake, sprinkle the top of
the cake with a little sugar. Citron peel can be
put on the cake either before cooking or
halfway through baking.

326 Victorian posy cake

Make the Madeira cake, but in order to have
a rather large shallow cake, bake for approximately 1 hour 10 minutes in a 8-inch tin,
or just over 1 hour in a 9-inch tin. Cool.
Cover with most of the butter icing.
Pipe the scroll or star design round the base
of the cake.
Make the marzipan and gradually work enough
cochineal or saffron yellow colouring into this
to make either pale pink or yellow. To make
the little shapes round the edge of the cake,
roll out the marzipan very thinly on a sugared
board and cut out with a fancy cutter. To
make the roses, cut out circles or heart shapes
in marzipan. Then proceed as for satin icing,
Recipe 166, starting from the centre of the rose
and building up each flower by adding another
petal. If the marzipan is very thin, you can get
a most realistic curl on the flower petals. The
leaves can either be made of the same colour
marzipan or a little can be put on one side
before you begin, then tinted a pale green.
Place the leaves and roses on a small gold
doily in the centre of the cake.

Victorian posy cake

327 Primrose cakes

Victoria sponge 1 or 2 (Recipes
30 or 59) *or fatless sponge*
(Recipe 130)
little jam
4 oz. desiccated coconut
glacé icing (Recipe 53) made
  with 3 oz. icing sugar
marzipan (Recipe 259) made
  with 12 oz. ground almonds,
  etc.

Make the sponge cake. Cut round shapes from
the sponge. Brush the outside of the cakes
with a little jam and roll in coconut, which
can be toasted. Decorate the tops of the cakes
with glacé icing, tinted pale green. You can
either tint the marzipan pale yellow before

rolling out or brush after moulding, see Recipe 329. Cut either rounds or heart shapes
of thin marzipan, allowing five for each cake.
Form into petals and arrange on top of icing.
The centres can be sweet mimosa balls or tiny
marzipan balls tinted deep yellow or brown.

Primrose cakes

328 To mould marzipan

Marzipan can be moulded into almost any
shape — little animals, flowers, fruits, etc.
You will find as you handle it that it may

become slightly oily, so have plenty of icing
sugar available to keep it reasonably dry. All
the recipes given are suitable for moulding.

329 To tint marzipan

In order to tint marzipan, put a few drops of colouring from the end of a skewer into the marzipan paste, when it is made. Alternatively, colouring can be blended with the egg yolk when mixing the marzipan. You will find it needs quite an amount of gentle kneading to get colouring evenly distributed throughout.

Another way to tint is to make the marzipan shapes, and before they have had a chance to harden, brush colouring (using, of course, proper culinary colourings) on to the marzipan with a fine brush. By adding this before the marzipan sets and hardens, you can produce rather softer colours.

330 Points to remember when using marzipan

Marzipan becomes oily when over-handled. You must therefore work quickly to prevent this and try to cut the handling to a minimum. If you know you are slow at kneading marzipan, the Australian Recipe 333, because of its lower ground almond content, is the consistency to use.
Ground almonds, like all nuts, can become

stale if kept for too long a period or in a damp place. This gives an unpleasant bitter flavour. If you are using ground almonds that have been kept for a very long time, be sure to taste them before using.
Marzipan becomes very hard when exposed to the air, so all marzipan-coated cakes must be put in covered tins as soon as possible.

331 Points to remember when using royal icing

Royal icing needs a great deal of beating to get a really good white colour and consistency, so do not shorten the time. An electric mixer is, of course, ideal for this purpose, but because it beats so violently and efficiently it can give the impression of a firmer consistency than actually exists. Make sure that you measure the egg whites and icing sugar with the greatest care if you intend to beat in the mixer;

i.e. do not put in the icing sugar first and then add what you think is the right amount of egg white. There have been cases when too much egg white has been used to too little sugar and the icing has become sticky and damp.
Royal icing hardens with exposure to the air: always keep bowls of icing made for piping covered with a really damp cloth or paper, and dampen again when necessary.

Australian Decoration

332

Basically the Australian method of decorating differs from usual in that far less piping is done and far more delicate moulding is used. This is illustrated in *colour plates 17 and 18*. The roses on this cake look almost real, for the petals are so delicate and fine.

In addition the cakes are not normally covered with royal icing, but with a plastic (or fondant type) icing.
Almond paste is very often used as a first coat, but because the plastic (or fondant) icing is so firm, this can be omitted if required.

333 Australian almond paste

2 oz. ground almonds
1 small egg yolk
6 oz. icing sugar
1 tablespoon sherry
few drops glycerine, optional

Although very similar to other marzipan recipes in this book, this is generally flavoured with a small amount of sherry and a higher percentage of icing sugar is used to give a

sweeter and less rich almond paste — e.g. marzipan 1, Recipe 256, would be altered as shown here. The method of handling and coating, and the total weight, is just the same.

334 Plastic icing or coating fondant

8 oz. icing sugar
1 dessertspoon water
1 teaspoon gelatine
just under 1 teaspoon glycerine
1 oz. liquid glucose

1 Sieve icing sugar into a bowl.
2 Put water and gelatine in a saucepan, stir constantly over gentle heat until gelatine is completely dissolved.
3 Remove from heat, add glycerine and glucose, stir well.
4 Leave mixture a few minutes to cool, then add to icing sugar.
5 Knead well.

6 Place on board lightly sprinkled with cornflour, knead well again.
Colour and flavour, but use colour sparingly. Keep all shades in pale tints. Continue to knead until colour is evenly absorbed and blended.
If icing is to be kept, store in an airtight container — *never* in the refrigerator.

335 To apply the plastic or fondant icing

1 Knead the icing well, form into the size for the top of the cake.
2 Press on top of the cake which has been brushed with egg white or a little sieved jam or put over a marzipan base.
3 If coating the top and sides of a cake, knead and roll out the icing to form a big enough

square or circle to completely envelop the top and sides.
This is similar to the coating with marzipan described in Method 3, Recipe 261, and gives a softer, rounder edge to the cake. If you wish a sharp edge to the cake, you must roll top and sides with a rolling pin or a jam jar.

21 Gâteau à la pêche

22 Valentine cake

23 Crown cake

336 To mould plastic or fondant icing

Many people use exactly the same fondant for moulding and icing, but because it is possible to have a slight diversity of ingredients, (some contain gelatine, some glucose, some glycerine), it does mean that you can choose exactly the icing you like best and find most convenient to handle.

Modelling or fondant icing, Recipes 338 and 339, is perfect for moulding, but can also be used for coating purposes.

337 Amounts of plastic icing or coating fondant to use

For the top of a 7-inch cake, thin layer	USE 8 oz. sieved icing sugar 1 dessertspoon water 1 teaspoon gelatine just under 1 teaspoon glycerine 1 oz. liquid glucose
For the top and sides of a 7-inch cake, thin layer	USE 1¼ lb. sieved icing sugar 1½ tablespoons water 1½ tablespoons gelatine just over 2 teaspoons glycerine 2½ oz. liquid glucose
For the top of an 8-inch square or 9-inch round cake, thin layer	USE 12 oz. sieved icing sugar 1½ dessertspoons water 1½ teaspoons gelatine just over 1 teaspoon glycerine 1½ oz. liquid glucose
For the top and sides of an 8-inch square or 9-inch round cake, thin layer	USE 2 lb. sieved icing sugar 4 dessertspoons water 4 teaspoons gelatine just under 4 teaspoons glycerine 4 oz. liquid glucose
For the top of a 9-inch square or 10-inch round cake, thin layer	USE 1 lb. sieved icing sugar 2 dessertspoons water 2 teaspoons gelatine just under 2 teaspoons glycerine 2 oz. liquid glucose
For the top and sides of a 9-inch square or 10-inch round cake, thin layer	USE 2½ lb. sieved icing sugar 5 dessertspoons water 5 teaspoons gelatine 4½ teaspoons glycerine 5 oz. liquid glucose

338 Fondant icing for modelling or coating

1 lb. icing sugar
1 egg white
2 oz. liquid glucose
flavouring
colouring

1 Sift the icing sugar into a basin and make well in the centre.
2 Add the egg white and glucose.
3 Beat, drawing the icing sugar into the centre from the sides of the basin until the mixture is a stiff paste.
4 Lightly dust a board with icing sugar and turn the mixture on to it.
5 Knead until of a fine smooth texture.
6 Add flavouring and colouring.

339 Modelling fondant

¼ oz. gelatine
2 oz. water
⅛ oz. glucose
1 lb. icing sugar

1 Add the gelatine to the water and dissolve over gentle heat.
2 Add glucose and cool, but do not allow to get completely cold.
3 Add approximately 2 oz. icing sugar, a little at a time.
4 Put into a plastic bag and leave several hours before using.
5 Knead in remaining icing sugar until desired consistency is reached.
This is generally used only for modelling.
Note: This form of decoration is so different that many people who have neither the time nor the patience for authentic piping, but have a great deal of artistic ability, can sculpture decorations for cakes.

340 Piping

Royal icing, as Recipe 267, is used for piping on to cakes. The only difference with the Australian method is that most of the piping is very fine and lacy.

341 Wire for moulding

You may be able to buy very fine green millinery wire but if this is not obtainable, use ordinary wire and then apply green culinary colouring to this with a fine paint brush.
Never use ordinary paint on decorations that come in contact with food.

cake as *Star Christmas cake* (Recipe 301)
fondant icing (Recipe 338) suitable for modelling and coating, made with 2 lb. icing sugar
royal icing (Recipe 267) made with 8 oz. icing sugar, etc. colourings
almond paste (Recipe 256) made with 8 oz. ground almonds *or* Australian almond paste (Recipe 333), made with 4 oz. ground almonds, optional
baby ribbon

342 Birthday cake

Make and bake the cake in a 7-inch square tin as Recipe 301 or Recipes 295 or 296. Coat with marzipan if liked. Coat with the fondant icing, leaving a reasonable amount for the moulding. Mould the flowers and the leaves as described below.
The writing is done as described in Recipe 87, with royal icing and a very fine pipe.
The base of the cake is decorated with a shell pattern in royal icing using a No. 5, 8 or 13 pipe, Recipe 319.
The lace pattern which is so typical of Australian cakes is made as described in Recipe 348. Pieces of very fine baby ribbon are placed on the cake and then the lacing stuck to this with a minute amount of royal icing.

To mould the flowers
Roses
1 Tint part of the fondant yellow and part very pale pink. Make the centre of the rose first from a tiny ball of the yellow fondant.
2 Take small pieces of the pink fondant and press and pull until absolutely wafer thin.
3 Cut or form into a petal shape.
4 Press to the centre yellow ball at the base.
5 Make more petal shapes; press into place.
6 When you are satisfied they are adhering firmly, turn the edge of the petals back to give the gentle curl of a perfect rose.
7 When enough petals have been added, turn the rose carefully upside down and remove any surplus fondant at the base.
8 Turn the right side up to dry.

Hyacinths
1 Tint a little of the fondant pale blue. Take a very small amount and work into a short cylindrical shape about ¾ inch long round a size 9 or 10 knitting needle.
2 Slip fondant off needle and cut down into six sections with very small scissors.
3 Insert a short length of wire down the middle of the flower and press around the base.
4 Bend the sections back to form petals and just snip round the edges with scissors to give a point.

Lilies of the valley
(a) buds
Form tiny pieces of white fondant into the bud shape and put on the end of fine wire.
(b) flowers
1 Shape tiny pieces of white fondant on the end of knitting needles to form a small cup.
2 Remove and cut round the top to give the shape of the flower.

Leaves
Tint the fondant pale green or use white fondant cut into a leaf shape and mark the veins. Brush the leaves with culinary colourings well diluted to give a very pale green.

The key
The key on a birthday cake could, of course, be an ordinary key bought from a stationer, but in this particular case it has been made and piped with the royal icing.
Draw the shape of the key on a piece of waxed paper. Put a little royal icing into a No. 1 or 2 writing pipe and pipe the shape of the key. Allow to dry. When quite dry brush with gold leaf colouring.
Illustrated in colour plate 17.

343 Flower shapes with fondant

Although only a few flowers have been described, any flower can be moulded in this fondant paste.

If you use a real flower as a model, it is not a difficult matter to work the tin paste into the right shape.

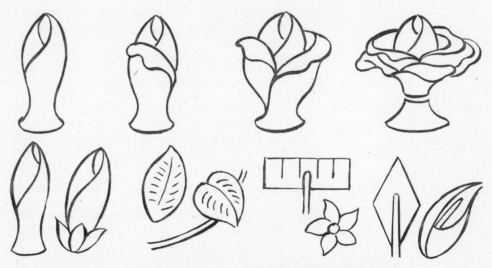

Flower shapes with fondant

344 To colour flowers

In some cases, e.g. the rose, it is best to work the colouring into the fondant at the start. If you are making a great variety of flowers, you may prefer to mould them all in a white fondant and tint by applying culinary colourings with a very fine paint brush. Remember that this will give a very much stronger colour, so it is important to try out the colour first. You may find it better to dilute the colouring with a little egg white or water.

345 Moulding

Flowers are the obvious things to choose for moulding, but you can use the same paste to mould a tiny cradle for a christening cake, or to mould animals and other objects.

346 To roll and cut out fondant paste

This modelling fondant is equally suitable for rolling out and cutting into fancy shapes, e.g. animals and doll shapes. You can then tint them with culinary colouring.

347 Lacework

This very delicate lace tracery is not as difficult to make as it may seem. It means using the finest writing pipe obtainable. This will vary. In Australia rather finer pipes are obtainable, but the No. 1 writing pipe is quite suitable.

348 To make the lace design

Put a piece of waxed paper on to a firm board or tin and secure this with a paper clip, drawing pin or transparent adhesive tape so that it cannot possibly slip.

Make the royal icing of a correct consistency so that it flows easily but not too rapidly.

Picture 1

This shows the most simple way to make the lace.

Start with a bow. Build up on this by adding two more loops. Then add tiny dots of the royal icing.

Picture 2

This shows two other very simple designs in this lace work.

To remove the lace work

Wait until the lace is completely dry and remove very carefully with the tip of a knife.

Because it is so fragile, it is more than likely that you will have a fairly high percentage of breakage in the icing, particularly when you begin handling this, so always make a great deal more than you need.

You can use ordinary lace as a pattern, piping the icing to match the design.

Either have the piece of lace beside you and copy it freehand or, if the lace is very fine, lay this on the waxed paper and pipe the icing on top. Allow to dry, then carefully peel from the paper and strip the lace away. This obviously requires an enormous amount of care and patience.

To apply to the cake

Pipe a little soft icing on the edge of the lace work you intend to put against the cake and press gently but firmly.

1 Building up a lace design from a simple bow

2 Two other simple lacework designs

Cream for Decoration

349

Freshly whipped thick cream can be used as a topping as well as a filling. It can be piped or used in any way like a butter icing.

350 Advantages of using cream in decorations

Fresh cream not only has a delicious flavour but can also have other flavours added to it.

351 Disadvantages of using cream in decorations

Cream keeps only for a limited length of time. This entails putting the cake in a refrigerator if it is to be kept overnight. It is best to use the cake on the day it is made.

352 Cakes suitable for decorating with fresh cream

Generally speaking, the type of cake on which cream is suitable for decoration is a rather light sponge cake, either plain or flavoured. It is also suitable for biscuit types of cakes.

353 Amounts of cream to use

This depends on the size of cake. For example, ¼ pint cream will give a good coating on the top of a 6½—8-inch cake. For piping with cream it is surprising how much you will need.

354 Mock cream

1 tablespoon cornflour
½ pint milk
1—2 oz. butter
1 oz. castor sugar

1 Blend the cornflour to a smooth mixture with the milk.
2 Put into a saucepan and bring slowly to the boil, stirring all the time.
3 Cook until thick.
4 Allow to become quite cold.
5 Cream the butter and sugar until very soft.

ON NO ACCOUNT WARM THE BUTTER.
6 Gradually beat in spoonfuls of the cornflour mixture.
7 The more you beat this, the better the cream becomes.
This gives quite a thin cream. For a thicker cream, use 2 tablespoons cornflour.

355 To use evaporated milk

Evaporated milk can be used as a light filling if the can is boiled and the milk whipped. It is unsuitable for piping.
A stiffer mixture can be made if the can is boiled for 15 minutes, opened while hot and 1 teaspoon of powdered gelatine, dissolved in 1—2 tablespoons of hot water, is added. Allow to cool, then whip.

356 Canned cream, etc.

This is extremely useful for emergencies. It can be used for whipping and piping, but in most cases you will need to pour off the whey. Packet toppings also whip and pipe easily.

357 Crème Chantilly

This is the name given to sweetened cream, lightly flavoured with vanilla.
1 Put the cream into a basin.
2 Using a whisk or a fork, whip it until JUST stiff enough to stand in peaks. Do not continue whisking.
3 Fold in sugar to taste (1 or 2 teaspoons for each ¼ pint) and a few drops vanilla, OR use vanilla flavoured sugar.
4 Whisk again very lightly if you are going to pipe it.
5 Never over-whip cream or it will separate and become buttery.
6 If cream is very rich (Jersey cream), and therefore a little solid when whipping, add just a tablespoon or two of cream from the top of the milk. Always do this before it becomes completely stiff.

358 To whip cream

Care must be taken to buy thick cream for whipping. In some places you may be given a choice of 'single' or 'double' cream and it is the 'double' whipping cream that is needed. Place the cream in a bowl sufficiently large so that it can be beaten with a fork or an egg whisk without splashing.
Do not over-whip. Directly cream begins to thicken, proceed very slowly otherwise it will either curdle or become thick and buttery.

359 To lighten cream

Once cream is whipped, a stiffly beaten egg white can be folded in for each ¼ pint cream.

360 To flavour cream

Because cream is such a light form of decoration, you must be very careful how you incorporate flavouring.

Almond and vanilla
Add a few drops of essence.

Chocolate
Use fine sweetened chocolate powder, blending this in very gently.

Coffee
Use either coffee essence or a little instant coffee powder, blended with a few drops of milk or water.

Fruit flavours
Fold crushed, dry fruit into the cream.

Chestnut cream
Use equal quantities of a thick chestnut purée and cream and add sugar to taste with a few drops of vanilla essence.

To make chestnut purée
Slit the chestnut skins, boil steadily for about 10 minutes, remove outer and inner skin while warm and put the nuts back again into a very little fresh water and vanilla, and cook until soft enough to sieve. It is important to remember that the extra stirring or beating needed to incorporate flavouring in cream could cause it to curdle.
It is therefore advisable to add the flavouring when the cream is just beginning to stiffen sufficiently to stand in very soft peaks. The sugar added to cream can be either castor or sieved icing sugar.

361 To spread cream

Spread and handle cream very lightly. In hot weather it is better to use a metal syringe for cream than a bag, since the warmth of your hands may make it wet and sticky.

362 Tasman apple shortcake

For the filling:
2 lb. cooking apples
little water
1 small lemon
sugar to taste
For the shortcake:
4 oz. butter
4 oz. castor sugar
6 oz. plain flour
pinch salt
1 level teaspoon ground
  ginger
1 tablespoon sherry,
  approximately
For the coating:
¼ pint double cream
1 oz. castor sugar
For the piping:
extra cream
To decorate:
angelica
glacé cherry

Peel and slice the apples and cook with as little water as possible with thin strips of lemon rind added. Remove the lemon rind, add sugar to taste and mash the apples to a fine pulp, or sieve; allow to become quite cold.
Cream the butter and sugar thoroughly, add the sifted flour, salt and ginger, then mix to a stiff dough with as much sherry as is necessary. Knead well, then divide the mixture into three equal portions. Roll each piece to an 8-inch round and bake in a greased sandwich tin for 10 minutes near the centre of a very moderate oven (325—350°F. — Gas Mark 2—3). Lift out before they set and allow them to become quite cold and crisp.

Place one round of shortcake on a suitable serving dish, spread with half the cold apple, then put another shortcake on top, then more apple and finally the third shortcake. Press top very gently to ensure that the apple is evenly distributed to the edges of the rounds. Whip the cream, add the sugar and completely cover the shortcake with it. Pipe an edging round base and decorate the top with leaves of angelica and a glacé cherry. Mark top of cake with a knife.
This is best prepared a few hours before it is required so that the shortcakes will soften slightly and so be less likely to crack when cut into wedges for serving.

Tasman apple shortcake

363 To pipe with cream

Cream is ideal for piping. Care must be taken that the cream is whipped to just the right consistency, that is when it stands in peaks. If it has been over-whipped even slightly, the moment pressure is applied in the bag or syringe you will find it will separate badly.

Use only a light pressure as the cream is much softer than ordinary icings and will therefore come through the pipe quickly.
Pipe on the cream decoration at the last minute or keep the cake in a really cold place once it has been decorated.

364 Tyrolean ginger gâteau

9 oz. flour (with plain flour
    add 2 level teaspoons baking
    powder)
7½ oz. soft brown sugar
½ level teaspoon salt
3 level teaspoons ground
    ginger
3 eggs
¼ pint corn oil
¼ pint milk
For the syrup:
6 oz. sugar
½ pint water
4 tablespoons syrup from
    preserved ginger
To decorate:
½ pint whipped thick cream
2—4 oz. chopped preserved
    ginger

Grease an oblong tin, approximately 7½ × 4 —
4½ inches and line the bottom with greased
paper. Sift all dry ingredients together into
a mixing bowl. Whisk egg yolks, corn oil
and milk together and add to the dry ingredients. Beat well to form a smooth slack batter.
Fold in the stiffly beaten egg whites. Turn the
mixture into the prepared tin and bake about
1 hour 40 minutes in the centre of a *very
moderate* oven (350°F. — Gas Mark 3). Cool
for a while in tin before turning out.
Boil syrup ingredients together briskly for
4 minutes. When the cake is cold, return to
the tin; pierce all over with a skewer and pour
the hot syrup over. Leave overnight.
Turn out the cake and cut through the centre.
Fill with whipped cream to which a little
chopped preserved ginger has been added.
Top with whipped cream and decorate as
liked with preserved ginger.

Tyrolean ginger gâteau

365 Peach blossom flans

Victoria sandwich 1 (Recipe
    30) made with 2 eggs
For the filling:
8 oz. raspberry jam
1 large can peach halves *or*
    fresh peaches
little extra warmed sieved
    apricot or raspberry con-
    serve or jam
¼ pint double cream

Grease 12—14 individual sponge flan tins
measuring 3¼ inches across the base.
Make the Victoria sandwich and divide the
mixture between the tins, smoothing level
with a knife. Place flans on baking sheets and
bake in the centre of a *moderately hot* oven
(400°F. — Gas Mark 5) for 10 minutes.
When the flans are cold, fill the hollow in the
centre of each with a spoonful of jam and place
the peach, cut side down, on the top. Brush
over the peaches with the warmed sieved jam.
Beat up the cream stiffly and sweeten to taste.
With a large star nozzle in a piping bag, pipe
stars round the edge of the flans.

Peach blossom flans

366 Gâteau marron

4 oz. luxury or softened
    margarine
4 oz. castor sugar
2 eggs
4 oz. self-raising flour
1 level teaspoon baking
    powder
For the filling:
¼ pint whipped double cream
2 heaped tablespoons
    chestnut purée (Recipe 360)
To decorate:
2 tablespoons heated and
    sieved apricot jam
2 oz. blanched, chopped
    almonds
¼ pint double cream, whipped
12 blanched, split almonds,
    browned
4 silver balls

Place all the cake ingredients in a bowl and
beat until well mixed. Place in two 7-inch
greased and lined sandwich tins and bake in
the centre of a *very moderate* oven (300 or
350°F. — Gas Mark 2—3) for 25—35 minutes. Turn out and cool on a wire tray.
Mix together the cream and the chestnut
purée and sandwich the cake together with
the mixture.
Brush the sides of the cake with the sieved
jam and roll in chopped almonds, see Recipe 7.
Place cake on board or plate. Spread three-
quarters of the cream on top of the cake and
make a ridge pattern across it with a knife.
Using a fairly large star pipe, pipe the remaining cream round the top edge. Arrange
the almonds on the top of the cake to form
four 'flowers' and use silver balls for the
centres of these.

Gâteau marron

367 Cherry ring

Victoria sandwich 1 (Recipe 30) made with 2 eggs
For the filling:
12 oz. fresh cherries *or* large can cherries
¼ packet jelly
just under ¼ pint hot water *or* syrup from the can of cherries
To decorate:
¼ pint double cream
½ teaspoon sugar
few drops vanilla essence

Grease a large ring mould, 8½ inches in diameter; place on baking sheet. Make Victoria sandwich; put mixture in ring mould. Smooth level; bake in centre of moderately hot oven (400°F. — Gas Mark 5) for 25—30 minutes. Leave in tin to cool; put on serving plate and prepare cherries. Dissolve jelly in enough hot water and syrup to make up to ¼ pint; leave in cold place. Put prepared fruit in centre of ring; when jelly is cold and starting to thicken, pour over cherries so that a little runs on to the sponge. Whip cream, sweeten and flavour; with a large star pipe in a piping bag pipe cream along edge where ring touches plate. The flan shown is decorated with washed leaves.

Cherry ring

368 Gâteau à la pêche

Victoria sandwich 1 (Recipe 30) made with 4 oz. margarine, etc.
To decorate:
2—3 tablespoons peach jam
¼ pint double cream
2 dozen sponge fingers
1 teaspoon arrowroot
¼ pint peach juice from canned fruit
1 large can peach halves

Make the Victoria sandwich and bake in two 7-inch sandwich tins, see Recipe 30.
Sandwich together when cold with the peach jam. Beat the cream until it is stiff enough for piping purposes.
Spread the sponge fingers halfway up with a little cream and arrange around the cake. Blend the arrowroot and a little of the peach juice together. Boil the remaining peach juice and add to the arrowroot. Return to the heat and boil, stirring, until it becomes clear. Allow to cool.
Arrange seven peach halves over the cake and pour the glaze over them.
When set, pipe large rosettes of cream over the top and sides, and tie round with a coloured ribbon, if wished.
Illustrated in colour plate 21.

Gâteau à la pêche

369 Butterscotch pie

To make pie crust:
3 oz. cornflake crumbs*
2 oz. butter or margarine
1 oz. castor sugar
To make filling:
4½ oz. brown sugar
2 oz. flour, preferably plain
¾ pint milk
2 egg yolks
1 oz. butter
½ teaspoon vanilla essence
To make topping:
¼ pint thick cream
shredded blanched almonds toasted
Or crushed cornflakes

Put crumbs into a basin and rub in butter. Stir in sugar and press mixture in a deep 7-inch pie plate. Bake in a moderate oven (375°F. — Gas Mark 4) for 18—20 minutes. Cool. To make the filling place the sugar and flour in a double saucepan, stir in the milk slowly and continue stirring until thick. Cover and simmer for 10 minutes.
Remove from heat, stir in egg yolks, return to heat and cook for 1 minute. Remove from heat, add butter and vanilla essence. Cool. Pour into pie shell. Whip cream until stiff and pipe over top of pie when cold. Spike the cream with almonds.

Butterscotch pie

370 Strawberry shortcake

4 oz. margarine or butter
4 oz. plain flour
2 oz. semolina
4 oz. castor sugar
To fill and decorate:
¼—½ pint thick cream
8 oz. strawberries
1—2 oz. castor sugar
little icing sugar

Rub fat into flour, add semolina and sugar and knead to a firm dough. Divide between two greased 8-inch sandwich tins, pressing the mixture in. Bake in the centre of a moderate oven (375°F. — Gas Mark 4) for 25—30 minutes until pale golden. Cool.
Spread half the cream on one piece of shortcake, add most of the strawberries, sliced, and sugar. Cover with second shortcake, cut into segments. Decorate the sides with rosettes of cream, using a bag with a large rose pipe, and whole strawberries. Dust the top lightly with icing sugar and place three strawberries in the centre.

Strawberry shortcake

Novelty Cakes

When you enjoy decorating and piping cakes, you will be able to work out a whole series of original decorations for special occasions. This section gives some you may care to try.

371 Beatle cake

4 oz. fine semolina
2 oz. flour (with plain flour use ½ level teaspoon baking powder)
1 level teaspoon baking powder (in either case)
pinch salt
6 oz. butter or margarine
6 oz. castor sugar
3 eggs
For the orange paste:
6 oz. castor sugar
6 oz. sieved icing sugar
6 oz. ground almonds
2 egg yolks
2 tablespoons orange juice
little melted jam or syrup
For the royal icing:
1 lb. sieved icing sugar
¼ teaspoon glycerine
2 egg whites
For the butter cream:
3 oz. icing sugar
1 level tablespoon chocolate powder
1½ oz. softened butter
1—2 teaspoons hot water
6 white pipe cleaners

Sift the dry ingredients. Cream the fat and sugar until light and fluffy. Beat in the eggs, one at a time; fold in dry ingredients. Fill two thirds of a well-greased 2-pint overproof pie dish and a bun tin with the mixture. Bake in the centre of a moderate oven (375°F. — Gas Mark 4), allowing 50—60 minutes for the large cake, 25—30 minutes for the small cake. Allow to cool.

Make the orange paste, see Recipe 256. Brush both cakes with jam or syrup. Cover neatly with the paste.

Make the royal icing, see Recipe 267, and attach the small cake (the head) to the large cake (the body) with a little of this.

Put on to a cake board and cover all over with royal icing. Leave to harden overnight. Make the butter icing, see Recipe 100, and with a writing pipe No. 2 or 3 put the hair, face and waistcoat on to the beatle.

The legs are six white pipe cleaners bent into shape and inserted at intervals along the side. A little of the paste can be put on one side and tinted and moulded into guitars and drums.

Beatle cake

372 Humpty Dumpty cake

4 oz. margarine
4 oz. castor sugar
2 eggs
4 oz. sieved flour (with plain flour use 1 level teaspoon baking powder)
lemon curd
butter icing (Recipe 100) made with 8 oz. icing sugar, 3 oz. margarine, 2 tablespoons milk, red colouring
7-inch square cake board
To decorate:
1 oz. desiccated coconut
green colouring
1 oz. plain chocolate
1 large plain chocolate Easter egg
almond paste (Recipe 256) made with 8 oz. ground almonds

Cream the margarine and sugar together until light and fluffy. Beat in the eggs, thoroughly, one at a time. Fold in the sieved flour. Place the mixture in a prepared 12 × 8-inch Swiss roll tin. Bake in the centre of a moderate oven (375°F. — Gas Mark 4) for 20—25 minutes. Cool on a wire tray and remove the paper while the cake is still hot. Trim the edges with a sharp knife and cut into three equal pieces. Sandwich these together with lemon curd.

Make the butter icing, tinting this pale pink. Cover the top and sides of the cake with this and put the cake on the board. Colour the coconut green. Spread a little lemon curd on the board and sprinkle on the coconut to represent grass.

Melt the chocolate in a small basin over hot water. Paint the melted chocolate on the cake with a small paint brush in a brick design. Mould one third of the almond paste into a shallow round, and curve the centre in the shape of a dish. Spread with lemon curd and place the Easter egg on top. Cut out the eyes, nose and mouth from the almond paste, rolled thinly, and coloured, if wished. Make the arms, legs, hat and bow from remaining almond paste and fix on to the egg. Fasten Humpty Dumpty to the wall with a little icing.

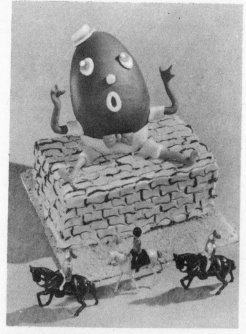

Humpty Dumpty cake

Victoria sandwich 1 (Recipe
30) made with 3 eggs
2 heaped tablespoons warmed
apricot jam
satin icing (Recipe 158), made
with 2 oz. margarine, etc.
red colouring
To decorate
apricot jam
1 large round chocolate biscuit
1 large round cake board
4 oz. desiccated coconut
2 thin pieces angelica or 2
cocktail sticks
4 oz. sweets
8 small biscuits
small piece cotton wool

Make the Victoria sandwich as Recipe 30 and place two-thirds in a lined 11½ × 7½-inch Swiss roll tin and the remaining third in a 6-inch square tin. Bake the Swiss roll in a moderately hot oven (400°F. — Gas Mark 5) for 10—12 minutes and the cake in the centre of a similar oven for 15—20 minutes. Roll up Swiss roll as Recipe 170, spreading with warmed jam. Make the satin icing, colouring three-quarters red and leaving the remaining part white.

Cut the square cake in half. From one half remove the centre, leaving a border of ½ inch all the way round. Put the centre on one side, and place the border on top of the other half of cake, sandwiching together with jam.

From one end of the Swiss roll, cut out half a circle, about 1 inch in width. Place this on top of the roll to form the cabin. From the centre of the square cake, cut out a step and

two funnels. Place the step under the cabin. Roll out the red satin icing into an oblong the length of the Swiss roll and as wide as the circumference. Brush the roll with warm sieved apricot jam and cover with red satin icing. Cover the truck, step and cabin in the same way. The funnels can be covered round with white satin icing and a circle of red satin icing put on top. Secure the chocolate biscuit to the front of the engine with a little jam, and decorate cab with circles of white satin icing. Brush the cake board with jam and cover with desiccated coconut, and make the railway line with the remaining red satin icing. Place the engine and truck on the cake board, joining together with angelica or cocktail sticks. Fill the truck with sweets, put cotton wool on top of one of the funnels and stick on the small biscuits, for wheels, with jam.

TO MAKE THE TRUCK

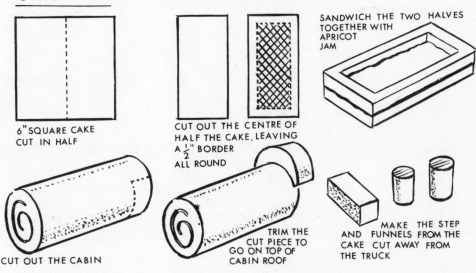

6" SQUARE CAKE CUT IN HALF

CUT OUT THE CENTRE OF HALF THE CAKE, LEAVING A ½" BORDER ALL ROUND

SANDWICH THE TWO HALVES TOGETHER WITH APRICOT JAM

CUT OUT THE CABIN

TRIM THE CUT PIECE TO GO ON TOP OF CABIN ROOF

MAKE THE STEP AND FUNNELS FROM THE CAKE CUT AWAY FROM THE TRUCK

To make the Party engine

Party engine

Victoria sandwich 1 (Recipe 30) made with 4 eggs and adding 1 tablespoon milk
chocolate butter icing (Recipe 103) made with 2½ level tablespoons hot milk, 12 oz. icing sugar, 5 oz. margarine, 3 tablespoons cocoa
almond paste (Recipe 256), made with 2 oz. ground almonds
glacé icing (Recipe 53), made with 8 oz. icing sugar
To decorate:
18-inch square cake board
little cotton wool
Christmas trees
animals

Make the Victoria sandwich as Recipe 30, adding the milk, and place mixture in a prepared 7½-inch square cake tin. Bake in the centre of a very moderate oven (300—350°F. — Gas Mark 2—3), for 1½—2 hours. Turn out and cool.

Make the butter icing by blending the cocoa and hot milk together in a small bowl. Cream half the sieved icing sugar and the margarine together until very light. Mix in the blended cocoa and the remaining icing sugar. Beat until the mixture is smooth and creamy.

Make the almond paste.

Cut a 2½-inch strip and a 1-inch strip from the cake. Cut the 2½-inch strip across diagonally and put the two halves together to form the triangular 'roof'. Cut the 1-inch strip into three equal pieces for the 'chimney'.

Cut the large piece of cake through the centre

and sandwich together with some of the chocolate butter icing. Then cover the sides with icing and smooth over evenly. Put on a cake board, spread icing over the top and place the roof in position. Stick the pieces of cake for chimney together with butter icing; cut an upturned 'V' from the bottom so that it fits on roof. Cover with butter icing.

Make the windows and door from almond paste rolled very thinly. Pipe the window frames from chocolate butter icing with a writing pipe. Make a porch from almond paste. Make the glacé icing of thick coating consistency. Carefully pour some of the glacé icing over half the chimney, roof and porch to represent snow. Make a footpath with the remaining chocolate butter icing and spread the remaining glacé icing over the cake board. Decorate with Christmas trees and animals.

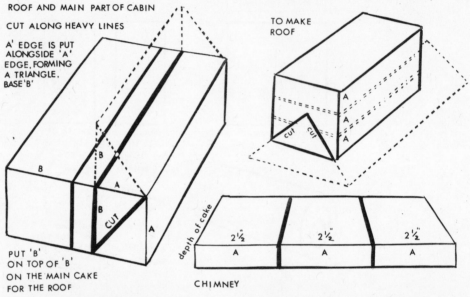

To make the Log cabin

Log cabin

375 Golden galleon

1 sponge cake baked in 2 lb. loaf tin (Recipe 59), made with 3 eggs
sieved apricot jam
8 oz. white chocolate
4 tablespoons water
yellow and blue colouring
approximately 1¼ lb. sieved icing sugar
gold and silver covered chocolate coins
white paper sails*
3 coloured drinking straws
*These can be made of ordinary white kitchen or writing paper or a double thickness of rice paper.

Scoop out the middle of the cake, making a 'melon' shape. Brush sides with jam. Melt white chocolate with the water in a basin over a saucepan of hot water. Remove from heat. Add a little yellow colouring to 4 tablespoons of the chocolate and set aside. Add some blue colouring and sufficient icing sugar to the remaining chocolate to make a rolling consistency. Knead the blue icing a little and roll out and coat the sides of the galleon. Attach coins along one side with jam. Place on a glass dish or cake board.

Using the yellow chocolate mixture, add sufficient icing sugar to make a piping consistency. Place icing in a piping bag and with a star tube pipe round the edge and ends of galleon. Crayon or pipe edging round paper sails. Put several blobs of icing on to drinking straws. Place sails in position stuck on the straws. Pile money in the galleon.

Golden galleon

376 Wagon cake

Madeira cake (Recipe 325) using milk, OR fatless sponge (Recipe 130), made with 6 eggs, etc.
little warmed jam
To decorate:
butter cream, (Recipe 100) made with 8 oz. butter
2 teaspoons coffee essence
yellow colouring
4 plain biscuits

Make the cake and bake in two lined and greased 12 × 8-inch Swiss roll tins and three paper baking cases. The paper cases should be half-filled and the remaining mixture then divided evenly between the Swiss roll tins. The larger cakes will take 10 minutes in a moderately hot oven (400°F. — Gas Mark 5), the smaller cakes a little longer. The fatless sponge needs baking as Recipe 130.

Turn one sponge on to sugared greaseproof paper, trim the edges with a sharp knife. Spread with warmed jam, and roll up quickly. The Madeira cake is not so easy to roll as the sponge; this must be done firmly. Cut a piece 7½ × 3½ inches from the other sponge to form the base of the wagon. Cut the shaft of the remainder of the cake, 2 inches wide and 11½ inches long. Two pairs of steps, 1 × 2 inches, can be cut from the small remnants from the side of the shaft.

Make the butter icing and divide in half. To one half add the coffee essence and beat well.

From the other half, take out one tablespoon and leave white, colour the rest yellow.

Spread the ends of the Swiss roll with a little coffee butter icing and mark downwards with a fork. Spread the remaining icing on the shaft and base. Place the base on top of the shaft towards the back, and stand on a cake board. Put the Swiss roll on top. Cover the Swiss roll with yellow butter icing and mark lengthways with a fork.

Put the white butter icing into a bag or syringe with a writing pipe, and pipe a zig-zag line where the coffee and yellow butter icing meet. Pipe two straight bands of white icing over the yellow butter icing about 2 inches from each end, to represent ropes.

Use the four biscuits for wheels, making spokes with yellow or white butter cream icing. Cover the steps with a little coffee butter icing and place at front and back of the wagon.

Toy cowboys and Indians add an exciting touch.

Wagon cake

377 Western corral

4 oz. butter or margarine
4 oz. castor sugar
2 eggs
5 oz. flour (with plain flour use 1½ level teaspoons baking powder)
1 oz. cocoa
butter cream (Recipe 100) made with 10—12 oz. butter, etc.
To decorate:
2 packets chocolate finger biscuits
small animals and figures

Cream the fat and sugar until light and fluffy. Add the beaten egg, a little at a time. Fold in the sieved flour and cocoa, adding enough warm water to make a soft dropping consistency. Bake in a prepared 9-inch square tin in a moderate oven (375°F. — Gas Mark 4) for 35—40 minutes. Cool.
Spread a little of the butter cream round the sides of the cake and a thick layer over the top. Mark the top of the cake with a fork. Arrange the chocolate biscuits round the sides as shown and put animals and figures in place.

Western corral

378 Sack cake

1 oz. glacé cherries
2 oz. chopped almonds
¼ pint water
5 oz. margarine
4 oz. currants
4 oz. sultanas
2 oz. mixed peel
rind ½ lemon
rind ½ orange
7 tablespoons condensed milk
½ level teaspoon bicarbonate of soda
5 oz. plain flour
pinch of salt
almond paste, (Recipe 259), made with 12 oz. ground almonds, etc.
glace icing, (Recipe 53), made with 6 oz. icing sugar
ribbon

Chop the cherries and place in a saucepan with the almonds, water, margarine, fruit, peel, grated rinds and condensed milk. Bring to the boil and boil for 3 minutes. Allow to cool. Add the bicarbonate of soda and then the flour sieved with the salt. Line a small 5—6-inch cake tin, allowing the greaseproof paper to come high up over the edge. Bake in the centre of a slow oven (275—300°F. — Gas Mark 1—2) for 1½ hours.
Make the almond paste and roll out to a large circle. Stand the cold cake on it and mould the almond paste up round the sides of the cake, making a roll round the top to resemble the sack opening. Coat in glacé icing.
Tie a ribbon round the neck of the sack. Make Christmas parcels either with squares of sponge cake dipped in glacé icing and tied with ribbon, or small wrapped parcels in Christmas paper. Pile in the centre of the sack.

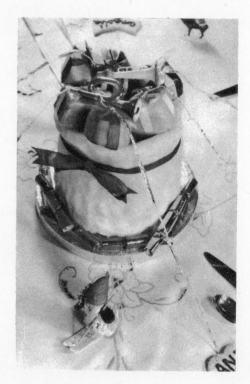

Sack cake

379 Cracker box

10 oz. flour (with plain flour
  use 2½ level teaspoons
  baking powder)
⅛ teaspoon salt
½ teaspoon mixed spice
6 oz. butter or margarine
6 oz. brown or granulated
  sugar
3 eggs
1 tablespoon warmed syrup
1¼ lb. mixed dried fruit
2 tablespoons milk
2 tablespoons brandy,
  optional
grated rind 1 orange,
  optional
almond paste made with 12
  oz. ground almonds, 6 oz.
  castor sugar, 6 oz. sieved
  icing sugar, strained juice ½
  lemon, 1 teaspoon vanilla
  essence, 1 egg or 3 egg yolks
beaten egg
royal icing, (Recipe 267),
  made with 1¼ lb. icing sugar
For the crackers:
2½ oz. flour (with plain flour
  use ½ teaspoon baking
  powder)
pinch salt
2 eggs
2½ oz. castor sugar
3 drops vanilla essence
1 tablespoon melted
  margarine
warmed jam
coloured crêpe paper
decorative seals
small cotton reel
thick cotton

Make the fruit cake by the method described under the Christmas or wedding cakes, i.e. add the dry ingredients to the creamed butter, sugar, eggs and syrup, then add the fruit, milk, brandy and rind at the end to give a smooth mixture. Put the mixture into a lined 12 × 8 × 3½-inch cake tin and bake in the centre of a very moderate oven (325—350°F. — Gas Mark 3) for 1 hour; reduce heat, if necessary, to slow (275—300°F. — Gas Mark 1—2) for a further 1—1¼ hours. Cover with greaseproof paper when top is brown enough. Make the almond paste, see Recipe 256, and roll out just under half on sugared greaseproof paper for the top of the cake. Brush the paste with beaten egg and place on top of the cake, press down well and neaten the edges. Roll out four strips for the sides of the cake and place in position in the same way. Neaten the joins. With the remainder of the paste, stick an edging 1 inch deep and ½ inch wide on the top of the cake with beaten egg. Allow to dry. Make the royal icing. Take out just under half and add a little water for a softer consistency. Pour in the top of the cake to cover the inside of the box. Use most of the remainder to coat the inside of the cake. Smooth the edges. Put

the remaining icing into a bag or syringe and with a No. 6, 7, 8 or 9 pipe, pipe a neat border round the edge of the box.
Make the crackers with the ingredients given in the method for Genoese pastry, see Recipe 134. Bake in a lined Swiss roll tin 13 × 9 inches, for 5 minutes in a very hot oven (475—500°F. — Gas Mark 8—9) using the centre of the oven.
Turn on to sugared paper, remove lining paper, trim edges and spread with warmed jam. Divide into half lengthways and into four across, making eight squares. Roll these up quickly and tightly.
From crêpe paper cut eight oblongs, 7½ × 5½ inches. Wrap each roll, when cold, firmly in the paper and secure with a decorative seal. Insert a small cotton reel at one end of the cracker and wind a piece of thick cotton round the paper between the roll and the reel, and pull tightly. Remove cotton reel and finish all the ends in the same way. Lay the crackers in the 'box'.
If you do not want the bother of making the crackers, you can buy a box of ordinary crackers and lay them on top of the cake.

Cracker box

380 Christmas grotto

butterfly cakes (Recipe 111),
  adding 1 tablespoon cocoa
royal icing (Recipe 267), made
  with 1 lb. icing sugar, etc.
13 chocolate finger biscuits
little cotton wool
Christmas trees
Father Christmas

Make as Recipe 111, folding the cocoa in with the flour and adding sufficient warm water to make a soft dropping consistency. Put the mixture into a greased 6-inch pudding basin and bake in a moderate oven (375°F. — Gas Mark 4) for 30 minutes and then reduce the heat to very moderate (300—350°F. — Gas Mark 2—3) for a further 45 minutes. Cool upside down on a wire tray. With a tablespoon, carefully scoop out a portion to form the cave entrance and remove all loose crumbs. Stand on a cake board. Make a stiff royal icing and spread evenly over the cake and around the edge of the board. Pull the icing in peaks, see Recipe 300, to give the effect of snow.
Cut the finger biscuits in half across and arrange 22 halves side by side around the base of the cake. Use the remaining 4 halves for chimney; add piece of cotton wool for smoke. Complete scene with Father Christmas and trees.

Christmas grotto

381 Ski jump cake

8 oz. butter or margarine
8 oz. soft brown sugar
grated rind 1 orange
12 oz. flour (with plain flour
    use 1½ level teaspoons
    baking powder)
4 oz. ground almonds
4 eggs
1 teaspoon treacle
2 tablespoons warmed golden
    syrup
2 tablespoons milk *or* 1 table-
    spoon milk and 1 tablespoon
    brandy
1 dessertspoon coffee essence
    or 1 teaspoon instant coffee
    with 1 dessertspoon water
8 oz. currants
8 oz. sultanas
4 oz. raisins
2 oz. peel
3 oz. glacé cherries
almond paste (Recipe 256)
    made with 10 oz. ground
    almonds, etc.
royal icing (Recipe 267)
    made with 1½−2¼ lb. icing
    sugar, etc.
To decorate:
little beaten egg
plywood 10 × 15 inches
little, figures, trees, etc.

Grease a 9-inch square cake tin, lined with double greaseproof paper. Beat the butter or margarine, add sugar and orange rind and beat again until lighter in colour and fluffy in texture. Sieve the flour, baking powder and ground almonds. Add eggs one at a time, together with a tablespoon of the sieved flour. Stir, then beat thoroughly. Stir in treacle, syrup, milk, brandy and coffee essence with 2 tablespoons of the flour; beat again. Add the fruit and the remainder of the dry ingredients. Stir thoroughly without beating. Put mixture into the tin, smooth level with a knife. Bake for 1 hour in centre of very moderate oven (325−350°F. — Gas Mark 3), then reduce heat to 275°F. — Gas Mark 1 — for a further 1½−2 hours, covering the cake with greaseproof paper when brown enough. Let cake cool; turn out on to cooling rack. When cold wrap in greaseproof paper; store in tin.

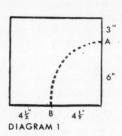

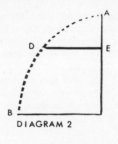

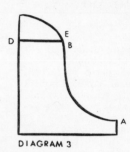

To make the Ski jump cake

Diagram 1
Mark the cake according to the diagram and cut through from A to B using a sharp knife. Turn the large piece of cake on end so that the edge measuring 4½ inches is uppermost.

Diagram 2
Cut the small piece of cake along line D−E.

Diagram 3
Place the small piece on top of the large one, using beaten egg to join the pieces of cake.

Roll out the almond paste on sugared paper. Brush the cake with beaten egg and cover the two larger sides first, then the back, followed by the run itself and the front of the cake.

Place the cake flat on greaseproof paper overnight and then stand it in an erect position for a few days to allow the almond paste to dry.
To finish
Get a piece of plywood 10 × 15 inches and cover with foil. Spread a thin layer of icing on it to represent snow. Stand the cake in position on the board so that plenty of space is left in front for the 'jump'. Cover the cake with icing, pulling it into points with a knife. Use a palette knife to make a smooth run down the cake. Place little figures and trees in appropriate places on the cake and board. *Illustrated in colour plate 25.*

382 'Kitty' cake

6 oz. margarine
6 oz. castor sugar
3 eggs
8 oz. sieved flour (with plain
    flour use 2 level teaspoons
    baking powder)
1 tablespoon milk
butter icing (Recipe 100)
    made with 3 oz. margarine,
    8 oz. sieved icing sugar and
    3 dessertspoons milk
To decorate:
6 oz. desiccated coconut
1 7-inch cake board
large sweets
almond paste (Recipe 256)
    made with 8 oz. ground
    almonds, etc.
2 long sticks spaghetti
small piece stiff white paper
red colouring
sugar mice, or use coloured
    almond paste, etc.

Cream the margarine and sugar until light and fluffy. Beat in the eggs, one at a time, adding a little sieved flour with every egg after the first. Fold in the remaining flour and the milk. Brush the insides of a ½-pint and 1½-pint pudding basin with melted margarine and put the mixture into these. Bake in the centre of a very moderate oven (300−350°F. — Gas Mark 2−3) for 45−50 minutes for the small cake and 1¼ hours for the large cake. Cool on a wire tray.
Make the butter icing. Cover the cakes all over with icing and roll in the coconut. Place the small cake on top of the large one and secure with a little skewer. Cover the board with a thin layer of almond paste, mark the edge with a fork and place the cake in position. The feet and tail can be made with moulded almond paste, covered with icing and coconut. Sweets or coloured almond paste are used to make the eyes, nose and mouth, and the spaghetti is used to make the whiskers. Cut the ears out of the stiff white paper. One side can be painted with red colouring, the other iced and covered with coconut. The cheese is made from almond paste, and although bought sugar mice can be used, these can also be made from moulded almond paste using a pipe cleaner for a tail, small sweets for eyes, and almond paste for whiskers.

'Kitty' cake

383 Clown cake

recipe as *Humpty Dumpty cake*
(Recipe 372)
2 heaped tablespoons warmed
  apricot jam
almond paste (Recipe 256),
  made with 1 lb. ground
  almonds, etc.
red colouring
apricot jam
To decorate:
1 5-inch biscuit
ice cream cone
4 or 5 glacé cherries
1 oz. desiccated coconut
3 cocktail sticks
7-inch cake board

Make the cake as Recipe 372 and bake in
a prepared 12×8-inch Swiss roll tin in a
moderately hot oven (400°F. — Gas Mark 5)
for 10—15 minutes. Roll up as Recipe 170,
using the warmed apricot jam. Cool.
Cut off 1½ inches from the roll for the clown's
head. Colour most of the almond paste red
and roll out two-thirds of this to cover the
body. Brush with apricot jam and roll the
almond paste round the larger portion of the
Swiss roll. Place upright on the cake board.
Cut a piece of red almond paste into a strip
1½×7 inches long. Place over the top of the
roll for arms. The hands are made from
uncoloured almond paste rolled thinly and cut
out with a small fluted cutter.
Place the large biscuit on top of the body for
the ruffle.
Mould the remainder of the uncoloured almond
paste round the small piece of Swiss roll for
the head. Stick on the ruffle with jam. Cover
the ice cream cone with red almond paste and
stick on to the head with jam for a hat.
The eyes, nose and mouth are made from the
remaining coloured almond paste.
Roll glacé cherries in coconut and fasten on
clown's body and hat with cocktail sticks.

Clown cake

384 Crinoline lady

Madeira cake (Recipe 325)
almond paste (Recipe 256)
  made with 4 oz. ground
  almonds, etc.
warm apricot jam
royal icing (Recipe 267) made
  with 2 egg whites
pink colouring
yellow colouring
china figure

Make the Madeira cake and bake in a greased
and floured 1½—2-pint pudding basin in a very
moderate oven (300—350°F. — Gas Mark
2—3) for approximately 2 hours. Cool.
Trim top of cake level and put this side
downwards on a cake board. Brush the cake
with warmed apricot jam. Make the almond
paste and cover the cake, pleating the front
slightly to indicate the front of the dress. Make

the royal icing and cover the cake. Allow to
harden. Put on figure, securing this with more
icing. Colour a small portion of the remaining
royal icing yellow, and the rest pink. Using
a No. 6 pipe, indicate the top layer of the dress
with pink stars placed close together. Finally,
outline the front of the crinoline skirt with
yellow stars.
Illustrated in colour plate 13.

385 Candle cake

Swiss roll (Recipe 170)
coffee butter cream (Recipe
  103) made with 4 oz. butter
  etc.
OR *mocha butter cream* using
  2 level teaspoons soluble
  coffee powder, 2 level tablespoons cocoa, 8 oz. icing
  sugar, 2—3 oz. margarine,
  2 tablespoons hot water
almond paste, (Recipe 256),
  made with 6—8 oz. ground
  almonds
little red colouring
3 tablespoons apricot jam
royal icing (Recipe 267) made
  with 12 oz. icing sugar,
  softened with glycerine
2 cloves
1 small cake board
flowers in round flower bowl

Make and bake the Swiss roll and fill with
either coffee butter cream or mocha butter
cream. To make the mocha butter cream, sieve
together the dry ingredients, mix to a cream
with the margarine and hot water. Make the
almond paste and put a very little on one side
for the flame.
Brush the sides and ends of the Swiss roll with
the jam, and cover with the almond paste. Fix
the roll in an upright position on the cake
board. Mould the edge at the top of the candle
to form a gutted ridge.
Make up the royal icing, using a few drops of
glycerine to soften. Coat the cake completely
with the icing, smoothing with a knife and
covering the cake board. Pipe drips of icing
from the gutted ridge and from the base up,
leaving gaps between, as the wax drips off
a candle unevenly.
Rough the icing at the base giving the appearance of wax drippings. Colour and shape
a small flame from the remaining marzipan and
stick the two cloves in the centre of the top of
the candle to support this.
Fresh flowers are used in the illustration to
decorate, but you could vary the decorations
to suit the occasion.

Candle cake

386 Christmas record gâteau

For each 'record':
Victoria sandwich 1 or 2 (Recipe 30 or 59) made with 2 eggs, etc.
butter icing, (Recipe 103) made with 8 – 10 oz. butter, etc.
chocolate flavouring
chocolate vermicelli
almond paste, (Recipe 256) made with 1 oz. ground almonds
holly decorations

Make the Victoria sandwich, bake in two 8 – 9-inch tins for thin layers, allowing about 15 minutes only, and allow to cool.
Make the butter icing and put a little on one side for piping. Flavour the remainder chocolate. Sandwich the cakes together with the chocolate butter icing; coat the sides and roll the sides in chocolate vermicelli. Coat the top. Mark grooves in the butter icing, either with a bowl scraper or with the prongs of a fork. Make the almond paste and cut a disc 3-inches in diameter with a ¼-inch hole in the centre to represent the label. Using a writing pipe, pipe on the name of the record with a little chocolate butter icing, and the snowflakes with the plain butter icing.
Decorate with holly, either real or imitation.
Illustrated in colour plate 19.

387 Derby winner

4 oz. cooking fat
4 oz. castor sugar
2 eggs
4 oz. flour (with plain flour use 1 level teaspoon baking powder)
¼ level teaspoon vanilla essence
1 dessertspoon milk
apricot jam
almond paste, (Recipe 256), made with 8 oz. ground almonds, etc.
red and blue colouring
7-inch silver cake board
3 small round biscuits

Place all the cake ingredients in a bowl and using a wooden spoon, beat for about 1 minute until well mixed. Beating will NOT make the mixture heavy. Turn the mixture into a greased 1-pint pudding basin and bake in the centre of a moderate oven (375°F. — Gas Mark 4) for 45 – 50 minutes. Cool. Brush the cake with hot apricot jam. Make the almond paste and colour half red. Cut out three triangles of each colour, approximately the depth of the cake. Arrange alternate colours on the cake, mould and trim carefully. Place on cake board. Cut out a red peak for the cap, trim with a length of yellow paste. Brush the biscuit tops with hot apricot jam. Add a few drops of blue colour to half of the remaining yellow paste. Make blue buttons to go on top and peak. Roll each colour into three long strips, trim to 1 inch wide, and pleat on the biscuits to form rosettes.
Place a round of different colour in the centre, and make numbers with third colour.

Derby winner

388 Honey wishing well

6 oz. self-raising flour
2 level teaspoons baking powder
pinch salt
2 oz. castor sugar
6 oz. cooking fat
3 eggs
2 level teaspoons coffee essence
4 level tablespoons honey
For the icing:
4 oz. butter or margarine
12 oz. icing sugar
1 lightly beaten egg
1 tablespoon coffee essence
To decorate:
5 oz. seedless raisins
piece cardboard, 8 × 10 inches
rose petal confetti or paper hearts
string
2 milk flake bars *or* sticks of barley sugar
cardboard heart

Sieve the dry ingredients and add the sugar and rest of the ingredients. Beat together for about 2 minutes until smooth. Put the mixture into two greased and lined 7-inch sandwich tins and bake just above the centre of a moderate oven (375°F. — Gas Mark 4) for 30 minutes.
Make the icing by creaming the butter and gradually adding the icing sugar and beaten egg and coffee essence.
Plump the raisins by covering with cold water, bringing to the boil, and leaving to stand for 5 minutes. Drain and dry.
From the centre of one of the cakes cut a round 5-inches in diameter. Spread the other cake with icing, lay the ring on top, and ice the sides and rim of cake with the butter icing. Press the raisins into side of cake.
Bend cardboard in half for roof, sticking on rose petals or confetti. Put over well by standing the milk flake bars or barley sugar sticks on either side. Hang the heart from the roof with a piece of string.

Honey wishing well

24 Pumpkin masks and Cat
on the moon gâteaux

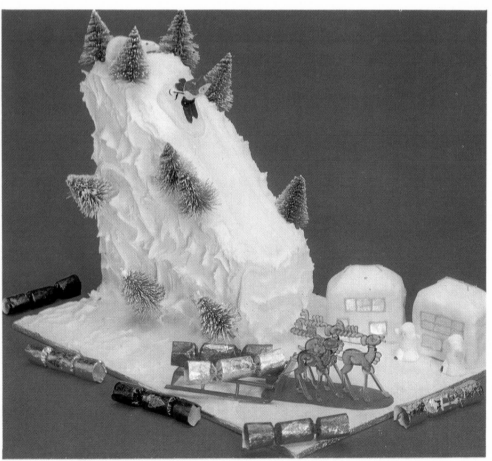

25 Ski jump cake

26 Chocolate orange gâteau (See Recipe 415)

389 Easter bonnet cake

6 oz. butter
6 oz. castor sugar
grated rind ½ lemon
1 oz. ground almonds
3 eggs
7 oz. plain flour
1 oz. cornflour
1 level teaspoon mixed spice
12 oz. currants
2 oz. chopped candied peel
1 tablespoon brandy
To decorate:
almond paste (Recipe 256)
    made with 8 oz. ground
    almonds
little apricot jam
12-inch round cake board
ribbon
artificial flowers

Cream the butter and sugar until light and fluffy. Add the lemon rind and ground almonds and continue beating. Beat in the eggs. Sieve the flour, cornflour and spice together. Add the currants, peel and brandy and mix all together thoroughly. Turn into a greased and lined 8-inch round cake tin and bake in a very moderate oven (300 or 350°F. — Gas Mark 2–3) for 2½–3 hours.

When cool, put on cake board and secure with a little of the almond paste. Brush the top and sides of the cake with warm apricot jam and cover the cake and board entirely with a very thin layer of almond paste. Mark downwards and sideways with a fork to represent straw, see Recipe 112. Tie a band of ribbon round cake and decorate with flowers.

Easter bonnet cake

390 St Patrick's Day cake

fatless sponge (Recipe 130)
    made with 2 eggs
butter icing (Recipe 100)
    made with 4 oz. butter, etc.
    flavoured with 2 tablespoons
    lemon or orange juice
2 bars milk chocolate
4 tablespoons water
approximately 1¼ lb. sieved
    icing sugar
apricot jam
yellow colouring

Sandwich the sponge cakes together with butter icing, reserving a little for decoration. Melt the chocolate and water together in a basin over hot water. Add icing sugar and beat until no more can be added by hand. Dust a board with icing sugar and knead the icing. Roll out to ⅛ inch thick, and cut a circle to fit the top of the cake and slightly overlap the sides. Brush the cake with apricot jam and place the icing on the top, pressing

firmly into position.
Cut heart shapes from the remaining icing and leave to set. Put on top of cake with apricot jam, in the shape of a shamrock as shown. Colour remaining butter icing yellow, and spread round the sides of the cake, drawing up into peaks. Pipe stalks on to the shamrocks with a No. 6 or 13 pipe. Make a shamrock with chocolate icing, on the side of the cake, in the same way as the top.

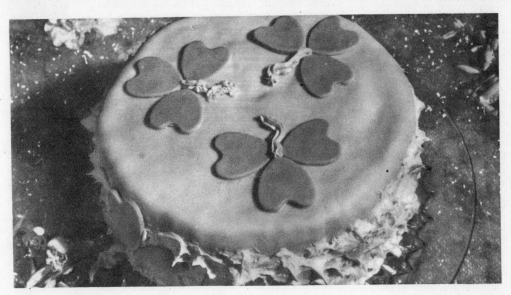

St Patrick's Day cake

391 Easter cake

ingredients for *St. Patrick's Day cake* (Recipe 390)

This cake is made in exactly the same way as the St Patrick's Day cake, except that groups of five heart-shapes of chocolate icing are placed on the cake to form a primrose.

The sides of the cake are coated with yellow butter icing as before, and the centres of the primroses are then piped with a No. 6 or a No. 13 pipe.

Easter cake

392 Lantern cake

Cracker box cake (Recipe 379), omitting the orange rind
almond paste made with 8 oz. ground almonds, 4 oz. castor sugar, 4 oz. icing sugar, 2 teaspoons lemon juice, ⅛ teaspoon vanilla essence, 3 dessertspoons beaten egg
warmed jam
little browning
½ packed strawberry jelly
1 teaspoon water
6-inch square cake board
butter cream (Recipe 100) made with 2 oz. butter, etc.
4-inch strip of angelica
holly sprays

Make and bake the cake as Recipe 379, in a 9×5×3-inch loaf tin. Bake for 1 hour in the centre of a moderate oven (375°F. — Gas Mark 4) and for 2 hours in a slow oven (275 or 300°F. — Gas Mark 1—2).

To shape the lantern, mark the centre of one end and cut away the four sides. The slope should start about 3 inches from the end.

Make the almond paste and cut off about a third. Roll out the larger portion on sugared paper and cut a strip about 5 inches wide and long enough to go round the cake. Brush the cake with warmed jam, and fit the paste in position. Leave about 24 hours to become firm. Also cut four triangles for top and leave. Make the remaining almond paste brown by kneading in gravy browning.

Roll out and cut four strips 4 inches long and 1 inch wide, also a strip 1 inch wide and long enough to go round the base of the lantern. Brush the strips with jam and fit the long one round the base, and the short strips down each corner, turning a little over on the top. Place the triangles for the top in position, cutting the edge to give the effect of tiles or slates. Cut eight strips about ¼ inch wide to form the window panes. Fix with jam. Cut up the jelly into small pieces and melt over a low heat with the water, taking care it does not burn. Pour a little jelly into each pane with a teaspoon and spread with a knife. Allow each side to set firm before turning over to do the next. Leave overnight. Put the cake on the board and put a little butter cream on the roof to represent snow.

Soften the angelica in hot water and bend into a loop, fixed with butter cream for the handle. Decorate with holly sprays.

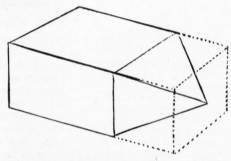

To make the Lantern cake

Lantern cake

393 Primrose cake

ingredients as for *Derby winner cake* (Recipe 387), omitting the vanilla essence and milk, and adding, 1 dessertspoon orange juice, $\frac{1}{4}$ level teaspoon salt and finely grated ring 1 orange
For the chocolate glacé icing:
  2 oz. plain chocolate
  4 dessertspoons hot water.
  2 oz. cooking fat
  8 oz. icing sugar
almond paste (Recipe 256) made with 4—6 oz. almonds
little chocolate powder

Make the sponge as Recipe 387, and bake in a prepared deep 8-inch sandwich tin in the centre of a moderate oven (375°F. — Gas Mark 4) for 30—35 minutes. Cool.

Break up the chocolate and put into a basin with the water. Stand the basin in a saucepan half-filled with hot water until the chocolate has melted and dissolved, but is not hot. Remove from the heat and beat in the cooking fat and the sieved icing sugar, until the icing is glossy and coats the back of the spoon. Coat the cake.

Make the almond paste, mould a primrose from part and five small stamens, or use stick sweet. Put on top of cake. Colour half remaining almond paste chocolate and roll both the uncoloured and coloured paste into long strips. Twist together and arrange round base.

Primrose cake

394 Cigarette box cake

Victoria sandwich 1 (Recipe 30) made with 4 eggs, etc., adding 7—8 drops vanilla essence
pinch of salt
chocolate butter icing made with 5 oz. plain chocolate, $\frac{1}{8}$ pint water, 4 oz. butter, 8 oz. sieved icing sugar, vanilla essence
40 sweet cigarettes

Make the cake and bake in a prepared 7-inch square cake tin in the centre of a moderate oven (375°F. — Gas Mark 4) for 1$\frac{1}{4}$ hours to 1 hour 20 minutes, covering the top with greaseproof paper when sufficiently brown.

When the cake is cold cut off the top to about a third of the way down. Make the chocolate butter icing as Recipe 124 and spread the sides of the box and the sides of the lid with about half. Mark this either with a fork or comb scraper to make ridges.

Build up the top edges of the cake by piping thick bands of butter icing on top of each other, so that a shallow box is formed. Fill the box with sweet cigarettes.

With a knife, mark from corner to corner of the lid, making four triangles. Fill each triangle in with bands of butter icing, using a No. 34 ribbed band pipe, starting from the centre and working to the base of the triangle. Finish the lid with a small knob of butter icing piped with a writing pipe.

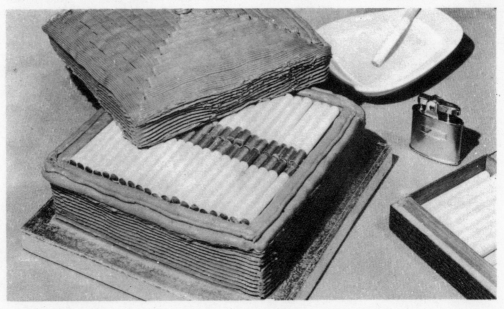

Cigarette box cake

395 Party hamper

ingredients as for *Cracker box cake* (Recipe 379)
almond paste as for *Cracker box cake*
royal icing, (Recipe 267) made with 1½ lb. icing sugar
little coarsely shredded coconut
12 chocolate liqueur bottles

Make the cake and bake in a prepared 8-inch round cake tin in the centre of a moderate oven (375°F. — Gas Mark 4) for 1 hour and in a slow oven (275—300°F. — Gas Mark 1—2) for a further 2 hours. Cool.
Make the almond paste and cover the cake as Recipe 261. From the trimmings, cut a strip of almond paste 1 inch wide and ¾ inch thick; place this round rim of cake, so there is a hollow in the centre. Allow to dry.

Make the royal icing, adding the sieved icing sugar gradually. When it is of pouring consistency, fill the hollow on the top of the cake. Stiffen remainder of icing and coat the rest of the cake.
With a fork, mark the rim and sides of the cake with downwards and sideways movements, to look like wicker-work.
Fill the hollow with the coconut and lay the chocolate liqueur bottles on the top.

Party hamper

396 Valentine cake

First cake:
2 eggs
pinch salt
2 oz. castor sugar
1 packet banana flavoured cornflour
½ oz. cornflour
Second cake:
2 eggs
pinch salt
2 oz. castor sugar
1 packet strawberry flavoured cornflour
½ oz. cornflour
butter icing, (Recipe 100) made with 4 oz. butter
glacé icing (Recipe 53) made with 1½ lb. icing sugar
To decorate:
ribbons and flowers

Separate the eggs and beat the whites with the salt until they are stiff, then beat in the egg yolks. Add the sugar and continue beating until the mixture is thick and creamy. Fold in the sieved cornflours and bake in a prepared 8-inch heart-shaped tin for 20—25 minutes in a moderately hot oven (400°F. — Gas Mark 5). When cooked, turn out and cool. Make a second cake in the same way, this time using the strawberry flavoured cornflour. Sandwich the cakes together with a little of the butter icing. Put the cake on a board and pour the glacé icing over, covering completely. Pipe an edging using a No. 8 pipe and the movement described in Recipe 319, with butter icing.
Decorate with ribbons and flowers.
Illustrated in colour plate 22.

Valentine cake

Madeira cake (Recipe 325)
To decorate:
almond paste (Recipe 256)
  made with 1 lb. ground
  almonds
apricot jam
orange colouring
chocolate powder
butter icing (Recipe 100)
  made with 2 oz. butter,
  etc., and green colouring

397 Pumpkin masks

Make the Madeira cake and bake in two prepared 5-inch round deep tins in the centre of a very moderate oven (350°F. — Gas Mark 3) for just under 1 hour. Sandwich the cakes together with apricot jam and trim the top and bottom edges to make a rough ball shape. Make the almond paste and colour most of it orange. Roll this into a circle approximately 12 inches in diameter, and after brushing the cake with apricot jam, mould the paste round it. The join of the marzipan should be at the base of the cake. Mark the

segment of the pumpkin with the back of a knife. Colour rest of almond paste brown with chocolate powder; cut out pieces for the eyes, nose and mouth. Fix with jam.
Make the green-coloured butter icing, and with a No. 10 pipe in a bag or syringe, make the petals or leaves on the top of the cake. Make each leaf from the centre down the cakes. When these are fairly firm, pipe the upright leaves or petals. Use same pipe but a shorter stroke so that the leaves stand upright.
Illustrated in colour plate 24.

Madeira cake (Recipe 325)
coffee butter icing (Recipe 100)
  made with 12 oz. — 1 lb.
  butter
2 oz. roasted flaked almonds
almond paste, (Recipe 256)
  made with 2 oz. ground
  almonds
yellow colouring
To decorate:
silver balls
1 large chocolate drop
1 small chocolate drop
1 oz. chocolate

398 Cat on the moon gâteau

Make the Madeira cake and bake in an oval tin or casserole approximately 9—10-inches long, in a very moderate oven (300—350°F. — Gas Mark 2—3) for 1 hour.
Make the coffee butter icing and, when the cake is cool, split through the middle and layer together with a little butter icing. Spread remainder of butter icing, save for a tiny portion, on sides of cake. Roll in roasted flaked almonds. Cover the top, marking by

drawing the end of palette knife across. Make the almond paste and colour this yellow. Cut out a large moon and small star and place on the cake. Place the silver balls in position. Make the cat by using the large chocolate drop for its body and the smaller one for its head. Melt the chocolate and blend with the small portion of butter icing remaining and pipe on ears and tail of cat.
Illustrated in colour plate 24.

1 heaped tablespoon cocoa
2 tablespoons hot water
4 oz. margarine
5 oz. castor sugar
2 eggs
4 oz. flour (with plain flour
  use 1 level teaspoon baking
  powder)
1 tablespoon milk
butter icing made with 1 heaped
  tablespoon cocoa, 1 tablespoon hot water, 6 oz.
  margarine, 1 lb. sieved
  icing sugar, 2 tablespoons
  milk, 1 teaspoon peppermint essence, green colouring
To decorate:
1 oz. chopped walnuts
  or 1 oz. roasted coconut
8-inch round cake board

399 Father's Day cake

Blend the cocoa and water together and leave to cool. Cream the margarine and sugar together until very light and fluffy. Beat in the cooled chocolate mixture, then the eggs, one at a time, adding a little sieved flour with the second egg. Fold in the remaining sieved flour and the milk. Bake in two 7-inch prepared sandwich tins in the centre of a very moderate oven (300—350°F. — Gas Mark 2—3) for 25—35 minutes. Cool.
For icing, blend cocoa and water together and leave to cool. Cream the margarine and half the icing sugar together until very light. Add remaining icing sugar, milk and pepper-mint essence. Beat until smooth and creamy. Colour half icing green and into the other

half carefully stir the cooled cocoa mixture. Cut through the centre of each cake and sandwich the four layers together with green butter icing. Cover the sides with green butter icing and roll in the chopped walnuts or roasted coconut. Place cake on cake board. Cover the top of the cake and the board with the remaining green butter icing. Smooth over evenly; mark top with a knife blade.
Using a writing pipe in a bag or syringe, write 'Father's Day' on the top of the cake, with chocolate butter icing. With a No. 6, 8 or 13 pipe make a shell design round top edge and base of cake, see Recipe 319. The dots inside the shell edge are made with a writing pipe.

Father's Day cake

Small Cakes and Biscuits

sponge as *Humpty Dumpty cake* (Recipe 372)
To decorate:
yellow colouring
4 oz. desiccated coconut
apricot jam
2 tablespoons water
almond paste (Recipe 256), made with 4 oz. ground almonds
green colouring
blue colouring
3 mimosa balls
3 small, paper parasols

There are many occasions, in particular at children's parties, when small cakes or biscuits will be more appealing than large cakes and some ideas are given in the following pages. Small cakes are better if decorated with a soft delicate icing. The best icings to use are glacé, fondant and butter. Because of their size, the decorations on small cakes should be clear cut and relatively simple. If marzipan is used as a coating it should be a little softer than for firm fruit cakes.

401 Easter parade

Make the sponge and place heaped teaspoons of the mixture in eight deep greased bun tins and the remainder in a prepared 7-inch sandwich tin. Bake the buns in a moderately hot oven (400°F. – Gas Mark 5) for 15—20 minutes and the sandwich in the centre of a similar oven for 25 minutes. Turn out to cool. Trim the buns with scissors, making one side pointed to represent a duck's tail. Cut out rounds from the sandwich with a 1-inch plain round cutter and trim into a ball shape for the ducks' heads.
Colour the coconut yellow and warm the apricot jam with the water. Sieve. Dip the cakes, both heads and bodies, in the jam and then toss in the coconut. Stick the heads and bodies together.
Colour half the almond paste green. Mould boy ducks' caps and girl ducks' bonnets and scarves from the green almond paste and stick on to the bodies with a little jam. The beaks can be made with yellow paste and the eyes from yellow paste with green centres. Roll little balls of almond paste in coconut and stick on girls' hats. Colour pupils of eyes with blue colouring; mark lines on boys' caps. Arrange on a plate with the boys following the girls and add a parasol to each girl.

402 Eggs for Easter

Make the sponge and divide the mixture between six greased dariole moulds. Place on a baking sheet and bake for 15—20 minutes in a moderately hot oven (400°F. – Gas Mark 5). Remove from tins and cool. Trim off any sharp corners with a knife.
Make the pastry. Roll out pastry and cut into rounds with a fluted cutter. Line twelve bun tins and place a teaspoon of jam in each. Bake for 20—25 minutes in a hot oven (425°F. – Gas Mark 6). Cool. Stick the jam tarts together, bottom to bottom, with a little jam. Make the chocolate glacé icing by breaking the chocolate and putting into a basin with the water. Stand the basin in a saucepan filled with hot water until the chocolate is melted but not hot. Remove from the heat and beat in the margarine and the sieved icing sugar. Beat till icing is glossy and coats back of spoon. Coat cakes with icing; place them in the 'egg-cups' formed by the jam tarts. Use empty sweet cases for hats and plaited wool for hair. Make faces of small sweets.

Biscuits should not be decorated until the day they are to be served. Most icings, even a butter icing, contain a certain percentage of moisture and this can, in time, soften the biscuits and spoil their crisp texture. Biscuits are better decorated with butter, glacé and fondant icings. Take care when making the icing to keep it of as firm a consistency as possible so it will not soak into the biscuits. Unless the recipe states the contrary, wait till the biscuits are cold before decorating.

Easter parade

sponge as *Humpty Dumpty cake* (Recipe 372), using only half ingredients
For tarts:
short crust pastry (Recipe 49), using 8 oz. flour etc.
raspberry jam
To decorate:
chocolate glacé icing made with 2 oz. plain chocolate, 4 dessertspoons hot water, small knob of margarine, 8 oz. sieved icing sugar
6 sweet cases
1 card yellow darning wool
small sweets

Eggs for Easter

403 Valentine shortbreads

6 oz. plain flour
2 oz. castor sugar
4 oz. margarine
For glacé fudge icing:
2 oz. margarine
finely grated rind 1 orange
3 dessertspoons orange juice
8 oz. icing sugar
orange colouring
To decorate:
little desiccated coconut
silver balls
mimosa balls
glacé cherries
angelica

Sieve the flour and sugar into a bowl and add the margarine. Knead together until it forms a smooth dough, leaving the bowl clean. Turn on to a lightly floured board and knead again until it becomes smooth and silky. Roll out to ¼ inch thick. Cut into sixteen shapes with a medium-sized heart-shaped cutter. Place a little apart on a baking sheet and prick all over with a fork. Bake in a very moderate oven (300—350°F. — Gas Mark 2—3) for 25—30 minutes. Cool.
Make the glacé fudge icing by heating the margarine, orange rind and orange juice together in a saucepan. Remove from heat; beat in sieved icing sugar. Colour orange. Sandwich the hearts together in pairs with a little icing. Put on wire tray over a sheet of greaseproof paper to catch surplus icing; pour icing over each to cover tops and sides. Pat sides with desiccated coconut. Decorate edge of each with silver balls. Arrange mimosa balls, glacé cherries and angelica in centre of each heart.

Valentine shortbreads

404 Coffee biscuits

4 oz. margarine
3 oz. castor sugar
1 egg
8 oz. plain flour
3 level teaspoons instant coffee
little milk
coffee butter icing (Recipe 103)
coffee glacé icing (Recipe 53)
walnuts
violets or silver balls

Cream fat and sugar, whisk in egg lightly and then beat until smooth. Sieve flour and instant coffee, add to the creamed mixture. Add a little milk if necessary to bind mixture together. Knead the dough lightly and roll on a floured board until ⅛-inch thick. Prick all over with a fork and cut into ovals, rounds or small fingers. Place on a greased baking tray and bake in centre of moderate oven (350—375°F. — Gas Mark 3—4) until golden brown, about 15 minutes. Cool.
Sandwich biscuits together with coffee butter icing and ice with glacé icing. Decorate with walnuts or violets before icing is set.

405 Coffee pinwheels

Mixture 1:
2 oz. margarine
1 oz. sugar
4 oz. flour
Cream fat and sugar, and knead in the flour.
Mixture 2:
4 oz. flour
2 teaspoons instant coffee
2 oz. margarine
1 oz. sugar

Sieve flour and instant coffee. Cream margarine and sugar and knead in the flour. Roll both doughs to equal-sized oblong pieces, brush the plain one with milk. Press the coffee one on top and roll up as for a Swiss roll. Cut off pieces ⅛-inch thick. Bake on greased tray in centre of very moderate oven (350°F. — Gas Mark 3) until pale golden.

Coffee biscuits and Coffee pinwheels

Meringue for Decoration

406 The purpose of meringues

Meringue is used with sponge cake and as a case, which is filled afterwards with delicious ingredients. Small meringues are often used for decoration.

407 To make meringues

2 egg whites
2 oz. castor sugar
AND 2 oz. sieved icing sugar
OR 4 oz. castor sugar

1 Whisk egg whites until stiff.
2 Beat in half the sugar.
3 Fold in the rest of the sugar gradually.
4 Pipe or pile small spoonfuls on to a well-oiled or buttered tin, or oiled or buttered paper on a baking tin.
5 Bake for 2—3 hours, depending on size, in a very low oven (225—250°F. — Gas Mark 0—¼) until crisp, but still white.
6 Lift from the tin with a warm palette knife, cool and store.
For the use of cornflour see Recipe 414. For firmer texture allow 1 level teaspoon of cornflour to each egg white, blending with the sugar.

The great advantage of a meringue case or tiny meringues is that they can be made, if necessary, weeks before being required and stored without any ill effect at all.

409 Disadvantages of meringues for decoration

Meringue sottens very quickly with cream or when added to cakes, so put them together at the last minute.

They are fragile, so handle with great care. They are very sweet for some people. If less sugar is used they do not become as crisp.

410 Gâteau suprême

ingredients for sponge as *Coffee layer gâteau* (Recipe 174)
4 oz. chocolate
coffee butter icing (Recipes 100 and 103) made with 4 oz. butter
small meringues (Recipe 418) made with 2 eggs whites
To decorate:
few blanched almonds
melted chocolate
angelica
glacé cherry

Make the cake and bake in an 8-inch tin, for approximately 30 minutes. When cool, cover the top with melted chocolate, Recipe 194. Allow this to set, then mark the lattice design on the top with a very fine skewer. Pipe the lines with a No. 6, 8 or 13 pipe. Spread a little butter icing on the side of the cake and press the meringues against this. Pipe rosettes (with the same pipe) between the meringues, round top edge of cake and fill in part of lattice work as shown.

Arrange split almonds in a rosette in centre; put a very little melted chocolate in middle of this, topped with angelica leaves and a cherry.

Gâteau suprême

411 Crown cake

4 oz. castor sugar
4 oz. margarine
4 egg yolks
2 tablespoons water
4 oz. flour (with plain flour use 2 teaspoons baking powder, with self-raising flour use 1 teaspoon baking powder)
meringue (Recipe 407 or 424) made with 4 egg whites, etc.
To decorate:
¼ pint thick cream
1 lb. fresh strawberries *or* raspberries *or* can of fruit cocktail

Cream the sugar and margarine until light and fluffy. Beat in the egg yolks and water, then fold in the sieved flour and baking powder. Bake in two 7-inch sandwich tins in a moderate oven (375°F. — Gas Mark 4) for 15−20 minutes. Cool.

Make meringue mixture, Recipe 407; pipe this on to two 7-inch circles of rice paper* placed on an oiled tray. Leave a 3-inch hole in centre; pipe, using a large ½-inch star meringue pipe, with a slightly sideways downward movement, round this space, building meringue up fairly high by using firm pressure. Use half the meringue for each circle. Set in a cool oven.

When both the meringues and the sandwich are cold, beat cream until it is stiff. Spread half this on first sandwich and place one meringue ring on top. Fill centre with a third of the fruit. Place second sponge on top; spread rest of cream over this, then place the second meringue in position. Pile rest of the fruit in the hollow.

This recipe can be halved, using one 7-inch sandwich tin, and making one meringue ring, and you will see a picture of this in the background.
Illustrated in colour plate 23.

By using rice paper, which is edible, you have a good support to the meringue. If by chance you have no rice paper, then put on to circles of well buttered or oiled greaseproof paper. When the meringue is set and cold, lift from the greaseproof paper by inserting a warm palette knife underneath.

412 To make meringue cases

When using meringue to make a case the secret is to cut out the shape first in greaseproof paper which will give you a guide. You can spread the meringue into the required round with a palette knife, but it will look more professional if the sides are piped.

413 To make cases without piping

Recipe 414 ring shows how a case is built up without piping. If you wish to make a base only, cut the greaseproof paper into a round shape and spread meringue carefully over top of this.

For a flan shape, work up edges to give a border. As the meringue case is very solid, it needs prolonged baking at very low heat to make sure heat has penetrated right through to centre.

To remove meringue cases or meringues from baking tins, dip a palette knife into very hot water. Shake reasonably dry and slip knife under meringue, loosening it carefully.

414 Blackcurrant meringue ring

3 egg whites
6 oz. castor sugar
3 level teaspoons cornflour
For the filling:
1 lb. fresh blackcurrants
3—4 oz. sugar
little water
1 packet raspberry flavoured
cornflour
2 eggs

Beat the egg whites stiffly and add half the sugar and continue beating until the meringue holds in stiff peaks. Mix the cornflour with the rest of the sugar and fold into the meringue. Spread the meringue with a palette knife into a 9—8-inch circle on a well oiled or buttered baking sheet. Build up the sides, using a fork. Bake 2—3 hours in a cool oven (225°F. — Gas Mark ½).
Make the filling by simmering 8 oz. of the blackcurrants, sugar and a little water together for a few minutes until the fruit becomes very soft. Rub through a sieve and make the purée up to ¾ pint with water. Mix the cornflour and egg yolks smoothly with a little of the purée and put the rest on to heat. Add the mixed cornflour and boil for 1 minute, stirring constantly. Remove from the heat. Beat the egg whites stiffly and fold in the cooked mixture. Leave to cool, then pile into the meringue ring and decorate with the rest of the fresh blackcurrants.

Blackcurrant meringue ring

Stores for Cake Decorating

415

If you intend to do a great deal of decorating, your store cupboard should be well filled so that you have a good selection of ingredients, decorations and cake boards to choose from. The following list may give you an idea of what is needed.

Angelica	Purchased by the ounce. Take care that you ask for long pieces of angelica, as these are more useful. Store in a dry, cool place to prevent becoming sticky. To make pliable, put in warm water for a short time. Most shapes can be cut from angelica with a sharp knife.
Candies and Sweets	Tiny chocolate drops, sticks of barley sugar and small sweets can be used as a quick decoration on children's cakes. Keep in a cool, dry place.
Chocolate	It is advisable to keep some chocolate in the house for decorating. Chocolate couverture is the best for coating, but ordinary plain chocolate can be used for grating. Chocolate powder should be used for chocolate butter icing, see Recipe 103. *Colour plate 26* shows how an ordinary plain Victoria sandwich, Recipe 30, can be turned into a Chocolate orange gâteau. Chocolate butter icing was used to coat the sides, using a fork or plastic cake comb for the lines. Flakes of chocolate for the top, Recipe 188, and canned mandarin oranges add the final touch.
Colourings	There a wide variety of colourings on the market.

The most useful would be:
Sap green
Clear blue
Carmine
Purvio
Saffron yellow
True red
Extract of cochineal
Store in tightly covered bottles. If they spill they stain badly.

Coloured strands	These are tiny sugar pieces which look very attractive on the top of cakes. They are quite cheap to buy. Keep in a cool, dry place. Often sold in plastic containers or polythene tubes.
Candles and candle holders	Tiny bright candles and holders keep indefinitely, so it is wise to buy these when you see them.
Crystallized fruits	These are expensive, but small pieces look very attractive on a cake. Store in a cool place. Can be bought in assorted boxes or separately. Crystallized ginger is one that is relatively inexpensive. Keep in a dry place to prevent it becoming sticky.
Christmas decorations	These become extremely difficult to get just before Christmas, so store carefully. If removed from the cake with care and washed, they can be used on several occasions.

Essences	One of the best ways of flavouring since you use very little to give a strong flavour.	**Canned fruit**	careful not to put them on to a cake designed to keep for a long period. Open the can, drain well and glaze, see Recipe 25.
	These often provide enough colouring and flavouring.	**Glacé fruits**	Use as crystallized fruits.
	Almond	**Jelly**	A layer of fruit flavoured jelly added when cold and just beginning to thicken looks most attractive on top of a sponge cake.
	Banana		
	Cinnamon		
	Clove		
	Coconut — rarely used since most people prefer adding desiccated coconut	**Nuts**	All nuts are excellent for decorations on cakes and, since they keep reasonably well in screw-topped jars, can be stored.
	Coffee		
	Ginger — rarely used since most people prefer adding powdered ginger	**Peel**	Use on top of cakes like Madeira, and finely chopped on biscuits. Keep in a cool dry place. For large impressive pieces of peel, do not buy cartons already chopped.
	Lemon		
	Nutmeg		
	Orange	**Sugared pieces of orange or lemon**	These are obtainable from confectioners and are considerably cheaper than crystallized fruit.
	Pear		
	Peppermint	**Silver balls**	A favourite decoration on top of a cake. Keep in a dry place otherwise the silver coating tends to rub off. Often called dragees. Coloured balls can also be obtained.
	Pineapple		
	Raspberry		
	Ratafia		
	Rose		
	Rum	**Hundreds and thousands**	Minute sweets which can be shaken over the top of icing for children's cakes. Apply when the icing has nearly set, otherwise the colour on these tiny sweets tends to run.
	Strawberry		
	Tangerine		
	Vanilla		
	Violet		
Dried fruits	Occasionally used for decoration as shown in this book, but of course a basic ingredient for cake making. Can be bought already washed, but if not wash and dry thoroughly for 48 hours before putting into cakes.	**Marzipan or almond paste**	It is possible to buy packets of almond paste or marzipan which keeps well in its waxed paper.
		Vermicelli	This is the term given to very fine strands of chocolate which you can buy from a good grocer, often in tubes. Do not store in a hot place as it will melt.
Fresh fruits	These are often an ideal way of decorating sponges and gâteaux. Be		

416   More aids to decoration

Cake boards	Any elaborate iced cake looks better on a board. These are generally silver, but for occasions such as a golden wedding anniversary you can buy gold-coloured cake boards.	**For christening cakes**	Model of stork
			Model of baby in cradle
		For birthday or wedding cakes	Vases for real or artificial flowers
			These are generally obtainable from first-class stationers or stores specializing in cake decorations.
Doilies	Many people like decorated cakes on a doily and certainly with a dark cake it tends to throw up and emphasize the colourings.	**Leaves**	Very tiny artificial leaves are obtainable from similar stores. You can often add real rose leaves or mint leaves at the very last minute.
	For weddings, both silver and gold doilies can be obtained.		
For wedding cakes	You will need some of the following	**Ribbon**	Attractive ribbon round the edge of a cake often saves the bother of elaborate piping. Line with a piece of greaseproof paper as Recipe 146. Instead of ribbon you may care to use cake bands and these are printed in various designs suitable for Easter and Christmas.
	Silver horseshoes		
	Silver shoes		
	Silver bells		
	Figures, i.e. bride and groom, and archways		

INDEX

Note. All references are to recipe numbers

ACKNOWLEDGEMENTS

The author and publishers would like to thank the following for their help and co-operation in supplying illustrations for this book.

American Foods
Australian Gas Light Company
Australian Home Cookery Service
Australian Women's Weekly
Belling Cookers Ltd.
Blue Band Margarine
Brown and Polson
Butter Information Council
Cadburys
Cadburys Milk Finger Biscuits
California Raisin Bureau
Camp Coffee
Colman's Semolina

Flour Advisory Bureau
Heinz
The Honey Bureau (Gales Honey)
Kellogs
Kraft Margarine
Kraft Cheese and Preserves
Mazola
McDougalls
Nestlé
Pascalls Marshmallows
P. R. Visuals (Coffee Information Bureau)
P. R. Visuals
Prestige
Proctor and Gamble
Spry
Stork
Tala
Tate and Lyle